COLONIALISM IN GLOBAL PERSPECTIVE

Kris Manjapra weaves together the study of colonialism over the past 500 years across the globe's continents and seas. This captivating work vividly evokes living human histories, introducing the reader to manifestations of colonialism as expressed through war, militarization, extractive economies, migrations and diasporas, racialization, biopolitical management, and unruly and creative responses and resistances by colonized peoples. This book describes some of the most salient political, social, and cultural constellations of our present times across the Americas, Africa, Asia, and Europe. By exploring the dissimilar, yet entwined, histories of conquest, settler colonialism, racial slavery, and empire, Manjapra exposes the enduring role of colonial force and freedom struggle in the making of our modern world.

Kris Manjapra is Associate Professor of History and founding Chair of the Department of Studies in Race, Colonialism, and Diaspora at Tufts University. He is the author of *M. N. Roy: Marxism and Colonial Cosmopolitanism* (2009), *Cosmopolitan Thought Zones of South Asia* (co-editor, 2010), and *Age of Entanglement: German and Indian Intellectuals across Empire* (2014).

COLONIALISM IN GLOBAL PERSPECTIVE

Kris Manjapra

CAMBRIDGE
UNIVERSITY PRESS

CAMBRIDGE
UNIVERSITY PRESS

University Printing House, Cambridge CB2 8BS, United Kingdom

One Liberty Plaza, 20th Floor, New York, NY 10006, USA

477 Williamstown Road, Port Melbourne, VIC 3207, Australia

314–321, 3rd Floor, Plot 3, Splendor Forum, Jasola District Centre, New Delhi – 110025, India

79 Anson Road, #06–04/06, Singapore 079906

Cambridge University Press is part of the University of Cambridge.

It furthers the University's mission by disseminating knowledge in the pursuit of education, learning, and research at the highest international levels of excellence.

www.cambridge.org
Information on this title: www.cambridge.org/9781108425261
DOI: 10.1017/9781108560580

First published 2020

A catalogue record for this publication is available from the British Library.

ISBN 978-1-108-42526-1 Hardback
ISBN 978-1-108-44136-0 Paperback

Cambridge University Press has no responsibility for the persistence or accuracy of URLs for external or third-party internet websites referred to in this publication and does not guarantee that any content on such websites is, or will remain, accurate or appropriate.

For Saugato

Wars. Wars thin like sea-smoke, but their dead
   were real.

Derek Walcott, *Omeros,* p. 29

Contents

CONTENTS

Illustrations

Acknowledgments

This work was possible only because of the assistance and contributions of many friends and benefactors. At Tufts University, I am grateful to my colleagues in the RCD, especially Lisa Lowe, Kamran Rastegar, Kendra Field, Kerri Greenidge, Amahl Bishara, Adlai Murdoch, Adriana Zavala, Heather Curtis, Kareem Khubchandi, Alexander Blanchette, Lilian Mengesha, Mark Minch, Matt Hooley, Nidhi Mahajan, Khury Peterson, and Ana Cruz. It is a rare privilege to think so collaboratively and profoundly, and over such a sustained period of time, with a group of such brilliant scholars. Thanks especially to Lisa, Adriana, Heather, Amahl, Lilian, and Mark for reading and commenting on versions of this manuscript, and to María Josefina Saldaña-Portillo. Special thanks, too, to Ayesha Jalal and Liz Foster in the History Department. I have deep gratitude for Deborah Kochevar's leadership in helping to establish the Department of Studies in Race, Colonialism, and Diaspora at Tufts.

I made a major start on the manuscript while on a fellowship at the Radcliffe Institute for Advanced Study. I forged transformative friendships at Radcliffe that strengthened me in important ways. Thank you, Joyce Bell, Ayesha Chaudhury, Tiana Kahakauwila, Alyssa Mt. Pleasant, Laurence Ralph, and Ross Gay for your grace, intelligence, and beauty. I also thank my undergraduate research assistants at the Radcliffe Institute, William Sack, Nicholas Santiago, Marguerite Solmssen, and Anes Sung. Over the course of writing this manuscript, I also benefited from the friendship and wisdom of Kari Polanyi Levitt, Demetrius Eudell, and Martin Kämpchen.

The work on the manuscript continued as a fellow at the Berlin Academy of Advanced Study, where I am indebted to Stefan Gellner for his heroic research assistance. In Berlin, I made many friends who inspired and instructed me. Thank you, Alice von Bieberstein, Zeynep Kivilcim, Barbara Hobson, Klaus Steinhoff, Felix Canditt, Daniel Schönpflug, Jeremy Wideman, Viktoria Serena, Sonja Mejcher-Atassi, Nimra Bucha, and Sian Gaston. A special thanks to Yassin Al-Haj Saleh and Om Barach for our conversations. My deepest gratitude goes out to Bo Forbes, Melissa Alexis, Betty Burkes, Melissa Bartholomew, Hammad Ahmed, and Jennifer Brown for your support and friendship in Boston. Bo, thank you for reading and commenting on my work with such care. Lucia Volk has been my steadfast friend throughout.

I am very grateful to all the students in the spring 2019 class of "Colonialism in Global Perspective" for reading and commenting on portions of this manuscript. Your feedback was essential and on point. And thanks, as well, to all the students in earlier iterations of the class, as well as my co-teacher in a number of its earlier avatars, Lisa Lowe. Thank you to Tathagatha Datta, Wendy Qian, Parker Breza, and Michael Mandelkorn at Tufts for assistance with editing.

This project would not have been possible without the gracious, careful, attentive, and patient insight and advice of Lucy Rhymer, my editor at Cambridge. It was a privilege to work on this project with you. And thanks as well to Emily Sharp for her generous contribution of expertise, and to Christopher Jackson for his careful eye and expert advice. The anonymous referees assisted me with their suggestions, critiques, and encouragements. And a special thanks to Christopher J. Lee for reading the whole manuscript and offering such meaningful recommendations; I'm truly indebted. While recognizing the many generous contributions of colleagues and friends, it is also incumbent on me to say that all the remaining errors and infelicities in this text are my own.

Finally, I thank my mother, Jeanile, for our cherished friendship and for all she has given me. And, Saugato, we travel together, and this book is for you.

Preface

Colonial formations are among the most important political entities of our contemporary times, as they function through nation-states, international regulatory regimes, and the amorphous clouds of global capital. But they have also supplied the webbing of global history for hundreds of years. This book has a simple objective: to provide a critical description of the different and interlocking aspects of colonial power, including the ongoing resistances to it, that inform the global history of our present.

We pursue two distinct approaches to inquiry: historical narratives, on the one hand, and sociological analysis, on the other. The first part of this book considers four distinct yet related histories of colonial power unfolding over long periods of time, which together describe the foundations for the making of the modern world. The second part considers five defining sociological aspects of colonial power and decolonizing resistance. This study does not constitute a comprehensive account, but a diagnostic venture to prompt further study. Furthermore, this book, both because of the limitations of the author, but also its motivating intellectual objectives, is not an exhaustive chronicle of colonial processes over hundreds of years. Rather, this book is a provocation.

Where possible, I sharpen arguments as opposed to softening them. Because, to me, the norms of traditional history-writing seem wanting in the face of the urgent intellectual, social, and ethical demands of our times, I find myself contesting these norms. Whereas traditional history-writing constrains itself to compartmentalized units of space (e.g. nation-state, area, world region, etc.), and of time (e.g. medieval, modern, contemporary, etc.), I break out of these containers and insist on connecting narratives across temporal thresholds and spatial divides.

The modern forms of colonialism I discuss in this book reverberate across different temporal periods, from the 1400s to the present, and across discontinuous spaces, from the Americas, to Africa, to Europe, to Asia and the Pacific. Only an assembled mode of history-writing is adequate to the task of describing colonialism's assembled histories of force and resistance. Traditional history-writing, because of its compartmentalizations, fails to grasp the relations between different histories, peoples, and sociological processes produced in and through modern colonialism. This book highlights the relations between histories that are often studied separately and in isolation from each other. Based on vivid and concrete historical examples, we see how colonialism is comprised of a diverse set of operations and logics, binding together distinct and non-equivalent communities in matrices of interdependence.

The idea for this effort emerged out of the changes I experienced first-hand on my university campus over the past decade. A major mobilization by Tufts undergraduates in 2010 for the transformation of the curriculum involved campus protests and a brief occupation of the president's office. Students demanded the creation of courses and programs centered on the critical themes of race, ethnicity, colonialism, and migration. Such courses were scant at Tufts University at the time, and are generally underrepresented in New England colleges, as they are in many other US institutions of higher education even today. One of the outcomes of the protests was the creation of a new Consortium of Studies in Race, Colonialism, and Diaspora in 2014, which sought to free the curriculum from the siloed and calcified conventions of "cultural diversity" and "multiculturalism" so favored in the 1980s and 1990s. We also established a Colonialism Studies Program, drawing on significant student demand. Faculty and students envisioned a new curriculum, bringing together powerful insights from Postcolonial Studies and Critical Race & Ethnic Studies. And we drew on the deep taproot of social critique found in the Black Radical Tradition. Finally, in 2019, the Consortium was transformed into the university's newest department: the Department of Studies in Race, Colonialism, and Diaspora (RCD).

Over the course of a decade, I saw the institutionalization of new ways of study, highlighting Southern narratives and globally entangled histories of colonialism and decolonization. The RCD Department connects the study of conquest, settler colonialism, slavery, empire, comparative racializations, gendered divisions of labor, colonial mobilities, liberal imperialism, biological–political management, and the experience and politics of diasporas and migrant cultures. Students explore relations among the histories of the Indigenous and Black Americas, Africa, Asia, and Europe in ways that catapult us out of the old ways of study into coalitional new ones.

Experiencing these changes alongside my colleagues and students shows me that the time for the twenty-first-century intellectual renewal of the humanities is upon us. This renewal involves disturbing the established disciplinary structures and narrative conventions in pursuit of spaces for interdisciplinary, comparative, and relational exploration. We are living in a moment of immense peril, promise, and transformation on worldwide societal scales. I write this book as a homage to and record of the great emergence I experienced first-hand on one university campus in New England over the past decade. Yet, I believe this text is also an imprint of our unsettled social and political world, of which my campus, situated on unceded Wampanoag land and on the plot of the old Ten Hills slave plantation, is but a fractal part.

Introduction

A STUDY OF COLONIALISM in global perspective starts with this
journey. Take tram number 44 from Leopold II Square in
Brussels to the end of the line, to the leafy suburb of Tervuren through
the lush Forêt de Soignes. The final stop leads to the Royal Museum for
Central Africa. Belgian King Leopold II (1835–1904), mastermind of the
colonization of Central Africa and its 20 million inhabitants, built the
ostentatious palace that today houses the museum. "The Congo Free
State has nothing to hide and no secrets," Leopold once proclaimed
from this palace, adding, "it is not beholden to anyone except its
founder." Of course, here, he was speaking of himself.

Today, the museum possesses 120,000 ethnographic objects, the
world's largest hoard of Africana. This includes an impressive collection
of African masks, one of the great ritual art forms of peoples in the Niger
and Congo basins. African dancers don these masks in ceremony to
expose and witness hidden truths, and to make ancestral spirits visible.[1]
Now these masks and the truths they are meant to reveal lie appropriated
and buried in the belly of the Tervuren museum. Also hidden away, as if
in a large tomb of secrets, is the history of Belgian colonial war and
atrocity, and its ongoing social legacies in Africa and Europe.

Yet, the Tervuren museum inadvertently confesses Belgium's violent
colonial history through a material inventory of thousands of objects
purchased or stolen from the Congo. Belgian schoolchildren clatter
through the museum's aisles every week on educational field trips. They
may gawk at Stanley's cap, Leopold's cane, or a gilded bronze statue
from 1922 entitled "Belgium Brings Civilization to the Congo." Yet the

museum also disguises its history in ways that betray the widespread syndrome of denial and deception characterizing many postcolonial societies today.

Consider this buried truth: many of the "objects" collected from Africa for the Royal Museum were human. Over the course of Belgian colonization of the Congo, the Royal Museum amassed skulls and skeletal remains from Africans starved to death, maimed, or murdered in genocidal colonial wars. Brussels' Natural History Museum took possession of this perverse ossuary in 1964. And today, the existence of these colonial remains is unknown to almost every living Belgian citizen.[2] Records of the identity, location, and means of acquisition of these African skeletons have officially "gone missing." Cultural institutions and political bodies actively relegate the existence of these human fragments and their histories to the abyss of the unknown.[3]

In Belgian national discourse, the ongoing historical legacies of colonialism in the Democratic Republic of the Congo (DRC) are equally unacknowledged. Belgian colonial exploitation and intervention has contributed to the legacies of poverty, debt, and political dysfunction in the Congo. Following decades of rabid Belgian colonial extractivism in the early twentieth century, followed by political mismanagement and overweening levels of foreign debt, the Congo is today one of the world's poorest countries. In 1960, the assassination of the first elected prime minister, Patrice Lumumba, ruptured the democratically elected Congolese government. European imperialists feared Lumumba's radical vision of social uplift. Covert Belgian security forces supported by the USA, along with local collaborators, masterminded Lumumba's assassination. Decades of political instability spilled from this act, compounding the original sin of colonial rule itself.[4] Belgium has never officially apologized for its colonial holocaust in the Congo or for its role in the assassination of Patrice Lumumba.

Recently, in December 2018, the Tervuren museum was remodeled and updated. Yet, the historical and present-day role of the museum in hoarding the corpses of African people, procured through Belgian colonial genocides, remains as unacknowledged as ever. An estimated 10 million people of the Congo died because of Belgian atrocities. The scale of this ongoing denial is not unique to the capital city of the European Union. In Paris and Lisbon, for example, no public memorial exists to commemorate the terrorization of societies in the French and Portuguese colonial ambit. In the United States, no national memorial has been built to acknowledge the genocides against Native peoples. In Japan, no museums stand to memorialize Japanese colonialism in Korea. To this day in Germany, no state memorial stands to the genocide of the Nama and Herero people of southern Africa. Britain has no national museum of colonialism to memorialize the histories of British war-mongering and its impact on more than 400 million colonized people across the globe, including nearby in Ireland. Some of the most prestigious universities of the Western world, such as Harvard, Yale, Cambridge, and Oxford, are built on the proceeds of colonialism and slavery, and full exposés are only now coming to light.[5] But on many of these campuses, the crests, statues, and endowed chairs of colonizers still stand. Colonizer societies eagerly and actively forget, forget again, and disavow their colonial histories. Even the material evidence of immense wealth from the colonies crystallized in imperial architectures, and the amassed bones of the colonized in the vaults of most every imperial city, cannot jog the public memory.

While many museums bask in the afterglow of imperial glory, few are built to acknowledge the legacies of colonialism. Empires are easily remembered. Colonial histories, on the other hand, are compulsively and continuously forgotten. They remain histories in disguise, actively repressed and masked. Colonial power seeks to disavow its historical contexts and to forget about where it stashed the bodies. Fundamentally, studies of imperialism focus on the infrastructures of incorporation and rule that operate across metropoles and contiguous or overseas "peripheries."[6] By contrast, the study of colonialism explores the excesses and disruptions arising at the sites of conquest, occupation, and forced displacement, including the varieties of transformative response and resistance.

All empires deploy colonial force on the ground, yet not all forms of colonialism are the outcomes of imperial infrastructure or statecraft. By studying colonialism, we describe and analyze forms of power that operate both within and beyond imperial states. And, importantly, colonial formations are among the most important political entities of our own times, operating at levels below and above nation-states, and through the apparatuses of nation-states, too.

Against a backdrop of colonial forgetting and evasion, this book's purpose is to engage in a practice of historical recognition and witnessing. Over the course of these chapters, we will witness colonial histories both hidden away at the center of empires and beyond them. According to the Oxford English Dictionary, "to witness" is "to furnish evidence about or to attest to something." The act of witnessing suggests an attentive and ethical mode of seeing and hearing that affirms what is true or real amid cultures of deception. The act of witnessing opposes the act of denial, and connotes a willingness to be present to – as opposed to absent or in hiding from – ethical experiences of understanding. Over the course of the chapters that follow, we will witness colonial histories that refuse to be masked.

THE MAT VERSUS THE MAP

The paragraph-length short story "On Rigor in Science" (1946) by Argentinian author Jorge Luis Borges concerns a map of empire. Borges tells us that in an unnamed empire long ago, the fever for mapping became so intense that the empire's cartographers developed "unmeasurably excessive [*desmurados*] maps," which overwhelmed the very things they were supposed to represent. The mapmakers' fever to define the boundaries of imperial rule on paper led to maps "whose size was that of the Empire, and which coincided point for point with it." Borges tells us that these imperial maps, yielded from the conquests of an archaic people, eventually succumbed to ruination. Future generations quickly perceived their absurdity and uselessness. The excessive and burdensome maps became tattered, and were claimed and repurposed as shelter for wandering animals and travelers. The maps, Borges suggests, reveal more about the folly of imperial lords, and the ingenuity of the lives they dispossessed and displaced, than they ever do about the "rigor" of empires.[7] The historical study of colonialism informs us about the grotesque and excessive falsehoods of imperial descriptions of reality, allowing us to witness the disparate and diverse ways that people, confronted with the conquest of imperial maps, defiantly re-arrange, reclaim, and recreate their own cultures and embodiments.[8]

This book is not a pursuit in mapping, but an exploration of history's matting. Jamaican author Erna Brodber, in her 2014 novel *Nothing's Mat*, helps me explain what I mean. At the center of the novel is the figure of a mat, made of sisal, woven by the narrator's aunt. The novel is interested in the interwovenness not just of the mat's history, but also of family history itself. The story spans multiple generations of a Jamaican woman's family, from the time of Emancipation in the 1830s to the present day. And instead of a map of occurrences, we see an interlocking weave of "recursions and iterations."[9] History, Brodber suggests, is not linear and chronological, but characterized by an interconnected relationship between different times and different places. Colonial histories are not linear or flat like the Mercator projection, but tangled and folded upon each other.

In the unfurling "mat" of history, interrelations are at play where the threads meet up, loop each other, and interlock. Brodber writes specifically of the generational history of an African Caribbean "fractal" family as it formed in and through the experience of slavery and racial colonial violence. Indebted especially to Erna Brodber's insight, and to the feminist scholarship of many women of color, I embark on the study of colonialism not as an exercise in mapping, but as an endeavor to trace the complex weave of historical fabric. Over hundreds of years, as colonizers nailed their maps on top of other people's geographies, the colonized have responded with counteractions to colonial force. The resulting tangling of different peoples' histories and communities on an increasingly planetary scale provides the bewildering and intricate mat for this book. Historical writing is about narrative construction and involves choosing ways to tell stories. History is a set of choices that provides an interpretation of what socially exists, yet always fails to fully represent what actually exists.[10] Colonialism, I propose, causes the knotting, folding, and meeting of juxtaposed processes, institutions, and practices held together in tension. And so, here, I seek to follow the most consequential loops and stitches of different and juxtaposed threads of global history.

APPROACH

This book unfolds in two parts. Part I considers interlocking colonial histories. We explore the differences and interrelations of distinct

historical trajectories across more than five centuries of colonial exploitation. We home in on histories of settler colonial warfare in the Latin
and Anglophone Americas; plantation slavery and the Atlantic slave
trade; and modern imperial expansion across Asia and resulting coerced
labor migrations and territorial occupations. Conversely, the distinctive,
unequal, and interlocking histories at the heart of this book also focus
on: Indigenous peoples' sovereign resistances and refusals; the liberation
politics of diasporic African peoples; and the contestations of oppressed
Asian communities and polities. We focus our attention on these histories because they tether together continents and oceans, and describe the
foundations of the modern world order, linking the Americas, Europe,
Africa, and Asia across the earth's seas. We have tended to study colonialism in silos, through the lens of one empire or one colonial process at a
time. This book adopts a relational and comparative approach. The
study of colonialism requires our curiosity about how different kinds of
histories are "cacophonous," to use Jodi Byrd's word, and entangled.[11]

Part II provides sociological analysis of five different aspects of colonial power and contestation. In this portion, we are concerned with
elementary aspects of colonial force, including its technologies and
strategies as they unfold over long periods of time. These dimensions
of colonial power rouse unruly responses and counteractions among the
colonized. We survey disciplinary, pedagogical, financial, spatial, and
biopolitical dimensions of colonial power, and consider how the tools
and scripts of the colonizers are variously refused, rearranged and
repurposed by the agencies of the colonized. The chapters in Part II
do not pretend to supply an exhaustive or complete analysis of all aspects
of colonial power. Instead, we take a diagnostic approach, describing
colonialism's major discourses, functions, scales of operation, and unfinished outcomes.

Our work here is not only to define and explore colonialism, but also
to experiment with a different way of knowing that is appropriate to the
task. This different way of knowing must contend with paradox and
contradiction, drawing relations between a multiplicity of discordant
perspectives. At the same time, this comparative way of knowing must
not impose sameness, or "speak for" others' histories, or flatten out
power relations, or obscure the differences among the many sovereign

groups that colonialism catches in its weir. This way requires intellectual humility.[12]

Studying a woven historical fabric to understand how it is put together demands a way of knowing, called *parallax*. Parallax, or the multiplied perspective, is the awareness that balances the many interrelated, yet different, perspectives on shared social experience.[13] Parallactic understanding beckons us to radically redistribute our ways of understanding the meanings of being human in the aftermath of centuries of colonialism, given the differential weights and vibrations of distinct legacies of survival and creativity among colonized communities on earth. The study of colonialism and the practice of parallax go together. Through this study, we trace relations among interlocking histories that are formed in and through each other, but are not the same.[14] This book highlights the intense relationships between peoples, places, ecologies, and things characterizing the emergence of the modern world order from the fifteenth century all the way to our present times.

RACIAL CAPITALISM AND COLONIALISM

I frequently refer in this book to "the new colonialism" as the form of colonialism emerging in and through racial capitalism. Allow me to define what I mean. This new colonialism accompanied the rise of capitalist empires from the 1400s onward, shifting into a higher gear by the mid 1700s. There is no consensus about what capitalism is, let alone when it began. This difficulty notwithstanding, I follow the lead of such authors as Andre Gunder Frank and Cedric Robinson in recognizing its historical origins in the 1400s, with drastic changes in transoceanic production developing from large-scale Native genocide in the Americas and the violence of the Transatlantic slave trade.[15] The historical emergence of capitalism progressed over the following centuries as the mercantile principle of profit-making penetrated deeper and deeper into the realm of human and ecological life.[16] Colonizers attempted to commodify, extract, and appropriate land and labor surplus from differentially racialized groups. Different forms of colonial coercion and racial differentiation were employed to "cheapen" the price of labor, and to dehumanize laborers in emerging capitalist economies. By the nineteenth century, the colonial forces of racial capitalism transformed the majority of human beings on earth into slaves, coolies, bonded laborers, or low-paid wage workers.[17] Racial capitalism did not arise after this new form of colonialism began – it was its animating spirit.

Scholarship on racial capitalism over the past fifty years is rooted in the Black Radical Tradition, and has general significance for the study of the modern world order. According to this tradition of social thought, the historical roots of capitalism intimately intertwine with racialized appropriations and the deadly treatment of oppressed racialized groups. These "primitive accumulations" have been constitutive of capitalist activity ever since the 1400s.[18] Scholars who contribute to the study of racial capitalism show that racialization is infrastructural to capitalism, with legacies that persist into our own time.[19] The analytic of racial capitalism disrupts historicist narratives of linear transition through time, and draws attention to intertemporalities, residues, and excesses of historical violence that derange the relationship between past, present, and future. Studies of racial capitalism also challenge the economism at the heart of classical Marxism.[20] Capital expropriates surplus value from labor not in universally uniform or homogeneous ways, but according to a highly differentiated racial division of productive forces. The production of economies, states, and citizenries in the modern world has the ongoing dispossession of racialized peoples as its condition. Degradation and destruction of racialized communities serve as the basis of value production for those dominant groups who claim to monopolize the category of "the human."[21] From the perspective of racial capitalism, the making of incarcerated, dispossessed, and disposable subjects is a necessary condition for the dominant social order.[22] The exercise of racialized violence is not extra-economic or episodic, but constitutive of how the modern capitalist world works.

The new colonialism, that is, colonial force arising through the history of racial capitalism, was more violent and more invasive than any other form of colonialism that the world had previously known. Vast amounts of Native lands were confiscated through genocidal wars. More African people were kidnapped, trafficked, and incarcerated under slavery than ever before or ever after (more than 60 million people over the course of

500 years). Almost 90 percent of all peasants and rural people worldwide eventually had their lands expropriated from them. Almost 98 percent of the globe's territory gradually experienced some degree of long-term colonial occupation. Wealth disparities developed that eventually allotted 10 percent of people on earth (mostly living in Europe, North America, and other European settler states) ownership of 85 percent of the world's wealth.[23] Centuries of new colonialism permanently changed life and economies on a worldwide scale.

RACIAL CAPITALIST DRIVES

The new colonialism we track in this book is animated by the basic drives of racial capitalism:

Capitalist war, fueled by principles of profit maximization, is the violent drive to subject peoples, including their lands, ways of life , and economic and cultural systems, to the accumulationist urges of dominant groups. Capitalist war arises from strategies to produce new value through destruction, and to hide away and disregard the debris and damage caused by such destructive force. This kind of war pursues the ever deeper penetration of the mercantile principle into the realm of life.

Racializing rule is the drive to impose the dominator's order on the rebellious and unruly domain of colonized social and ecological life. This drive involves the ongoing and anxious compulsion of colonizers to sequester, categorize, contain, arrange, commodify, and manage colonized peoples and communities. Racialization allocates safety and quality of life to dominant and "normed" social groups by consigning selected groups of people to direct experiences of, or enhanced vulnerability to, neglect, exploitation, social abuse, and premature death.[24]

Moral deception names the psychological impulse of colonizers to disguise and disavow their warring acts and legacies with alibis of cure, safety, civility, health, enlightenment, development, and progress. The colonial force animated by racial capitalism is not just practiced with guns, swords, and pen and paper, but also with smoke and mirrors.

Transformative resistance is the inherent impulse of contradiction and transformation that operates from within systems of racial capitalist oppression, always opening up instabilities and interruptions that exceed the objectives of rule. Histories of colonialism always exceed the terms imposed by colonial forces. As colonial rule arises, the colonizers invent new strategies of control and domination as the fretful counter-response to ongoing acts of resistance and freedom among the colonized.

The poet Derek Walcott saw the "rancor of hatred" hiding in the apparently pastoral dreams of colonizers. Furthermore, amidst the supposed peace and quiet of colonial regimes, he perceived the "silent screams" of all the people held on the edges of the ruling order.[25] In the United States, for example, Black families are almost three times more likely to live below the poverty line – and Latino families almost twice as likely – than White families. In Britain, Black and Asian migrants are almost twice as likely to end up in prison as White Britons. In France, where the state claims to be "color-blind" and does not collect race-based data, French persons whose families experienced French colonialism are three times more likely than White French people to be unemployed, while French children of color are five times more likely to report difficulties in school than their White counterparts.[26] These racial social constructs of our time define real social experience, and they are rooted in deep, and still ongoing, historical legacies of colonial history.

From the start, colonialism generates a spectrum of racializations in different contexts and societies. By continuously separating human communities across lines of dominance and subjection – lines of racial and colonial difference – the colonized are made disproportionately more socially insecure as individuals, communities, and intergenerational groups. Yet, conversely through this process, the subjugated create their own means of endurance and strength, and their own visions of the future. Racialization is as much about the fact of survival and vital reclamations among the colonized as it is about the social violence inflicted by colonizers.[27]

Racialization, when understood through the lens of colonialism, can be studied in comparative and global perspective. Native peoples were racialized as vanishing and disappearing, supposedly making way for the expansion of White settlers to take over their lands. Meanwhile, African peoples were racialized as morally indebted, as fit for toil as slaves, as permanently punishable, and as radically unassimilable into White settler society. Chicano and Latino people, in the course of Anglo-American Westward Expansion during the nineteenth century, were racialized as trespassers and migrant threats to Anglo-settler manifest destiny. In the Hispanic Americas, Indigenous peoples constituting large peasantries were racialized as backward and primitive in relation to families claiming

European descent. Asians were racialized as permanent outsiders in colonial societies, while European migrants were also differentially racialized as White "settlers" and "pioneers," or as "the White working class" and "the poor."[28] Meanwhile, Eurowhiteness emerged among the populations left back home, as colonial extraction and consumption nourished the growth of European national cultures. These disparate racializations exist because of colonialism. They function in a relational matrix with each other, and thus continually reference each other within systems of social power.

Race functions within a matrix of constructed social differences. These different racializations do not lead us to equivalent histories and experiences of colonial domination and decolonizing response. Rather, they involve *differential* experiences of vulnerability, exploitation, and resistance.[29] The oppression of Native people is not the same as the oppression of Black people, just as the ongoing legacies of settler genocide are not the same as those of anti-Black racial slavery. Anti-Muslim racialization is not the same as anti-Jewish racialization, even though they both have enabled practices of genocide. The West's Islamophobia is not the same as its Afrophobia. Yet, these racializations conspire together to provoke interlocking histories of oppression and resistance, and radical and coalitional possibilities for liberations still to come. We cultivate parallax by learning to recognize how these different threads hold together.

Colonized peoples, for their part, continuously contest the racialized containment imposed by colonial powers, perpetually skewing the plot by their own emancipatory acts. Small and large acts of emancipation create the counterpoint of new forms of culture, new claims to human meaning, and new modes of community and belonging that cannot be anticipated. Colonial power, as Patrick Wolfe said, is a reverse "imprint" of the ongoing, uncontainable agency of the colonized.[30] Colonialism is the story of conquests and occupations, but also of runaways, rebels, strikers, preachers, artists, community organizers, healers, futurists, revolutionaries, and chosen kin who continuously resist the ruling designs.

COLONIAL FORMS

Although we are interested here in the new kinds of colonialism emerging during the 1400s that still live on today, we also recognize that colonialism is itself ancient. Colonialism as the conquest, occupation, and rule of peoples and territories by dominant groups has had a long history. In order to understand the newly emerging colonial expressions of the 1400s – colonialism under racial capitalism – we should also consider what was already old then, too. For example, the Roman empire existed a millennium earlier and occupied scores of colonial domains stretching from today's Bulgaria to Britain. From the 1200s to the 1800s, other tributary empires proliferated across Asian domains.[31] They derived their wealth from farming revenues, tributes, tithes, and taxes from disparate colonized peoples. Consider, too, the many Asian mercantile empires, such as the Chola or Omani, amassing wealth from lucrative colonial trade in sugar, spices, and slaves across distant port cities of the Indian Ocean.

So, what was so different about a subset of emerging empires beginning in the 1400s? As explained in detail earlier, a specific new characteristic emerged: capitalist interests sought to drive the principle of profit-making deeper and deeper into the realm of life by using racial differentiations.[32] Out of this new colonialism, novel political, economic, and social formations arose. States transformed from small, relatively uncoordinated entities waging scattered wars, into large, centralized, profit-seeking national and imperial states deploying well-coordinated and persistent warfare. European statecraft increased its administrative capacity to forcibly promote long-distance capitalist expansion. Colonial force eventually bored into subterranean mineral reserves, rocketed up into the skies, and penetrated deep into the bodies of humans, plants, and animals. Colonies do not collect on shadowy margins of the earth. The wealth they generate, and the social and ecological entanglements they comprise, are the dispersed centers of our shared global history.[33]

Across the arc of 500 years of history, we note the rise of different kinds of colonies. *Plantation and extraction colonies* are sites of the intense exploitation of enslaved or bonded laborers on enclosed and exploited lands. A few major examples include the plantation colonies of Jamaica, Saint Domingue (today's Haiti), the Mississippi Delta, and the mining centers of Potosí, Bolivia and Guanajuato, Mexico. *Settler colonies* are territories on which mercenary arrivants seek to eliminate and replace Indigenous peoples through the confiscation of lands, and the imposition of settler laws and maps. Here we think, for example, of the United States of America, Argentina, Australia, and the Israeli state. *Entrepôt* and *port colonies* are the transfer points through which colonial laborers and resources pass into interoceanic webs of colonial capitalism. We think here of Hong Kong, Acapulco, and Elmina. *Protectorate colonies* are yet another form of colony, emerging primarily from the eighteenth to twentieth centuries, in which centralizing imperial states impose dictatorial "protection" onto overseas colonized societies. The British Crown Colonies, the Dutch East Indies, and the American Pacific are some examples. Finally, *militarized zones* and *penal colonies* mushroomed across land and sea from the 1600s onwards as colonial militaries divided, displaced, and incarcerated colonized peoples upon their own lands. Just a few examples include Diego Garcia, the Andaman Islands, and the vast prison-industrial complex of the United States of America.

Such categorization highlights the dissimilarity and asymmetry of colonial forms, but also the failed comparisons imposed by these categories themselves. Different colonial forms nest in each other and fuse with each other. Port colonies and protectorate colonies can nest in settler colonies. And extraction colonies and militarized zones can wedge into protectorate states. But, more importantly, the colonial experience of Elmina is not equivalent to that of Acapulco; nor is the experience of Native North America the same as Aboriginal Australia. Colonial formations tangle up different kinds of subjects and legacies, from dispossessed and forcibly removed Native peoples, to kidnapped and enslaved African peoples, to bonded and policed Asian labor migrants, to the socio-economically exploited populations of the Global South. We have to work parallactically to explore these interwoven histories, while also striving to avoid the imposition of false equivalences. We struggle against the limits of flat comparisons to witness the textured mattings of history. These textures have implications for our ethical responsibility to each other, to our living pasts, and to our vibrant futures.

BEARING WITNESS

Each of the following chapters bears witness to artifactual evidence – evidence I stumbled across in an archive that stopped me in my tracks, and asked me to look again, and to recognize something that seemed initially hidden from sight. These objects shed light on the colonial logics under discussion. I think of these objects as glyphs, or small condensates of colonialism's processes of camouflage and cover-up, but also to the quiet survivals and resilience that colonialism engenders. Throughout these pages, we will pause to consider these objects as puzzles. Our aim is not to solve the puzzle presented by colonial materials, but to think with and through them. Objects mediate relationships between historical processes, temporalities, and peoples. Objects also exercise a kind of gravitational pull on our interpretive world. They want to speak to us, but we must also wish to hear. And by 'deciphering' objects, we confront the limitations of dominant frameworks of historical understanding. The historical meaning of material objects can be unknotted, but only in ways that also tell us about ourselves, our blindspots, and our own limits as interpreters.[34] Following the inspiration of approaches to historical study provided by Saidiya Hartman, with her concept of "critical fabulation," and Lisa Lowe, with her call for critical inquiry into "what could have been," I am interested in asking questions of archival objects that evoke what is hidden, but eminently alive and present, all around us.[35]

Through their confrontation with colonial power, disparate colonized peoples were actively made into new kinds of subjects in relation to each other. Differently racialized groups reclaimed themselves as new subjects in creative response to their confrontation with the colonial force of racial capitalism. This emerging subjecthood of the colonized – their agency and action within interoceanic and global fields of relation – is an unintended living consequence of colonial domination. Colonialism is not just a set of "strong" acts and top-down impositions. It is also the responses, contestations, and creativity among the supposedly "weak," as their underground and grassroots disruptions shake anxious and fragile ruling orders to their core.

When considering colonialism, we bear witness to stories and processes from which we cannot turn away. Our world is created in and through colonial force and the multiplicity of resistances to it. Active witnessing, as a mode of historical study and of critical reflection on our present, prompts us both to call out ongoing processes of colonial war, racializing rule, and moral deception, and to confidently play our part in transforming our shared history on earth in relation to our unbound and unruly futures.[36] This is a journey for us to continue on together, for history has already interwoven our pasts.

PART I

INTERLOCKING COLONIAL HISTORIES

CHAPTER 1

War

TRAVEL ACROSS THE HEMISPHERIC AMERICAS to notice the repeating architecture of the Spanish colonial square. From Havana, to Cuzco, to Mexico City, to Port of Spain, you observe the recurring architectural design of *la traza*, with government buildings (*cabildos*) on one side of a green plaza, and a great cathedral opposite. Not far from the council buildings and the church is the court and jail. Spanish colonial power asserted itself through this trifecta of governor's building, church, and court. This familiar architectural pattern is reiterated across colonial towns established by the Spanish in the Americas, marking the places where a colonial frontier once cut into sovereign Indigenous societies. The innovation of the Spanish colonial square actually adapted urban architectural design from Indigenous imperial cities, such as at the Aztec capital of Tenochtitlan.[1] Eventually, over the coming centuries, this colonial town plan made its way to Europe, spreading across European cities.[2] The *traza* commemorates and propagates the myth of conquest brought to the Americas by weapon-carrying men from the Atlantic European fringe.[3]

Myths are the stories that social groups tell themselves in order to affirm their community identity. Native American peoples' myths were often rooted in their earth, as they believed themselves to be formed out of the clay, rocks, and soil of their environment. Spanish mercenaries, on the other hand, believed in the myth of their calling to bring civility and salvation to "savages," and to impose law and order on a wild and empty space. This is why Spanish settlers so often built their massive cathedrals on the sacred grounds of the Indigenous: they needed to ritually reaffirm the precarious myth of their supremacy.[4]

Frontiers play an important role in colonizers' myths, marking the boundaries that colonists draw first in their minds and then project outward on the world beyond, in which they see only emptiness and savagery. Colonizers imagine frontier spaces as the sites of violent conquest. They claim to advance their colonial frontiers in order to protect themselves, or improve the earth, or spread civility, or carry out the will of God. Efforts in accumulation and aggrandizement by one people through the exploitation, displacement, and dispossession of other peoples unfolds on colonial frontiers.[5]

The conquest of the Inca empire by mercenaries of the Spanish king beginning in the 1530s resulted in the imposition of a *traza* grid – with a viceregal palace, church, and court – centered in Lima. The Spanish colonial square was imposed over the existing political and spiritual geography of the Andean people, radiating from the nearby Indigenous *huacacuna* (sacred shrine) of *Pachacamac*, the "place that charges the world with being."[6] The Inca saw divinity in the landscape, in geological formations such as hills, rocks, and mountains, in burial sites for ancestors and sculptures, and in different human, animal, and vegetal beings. Their sacred places were contact points between the natural and supernatural realms. But where the Inca saw a changing, multidimensional landscape of spirits and spacetimes marked by *huacas* (extraordinary places) and *ushnus* (places of offering), the band of invading European mercenaries saw opportunities for plunder, expansion, and resource extraction. *Conquistadores* such as Francisco Pizarro and his brothers were unwilling to countenance sovereign Indigenous political power when they plundered temples and beheaded kings in the Incan empire in the 1530s. They vanquished Indigenous regimes – some of which were themselves imperial systems dominating weaker polities – and established governance over territories they would call *América Latina*.

The system of rule anchored by Spanish colonial squares protected the cultures of feudal lordship emanating from southern Atlantic Europe at the time. In this system, social station was not only determined by landed wealth, but also by customary privileges and feudal command over peasantries. Powerful men held large landed estates, called *latifundia*, and wielded power over obligated peasants and laborers.[7] Peasant families paid the *capitación*, or head tax, to the feudal lord, and submitted to seigneurial right. And status was also pegged to aristocratic ranks and titles, codes of dress and etiquette, and carefully rehearsed performances of prestige.[8]

This feudal system of landed estates and customary lordship over people was not unique to Atlantic Europe in the 1500s, but was practiced in diverse forms across the Eurasian continent and Asia. However, elements of feudal command traveled, expanded, and combined with new social and economic systems of oppression in the Spanish and Portuguese American colonies. The combination of hunger for land and labor, feudal and patriarchal license, and state intervention generated a noxious mix of colonial violence that confronted Native peoples across the Caribbean and southern and central America in the decades after 1492. These colonial activities differed in scale from other forms of colonialism experienced anywhere else ever before. When Admiral Christopher Columbus first set foot on the island he called *La Española e La Isabela*, the place that Natives called *Ayiti*, he pressed a figurative lever that put European colonial violence into overdrive.[9]

Spanish and Portuguese colonists sought to replicate ideals of European feudal prosperity from southern Europe, but with a difference. Their endeavors were increasingly infused with the spirit of early capitalism. The very word "colony" evokes pre-capitalist, feudal, political, and economic arrangements, coming from the Latin term, *colonus*, meaning "tiller, farmer, cultivator, planter, or settler." Lordship over large *latifundia*, or landed estates cultivated by coerced and bonded laborers, had existed ever since the time of the Roman empire.[10] However, New World capitalism was never interested in farmland alone, but in capitalist conglomerations of ownership and exploitation over land and sea.[11] Forever changing the trajectories of colonialism from the late 1400s onwards, colonial capitalism constructed new frontiers of conquest in order to extract wealth from land, to commodify the sea, and to profiteer from the recombined labors of peasants and unfree peoples across oceanic distances.

Commodities are priced goods traded on markets. Commodities, by definition, are tradable units of owned things: their owner is the one who purchases them for a stipulated price and has the right to sell them for a price.[12] The price mechanism of capitalist markets determines the value of commodities in terms of the amount of money they can be exchanged for, disembedded from social context. Commodities were certainly not new in the 1400s. But colonizers came to commodify many more kinds of entities beginning from that time, and used unprecedented levels of intense violence to force commodification on sovereign people and ecologies.[13] Indigenous peoples were variously transformed into landless laborers, dependent peasants, bonded workers, or the enslaved, by the pressure of colonial governance. Colonial forces from Atlantic Europe projected the mercantile principle of profit-making over the seas, and deep into realms of Native life across the "New World," including the land and seascapes of the Americas, the Pacific, and west Africa.

FRONTIERS OF THE SEA

For hundreds of years before 1400, commodification fueled historical developments across many domains of Asia. Mercantile interests, or the commercial principles that govern the decisions of traders, reached a remarkable height across the whole Indian Ocean world from about AD 900 onwards.[14] The world of the Indian Ocean, for a millennium, was perhaps the most active and lucrative trading domain of the world. Indian Ocean trade overshadowed the level of commerce across the Mediterranean and Atlantic European coasts up to the 1700s.[15] European markets prized goods from the commercialized economies of Asia for centuries – spices, fine textiles, and luxury craftwork – with Venice serving as one of the major European terminals of the Asia-to-Europe overland caravan routes. European ports like Venice also tied into Islamic seafaring networks connected to Asian markets. Venice looked towards the East, and received both goods and learning from Asia. These interests of buying, selling, and making profits through trade and money exchange drove merchants across land thoroughfares and sea routes, as they moved goods, services, and people from regions of supply to regions of demand.[16]

Up until the 1800s, Europeans were only small players in the big sea of the Indian Ocean merchant world. The 1299 account of Marco Polo's travels from Venice to Armenia, Persia, India, Tartary, and China is at least partly a catalog of Asian commodity delights. He enthusiastically itemized goods hungrily desired in European markets. Polo's brimming inventory included gold and silver, fine wines, handsome carpets, large fish, silks, muslins, date trees, coconuts, lapis lazuli, goshawks, nut oils, precious stones, pearls, and various drugs and spices.[17] Just as Marco Polo embarked on an overland voyage to Asia, the Vivaldi brothers of Genoa, in 1291, attempted to circumnavigate Africa in order to dip into the rich trade emporia of the Indian Ocean. European consumers dearly desired Asian products. And European merchants took up their marine mandates, scouting to satisfy this desire. Eventually, they transformed themselves into gun-toting soldiers of fortune.[18]

By the 1400s, Atlantic European states – especially Spain and Portugal – began designing frontiers of conquest across the distant seas of Asia, just as they would draw frontier lines across the lands of the New World Americas. In this period, the royal courts of Spain and Portugal pursued administrative centralization and the imposition of state monopolies. These courts thus sought to assert command over oceanic trade not just nearby, such as across the Mediterranean and the Atlantic coasts of Africa, but also far, far away. In this context, mercenary entrepreneurs made increasingly daring travels from the Iberian coast.

Bartolomeu Dias, driven by the wish to gain access to the vast trading emporia of Asia, circumnavigated the Cape of Good Hope into the Indian Ocean in 1488 primarily in pursuit of commerce. Vasco da Gama and other generals, such as Alfonso Albuquerque, became the first Europeans to travel by sea from the Horn of Africa across the Indian Ocean to establish Portuguese trading centers on the coasts of South Asia and Southeast Asia. Vasco da Gama sailed across the Indian Ocean in 1497 and formed outposts on the coasts of east Africa and southern India, in such places as Mombasa, Goa, Cochin, Malacca, and Ormuz. The Portuguese soon established additional trading posts across the Bay of Bengal in Nagapattinam, Galle, and Aceh. A few years earlier, in 1492, the same pursuit propelled Christopher Columbus to reach the "Indies" via a rumored western route, bringing his expedition to the Caribbean instead.

In the early 1400s, under the patronage of Infante Dom Henrique of Portugal, maritime plunder of and territorial incursion into west-coast Africa picked up. Under Henrique, the Portuguese court innovated a new procedure, the precedent of the *cartaz* system, to extend colonial power over sea routes both near and far.[19] Militarized Portuguese entrepreneurs first used the *cartaz*, or the state-issued license, off the coast of western Europe and Africa, and then later across the Indian Ocean littorals, in order to make money not only from trade, but also from the policing of trade across newly imposed boundaries. Under the introduction of this *cartaz* license system, the Portuguese state claimed distant seas as its own property, placing the profits from those corresponding sea trades under the jurisdiction of the Portuguese crown.[20]

Portuguese rulers and merchants envisioned a domain called the Portuguese *mare clausum* – or closed sea – stretching from the coast of Portugal all the way down to the west coast of Africa. Portuguese seaborne mercenaries and merchants soon dreamt of creating Portuguese "closed seas" in other, distant arenas. Where the sea could be designated as closed, a monopoly could be imposed, along with new opportunities for conquest and profit. If a ship did not have its license while in the *mare clausum*, it could be commandeered or destroyed. When the Portuguese traveled by sea after this time, they not only sought contact with other coasts and peoples, but also command over those coasts and peoples.[21]

As European merchants and mercenaries started colonizing other peoples' lands in the Americas and in Asia, they busily designated whole regions of the Atlantic Ocean, and soon the Indian Ocean, as their own closed seas. The *cartaz* made the concept of a closed sea a reality and allowed it to be enforced. By seeking to command maritime trade, and not just to participate in it, the Portuguese differentiated themselves from the many polities and merchant groups that were historically involved in Indian Ocean commerce. The income from the selling of *cartaz* went directly to the coffers of the Portuguese state.

One Portuguese *cartaz*, issued in 1570 for ships in the Indian Ocean, asserted authority over ocean traffic: "Christians, the Gentiles who favor Christendom in parts of India, can navigate from one part to another."[22] The document made allusion to a presumed divine right bestowed by the Christian God. References to God and divine right appear, even today, as justifications for colonization and settlement. Whether gods mirror the actions of their devotees, or devotees mimic their deities, colonialism infuses the Christian sacred imaginary, not unlike those of other major religions.[23]

Meanwhile, in the 1500s, the Spanish crown imposed another kind of license regime on the seas with the *asiento* or "station" system, licensing ships for the new Atlantic trade in kidnapped and enslaved Africans. With the *asiento*, as with the *cartaz*, coastal European governments established militarized monopolies on sea trade. In one case, licensing allowed for the Portuguese to skim profits from the trade in textiles and spices in Asia; and in another, the Spanish crown made profits from the trade in captive African peoples.[24]

A century later, in 1609, the Dutch legal scholar Hugo Grotius wrote a famous treatise, *The Freedom of the Seas*, opposing the creation of closed seas. In a fundamental contribution to early maritime and international law, Grotius insisted that the sea could not be owned as dominion, but ought to be recognized as a realm of free transit. Grotius was a legal consultant for the biggest colonial enterprise of the Netherlands, the Dutch East India Company. The main interest informing Grotius' work was not freedom for freedom's sake. In fact, he sought to justify the efforts of the fledgling Dutch Republic, and its biggest incorporated firm, the Dutch East India Company, to compete in the Indian Ocean arena then dominated by the Portuguese. European powers were struggling to rewrite, to their respective advantage, the laws governing naval travel. In a pattern that recurred for centuries, newcomers to the Indian Ocean trade argued for the "free seas," while the old claimants of dominion over that trade argued for "closed" ones. Eventually, the newcomers would start to exert possession over their own swathes of sea and coast.[25]

The composite acts of Portuguese seaborne colonialism established the *Carreira da Índia* (the India trade). The Portuguese presence in the Indian Ocean eventually came to be known as the *Estado de Índia*, the Portuguese Indian Ocean empire. By the mid 1500s, the *Nao de China* began – the Spanish seaborne trade with Asia.[26] Small ships such as caravels and large ones – carracks, cocas, and galleons – became the new merchant-shipping technologies of the 1500s.[27] One of the main sites of the new colonialism floated on water: the decks of mercenary vessels.[28]

Ship improvement was an increasingly lucrative investment opportunity out of which profit could be obtained. Trade relations began to extend farther, take place faster, and be more handily manipulated and controlled by the investors who stood to profit from the Asian trades.[29]

MARINE MILITARISM

By the 1500s, the western and central portions of the Eurasian continent were war-addled. Christian European kingdoms used warfare as a language of statecraft. The conclusion of the Hundred Years War in 1453, with its epicenter in French lands, led to new wars from the 1400s to 1600s: the Wars of the Roses that shredded the peace in England; the Habsburg–Valois Wars between the Spanish and French crowns on Italian soil; the Wars of Religion that unsettled German principalities in the 1500s; the Eighty Years War between the Netherlands and the Spanish Empire; and the regicidal English Civil War of the 1640s. These wars projected violence outwards into seaborne dealings.

Christianity wove together with militarism to promote state consolidation. European monarchs pursued the stations of their Christian cross not only for the indulgences of heaven, but also to expand the territorial and naval capacity of their states and to centralize their powers. The "re-conquest" (the *Reconquista*) by the Christian rulers of Castile and Aragon culminated in the War of Granada of 1482–92 against Iberian Muslims and Jews, defeating the Islamic court in the southern Iberian Peninsula. The "Inquisition" also unfolded at this time, as Ferdinand V of Aragon and Isabella I of Castile (r. 1474–1516), the "Catholic King and Queen," colluded with leaders of the Church to shore up the social order. At the same time, royal houses across continental Europe participated in a coordinated offensive of Christian courts against the expanding prowess of the Ottoman empire.[30] In 1571, an alliance of European crowns celebrated their military success at the battle of Lepanto on the borderlands between Austrian and Ottoman territories as a vindication of Christianity over Islam in the eastern Mediterranean.[31]

Intra-European warfare prompted the creation of the first great naval fleets of Europe, the Armadas of Spain and England, and the *tercios* of the

Spanish Habsburg empire – the first standing armies.[32] The Spanish Armada contained 130 ships in 1588, a gigantic assembly. And the Spanish *tercios* were huge, permanent, armed groups of up to 3,000 men each. Such weaponized formations were widely in place by the 1600s. Eventually, smaller and more agile standing military forces became the European norm. The rise of armed brotherhoods also led to an exportation of cultures of war beyond European principalities, in pursuit of colonial ventures in Africa, the Americas, and Asia.[33]

MISSIONS AND THE NEW COLONIALISM

Beginning again at the roots, we observe how, in addition to militias, official Christianity played an important role in the advance of the new colonialism. Initially organized through orders and fraternities of the Catholic Church, missionaries wielded a particular weapon of conquest alongside the sword: the lettered word. Spanish and Portuguese colonialism in the Caribbean and South America, on the one hand, and in Africa and Asia, on the other, was associated not only with mercenaries and entrepreneurs, but also with European keepers of the Christian Book, as well as the more mundane books of registration and governance produced by colonial rulers. In fact, there is nothing mundane about the power of language, whether it is the language of the people or of the lords. Societies across the earth see language as a vessel of the transcendent and the divine. And European missionaries believed that not only their own Latinate spoken tongues, but also their Roman alphabets and their sacred and profane books were vessels of moral and spiritual content: gifts of divine being for the colonial "savages."[34]

The first Christian missionaries, members of Catholic orders such as the Jesuits and Dominicans in the 1500s and 1600s, believed they were bringing knowledge about the Christian God to idolaters. And they also thought they were conferring an advanced form of language on savage peoples. Colonial missionaries were convinced not only of Christian salvation, but also of the superiority of European forms of linguistic expression.

The history of missionary encounters with the Indigenous people of South America contrasts with the scorched-earth approach to cultural interaction that characterized colonial settlement in North America, as we shall see in the next chapter. The Spanish recognized many Indigenous peoples as literate, and trained Indigenous elites in the Spanish language. They translated many Christian religious writings into Nahuatl and Quechua. They immediately brought Indigenous nobles into the priesthood, although relegating them to subordinate ranks. Priests and missionaries also taught many Indigenous peoples in their own mother tongues, now with hispanized alphabets. Spanish colonial scribes produced many manuscripts in Indigenous languages for Indigenous folk to read.[35]

Yet, Christian missionaries believed Indigenous cultures were less civilized than their own because they did not have the same kind of alphabetic writing. In fact, Indigenous cultures right across the Americas cultivated many ways of writing that combined glyphs and syllabics. On Abya Yala, on what came to be called America by the colonists, Native communities wrote about sacred and temporal matters using a variety of technologies. The Mayans, Mixtecs, and Aztecs wrote with glyphs, while the Inca wrote with *quipu*, colored cotton and woolen cords, spun and knotted in ways to record knowledge.[36] The forms of literacy among Native peoples differed from what developed in European culture, and oral cultures of storing and transferring knowledge also had a place of privilege.

Even as tropes of the "savage" and "wild" Native circulated, missionaries confronted and tarried with the on-the-ground complexity. For example, the Spanish Jesuit missionary José de Acosta (1539–1600) recognized that Indigenous peoples had their own civilization and political cultures, as documented in his *Natural and Moral History of the Indies* (1590). Nevertheless, he was still assured of his own cultural superiority. Acosta, who spent a long time in Peru, maintained that "no nation of Indians has been found to have the use of letters." While acknowledging that Indigenous peoples used other kinds of "signs, ciphers, and characters," he emphasized that they "lacked an alphabet."[37] This European missionary conception of the Indigenous lack of letters underpinned the commonplace European tropes about Indigenous peoples as "without history" and "wild." Spanish missionaries thus were not only endeavoring to turn souls towards their Christ, but, more centrally, they wished to impose their system of language onto other human systems.

Spanish missionaries, for many centuries, endeavored to plant the beneficent kernel of Castilian Spanish in the colonies and have it flourish on the tongues of Indigenous elites. By the 1600s, French, British, Dutch, Danish, Swedish, and German missionaries embarked on their own colonial campaigns. They saw themselves as planters of alphabetic seed. And by sowing their languages, missionaries, and the colonial states they represented, saw themselves as gift-givers, as opposed to thieves.[38] Here was a particular impairment of vision among European colonizers in the Americas: as they disavowed their own thieving practices, they saw only deficiency among their colonial Others.

Colonists in the Americas wielded words like weapons. The term *América Latina* emerged from the Creole community, among the European descendants of colonizers. Native communities, of course, had their own names for the continent: Tawantinsuju (among the Inca), Abya Yala (among the Guna), Anahuac (among the Mexica), A'nó:wara tsi kawè: (Turtle Island) among the Haudenosaunee people. The term "America" was an imposition by a German cartographer, Martin Waldseemüller. In 1507, he designated the new landmass after the name of an Italian seafarer, Amerigo Vespucci. Vespucci was a Florentine merchant and traveler who resettled in Castile and led his first maritime voyage to the coasts of northern Brazil in 1502. If Columbus believed that the shores he reached were the eastern climes of Asia, Vespucci corrected this view for European audiences and identified a new continent that lay between Europe and Asia. Amerigo Vespucci's name stuck. As Derek Walcott once wrote, in the eyes of the new colonizers "[all things] have only Christian names."[39] All these monikers, "Hispaniola," "West India," and "America" carry in their very usage the reverberations of centuries of colonialism. The "Americas" emerged as one of Europe's first racialized "Others," and as a vast domain in which Creole and settler Europeans continuously produced colonial value on advancing frontiers of war against Native peoples and ecologies.[40]

EXPANDING COMMODITY NETWORKS

Colonialism, at its core, involves taking possession of other peoples' wealth, and of the earth's geophysical bounty.[41] But more than this, by the turn of the 1500s, the new colonialism also involved taking possession of other people's sovereign domains in the pursuit of commodification. Cultural critic Macarena Gómez-Barris defines extractivism (*extractivismo*) in the Latin American context as "an economic system that engages in thefts, borrowings, and forced removals, violently reorganizing social life as well as the land by thieving resources from Indigenous and Afro-descendent territories."[42] Early extractive capitalism across the Spanish Americas converted silver, water, timber, and rubber into commodities for transoceanic markets. As happens so often in history, new economic impulses do not supplant old ones, but absorb them and direct them to new ends.

In the 1500s and 1600s, the Spanish and Portuguese crowns gave large land grants to colonizers in the Americas. These large manors were devoted to new ends: to industrious activity for emerging transoceanic production and distribution networks. Spanish colonial wealth and prestige were based both on the old economy of head taxes and on the new economy of mining, textile spinning, and sugarcane cultivation for transoceanic markets. Command over land and bonded laboring peoples combined with colonial capitalist production and the long-distance shipping trade. In other words, the economy in Spanish colonial America wedged aspects of old feudalism into new emerging capitalism.[43]

The Spanish and Portuguese crowns set up vast bureaucracies to administer this emerging capitalist system. Economists call this system "mercantilism," or the marriage between advancing commodification, on the one hand, and expanding state centralization, on the other. For example, the *Casa de Contratación de las Índias* (House of Trade of the Indies) was established in Seville in 1503, a couple of years after the formation of the *Casa da Índia e da Guiné* in 1501. Both of these institutions sought to manage the overseas trade of Spain and Portugal in the sixteenth century. All the metals brought back from the Spanish colonies, mostly gold in the first decades (1494–1525), and then mostly silver thereafter, had to pass through Seville. Known as the *quinta* system, the Spanish crown claimed one-fifth of all profits on trade. In both cases, the Portuguese and the Spanish sought to extract revenue from emerging colonial commerce by imposing monopolies and duties, just as they asserted monopolies on the sea trade across the Indian Ocean and the Atlantic with the *cartaz* and *asiento*.[44]

Spanish military men in the Americas set up new towns for settlement. These towns, laid out on a regular *traza* grid with a central plaza anchored by a church, served as transport hubs and centers of government. Spanish colonists often established their central squares on the most sacred land of the Natives – on their burial grounds or on the site of the Indigenous sovereign's seat. For example, the Spanish square in Port of Spain, Trinidad, was built on Taíno burial grounds; the main square in Mexico City, meanwhile, was built over the ceremonial center of the Aztec city of Tenochtitlan.

The *encomíenda* system was initially employed in order to organize the land claims of Spanish settlers, and to obtain the labor for silver mining. *Encomíendas* were "atomized towns," individual Indian communities assigned to conquistadors by the crown. The *encomíenda* system developed from the feudal idea that both people and land belonged to landlords.[45] The *encomíenda,* or "land trust," granted by the Spanish colonial state, gave Spanish settlers large tracts of land, along with control over up to 300 Indigenous persons each. The *encomendos,* or settler lords, had the right to impose a head tax and command the labor of Indigenous people. The *encomíenda* system was replaced by the *repartimiento* system, or tribute labor system, in 1542, in which Indigenous peoples were dispossessed in a different way and made into forced laborers who had to work for their masters without pay for specific periods of time. Indians were required to wear specific costumes as a means of surveillance. And the new hierarchies of Spanish administrators and local councils undermined Indigenous social structures.[46] Eventually, by the 1550s, the *hacienda* system was put in place. It foreshadowed the plantation system, in which workers were forcibly moved onto land enclaves and incarcerated. Enslaved Indigenous laborers could be bought and sold for a price.[47] Eventually, over the course of the 1600s, kidnapped Africans were brought onto the *haciendas* in large numbers.

The colonist, according to European legal traditions of "Natural Law," is said to lay claim to the land title in order to settle and cultivate it by the act of *inventio,* or discovery.[48] The Creole Spanish practiced *inventio,* or the forceful confiscation of other peoples' lands and bounties, in order to put it to their own use. In the Spanish colonial economy, land bounty was conceived in terms of the expanding transoceanic mercantile market. The Spanish extracted vast amounts of mineral and metallic wealth from their new colonies. Beginning with place mining, or the mining of riverbeds rich with gold sediment, Spanish colonists soon began a more industrial form of mining and extraction. Colonists operated mines using the labor of tens of thousands of enslaved Indigenous people. Rich deposits of silver were found in the city of Potosí in Bolivia in 1545 and at Zacatecas, in southern Mexico, in 1548. At Potosí, in particular, an immense deposit of silver under the mantle of a mountain would soon become the most important site of silver ore mining in the emerging capitalist world system.[49]

The Spanish colonized silver-rich Zacatecas in 1540 during the Mixtón War. They also established copper and diamond mines, interrupting the pre-existing economy. The Spanish empire soon became the world's leading silver producer. Over the coming decades, stocks of silver in Europe were doubled. A price revolution in Europe resulted from the influx of silver bullion from the mines of Potosí and Zacatecas.[50] As we shall see, up to the 1800s, most of this silver eventually ended up in Asia. The colonial system took possession of other peoples' lands, extracted resources, and shipped them to distant markets in order to fund new trading opportunities and new possibilities to profiteer.

Just as silver mines were exploited in Mexico and at Potosí, Japanese silver mining also expanded, exported from the port of Nagasaki. Japanese silver was long part of inter-Asian trade networks. The boom in Japanese silver production came in the 1500s in the context of rising demand for silver bullion from Europeans doing business across the Pacific. Portuguese and Spanish merchants purchased Japanese silver in the marts of coastal China, where they also bought silks, porcelain, and handicrafts.[51]

The explosion in silver production contributed to a rise in prices in Europe, as silver specie came to circulate on markets much more freely than ever before. Great amounts of silver coin were kept in circulation. Given the exploding demand, new technologies and labor regimes developed to increase the yield from colonial mines. Colonial metallurgists used mercury, or quicksilver, to refine metal more effectively. In the 1550s, the addition of mercury from Almadén, Spain, was first introduced to the refining process at Potosí and in southern Mexico.

A huge expansion in production resulted, allowing for the purification of residual silver from refuse ore.

Indigenous people supplied the technical know-how needed for this mining. And Indigenous chemistry was combined with expertise coming from central European metallurgists of the "ore mountains" of today's Hungary, Czech Republic, and northern Italy. A new world of enterprise came to village towns across the Andes and Sierra Madre mountain ranges through the physical digging up of metals, the colonial laboratories of metallurgy, the refining and minting houses, and the distribution networks across the oceans.

But the introduction of mercury and metal amalgamation into the production process also meant more intense labor conditions for enslaved Indigenous peoples in the mine pits. Mine owners forced workers more aggressively down the shafts. Workers then climbed up long ladders, carrying baskets of ore weighing three times their own bodyweight. Silver ore had to be arduously crushed, mixed, and soaked in the sun for weeks on end as part of the refining process. To find more labor reserves, colonial capitalists expanded the *mita* system, a regime of rotational compulsory work. By the 1560s, one-seventh of the total 91,000 eligible men aged 18 to 50 living in the area of the Potosí mines were put in bondage every year. Bondage lasted for a period of time before workers were relieved by replacement laborers from their home villages. When the *mitayos*, bonded mine laborers, moved to the mines, so too did women and children. The *mita* system forcibly displaced people from their homes, and the failure of *mitayos* families to return home devastated Native communities. It was not uncommon for workers to be worked to death on the "unending frontier" of the mine.[52] The notorious "man-eating mines" of Potosí caused the systematic depletion of Indigenous communities. Andean peoples responded with mass exodus and escape. The population of the areas surrounding Potosí plummeted by more than two-thirds in less than a hundred years, as people fled the control of the colonial *corregidores* (municipal administrators).[53] Yet sections of Indigenous society also became merchants and traders in the silver nexus. At Potosí, Indigenous merchants, called *qhateras*, played an important role in bringing silver to the oceanic markets, and were simultaneously embedded in transoceanic trade and in local cultures and technologies.[54]

GALLEONS

By incorporating Indigenous middle classes and subjecting Indigenous peasants to labor bondage, the Spanish economy produced great metallic bounty. European colonists used this proliferating bullion wealth to extend their dominance over new trade domains. Beginning in the last decades of the 1500s, Spanish American merchants sent coin directly to Asia in specially authorized galleon ships. A triangle of colonial trade emerged that linked Europe, Latin America, and sites across the Philippine archipelago, coastal China, and islands of the Pacific Ocean (see Figure 1.1).[55] For example, the trade route of the Galleon of Manila, also known as the Galleon of Acapulco, was in place from 1565, and continued until about 1825. Alexander von Humboldt, writing at the end of the galleon system, called it the trade in "silver and friars" with Asia.[56] Cargoes of silver were regularly sent from Acapulco, Mexico, to Manila, Philippines, and shipments of luxury Asian goods came in the other direction.

This created trading routes between Spanish America and what the Spanish initially called the "Islas del Poniente," or the Islands of the West. By the early 1600s, at least 100,000 kilograms of silver annually circulated through the port of Manila, with profit ratios of 300 to 400 percent on the transactions taking place there. Latin American mines, and the Indigenous enslaved people that manned them, became major sources of wealth used to leverage trade with China, India, and Persia. The Spanish in Mexico became the middlemen and merchants organizing trade between Manila and Lima. This trade provided an essential motor force for ongoing Spanish colonialism from the 1500s to the 1600s, precisely in the hard and mean centuries of European internal warfare.[57]

In 1542, Ruy López de Villalobos traveled with 1 galleon, 2 flat-bottomed boats, and 370 men, including several Augustinian priests, from Acapulco to the emporia of the South China Sea. After a two-month journey, he arrived at the shores of the island of Leyte in today's Philippines. De Villalobos, replicating a practice that was common among Spanish seaborne mercenaries, proceeded to name the whole archipelago according to his whim, calling it the "Philippine Islands" in honor of Prince Philip of Spain. Andres de Urdaneta successfully led the

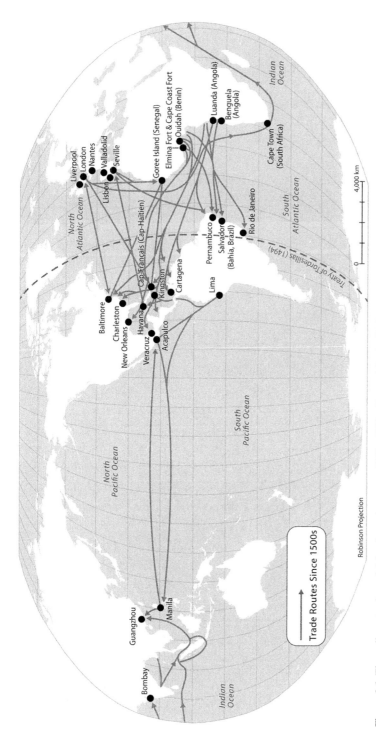

Figure 1.1 The galleon trade and Atlantic trade routes, 1500s–1800s. Created by the Tufts Data Lab: Carolyn Talmadge, Deirdre Schiff, Patrick Florance.

tornaviaje, or "return route home," from the Philippines to Mexico across the Pacific Ocean, as the galleon trade took shape.[58] In 1570, Spanish boats arrived at the ports on the island of Luzon, where they encountered the Islamic polity ruled by Raja Suleiman III, with its capital in Manila. The Spanish waged war, took violent possession of the beachhead, executed the Indigenous ruler and his family, and founded a settlement colony. As the mercenaries stepped off the boat with their war swords, Catholic priests disembarked too with their crosses, catechisms, and writing instruments to keep records for the Spanish crown. The sword was married with the baptismal font in the Spanish conquest of the Islamic kingdom of Manila.

As they settled around Manila, the Spanish encountered the fertile and densely populated areas of Pampanga and Bulacan. They engaged in their *inventio* by taking possession of territory, and waging bloody and devastating wars against Indigenous communities in Haganoy and Macabebe. Yet, Spanish incursions were confronted by an ongoing series of uprisings and acts of resistance by Native communities. In the first decades of Spanish colonialization, this included the Dagami, the Lakandula, the Pampanga, and the Magalat revolts. As would happen again and again in the history of colonialism, the Spanish killed off large segments of the Indigenous population (more than 300 people during the first sortie alone), and captured others in a program of pillage and plunder. By 1572, Indigenous towns in the area were assigned as *encomiendas*, and Native communities were forced to serve Spanish settler mercenaries.

The Pampangan people were employed in extracting timber to build ships. They were also conscripted by vigilantes and mercenaries into militias to advance the conquest of upland areas through raids and small wars.[59] The Spanish laid the foundations for a Transpacific slave trade between Manila and other Asian outposts, such as Guam, and the South American hubs of Acapulco and Mexico City. Enslaved laboring people from the Philippines, Guam, and coastal China were pressed into the urban economies of such cities as Mexico City from this early time, and came to be known locally as *Chinos*.[60]

Already by the 1590s, Manila served as a major Spanish colonial port city for the main trades in silk, spices, and silver. The Asian trade extended from other important port cities, including Zhangzhou,

Guangzhou, and Nagasaki. Again, here, Europeans sought to penetrate into rich trading environments that long pre-dated their arrival. But they did so now with the special powers provided by the silver of the Americas, mined by the labor of enslaved Quecha, Aymara, Ashanika, Aonikenk, Huarpe, Mapuche, Guarani, Caxcan, and Zacateco peoples. Two continents (Europe and the Americas) were linked in the production of Spanish colonial silver, and four continents, three oceans, and many seas were bound together by trades stimulated by the colonial silver spewing from the veins of Potosí.[61]

One of the largest and earliest trade diasporas of Europeans in Asia resided in the port city of Manila, linking markets in Europe, China, and South America at the time of Spanish colonial expansion.[62] The Spanish part of Manila was called *ciudad de Espagnoles*. Spanish settlers, especially from Mexico, devised a special body of law for themselves. On average, about 200 Spaniards came to Manila every year by the late 1500s. In the architectural design of the port city, the same kind of colonial square was used as in the Spanish colonies of South America, with rectilinear streets anchored by a cathedral at the center. The Spanish were not satisfied with being traders on the fringes of an Islamic, Tagalog-speaking people. Instead, they insisted on asserting the dominion of their Christian temporal and spiritual order. Spanish missionaries settled on the perimeters of the central square, just as their practice was in the colonial Americas. This placed them in a spatially intermediate position between the Spanish mercenaries and traders, on the one hand, and the locals, on the other. Missionaries facilitated the galleon trade through the cultural and interpretive services they provided across colonized territories in Asia. They were translators, surveyors, spies, administrators, judges, cultural diplomats, indoctrinators, and the keepers of ceremony.[63]

Manila became a bazaar for the Asia trade. As an emporium for the spice trade, it received shipments of cinnamon from Ceylon, pepper from Sumatra and Java, and cloves, nutmeg, and other spices from Malacca. Along with the spices, merchants in the city also traded in fine textiles: Persian silks, woolen carpets from Hormuz and Malabar, draperies and textiles from Bengal, balm and ivory from Cambodia; and perfumes, silks, woven velvets, gold-plated articles, embroideries, and porcelain from coastal China. Silk fabrics were in high demand: crêpes,

Figure 1.2 Capa pluvial bordado en seda. Cantón, China, eighteenth century. Used with permission of Museo Oriental, Valladolid.

taffetas, damasks, and brocades. The galleon trade also procured goods from Japan, such as lacquered furniture and silver vessels.[64]

The silk brocade garment depicted in Figure 1.2 is an artifact of the colonial galleon trade and the transoceanic social, economic, and cultural relations that it generated. It is a chasuble, a religious garment used by priests in the Roman Catholic mass. Spanish missionaries in Manila commissioned this garment from Chinese weavers. The production of this chasuble was predicated on war-making, conquest, settlement, and the subjection of Indigenous peoples in South America and Manila. What histories do you see woven into this fabric? Look closely. Histories of Tagalog shipbuilding and dock labor, Chinese artisan labor, and Indigenous American enslaved mining labor condense into its embroidery. Native Tagalog peoples were forced to work as shipbuilders, personal servants, and dockworkers for the galleons. Meanwhile, in Peru and Bolivia, a slave-labor regime extracted, refined, and minted the silver bullion. The chasuble makes visible an interwoven and transoceanic history of colonial violence and commodification.

These highly detailed embroideries took immense amounts of time to weave. An embroidered silk chasuble might take two Chinese artisans up to two years to finish. There are some 20,000 stitches in just 4 centimeters of such cloth.[65] New kinds of patterns and decorative elements were used in the garments commissioned by the galleon trade and paid for with silver from the Americas. Artisans mixed Chinese and European styles according to the tastes of the Spanish commissioners. The chasuble, for example, employs the "eternal knot," a Buddhist symbol, as well as the dramatic chrysanthemum flower pattern. But note, too, the ornamentation and embellishment prized by the Spanish Catholic buyers, in this case the Augustinians, such as the heart symbol, the cross, and the eagle. Overall, the decorations are meant to connote the grandeur and authority of Catholic authority, but with an opulent and ostentatious "Oriental" flair. The chasuble also bears witness to the history of Filipino colonial interpretations of Christianity and the ways it combined European and Native elements to create new cultural expressions. The Spanish could not have anticipated how Native Tagalog-speaking peoples would use Christianity in their own ways and to their own ends. The Filipino church became an important site of identity and cultural survival for colonized and creolized Filipino communities.[66]

Missionization, as we saw earlier with relation to the weaponry of words and letters, was an aggressive profession. By 1591, 79 Augustinians and 42 Franciscans resided in Manila and its environs, and they had baptized more than 6,000 Filipinos. By the middle of the 1600s, Manila had more than 42,000 inhabitants.[67] The number of missionaries expanded quickly, and as they grew they spread their sense of Christian cultural superiority. Priests and friars served as governors and judges for the Spanish colony, as they worked to assimilate the local society to Christian norms and to suppress local religious and cultural traditions. In this way, the chasuble captures the close entwinement between mercantile trade, capitalist penetration into the realm of production, and plunder, but also the history of Indigenous cultures of adaptation, resistance, and response.[68]

The chasuble allows us to reflect on the intertwined colonial histories that link the coast of Manila, Canton, Acapulco, Potosí, and Seville in a transoceanic complex of production, distribution, exchange, consumption, and social transformation. The emergence of this economic system, along with the cultural currents and countercurrents imbricated in it, comprised the new colonialism. Materials such as silver bullion, excavated by Indigenous peoples in South America, passed through the purses of the Spanish and ended up on the accounts of Chinese merchants. Meanwhile, textiles sewn by Chinese weavers traded by Spanish merchants and donned by Augustinian priests helped to spread religious teachings that the Indigenous would transform through their own practice. Colonialism is comprised of long chains of interrelation defined by asymmetry, inequality, violence, and the tangling of distant peoples, geographies, economies, and intelligences. The outcomes are always more than what could be anticipated.

CREOLIZATION AND RESPONSE

Spanish colonial rule unintentionally generated alchemical contact zones of cultural exchange, ethnic interweaving, and political innovation. European colonists, known as the *peninsulares* because they came from the western European peninsula of Spain and Portugal, became deeply interdependent upon Native communities and cultures for their knowledge, their labor, and their resilient ways of life. Peninsular European conquerors found themselves overcome by the forces of history that they themselves helped to unleash.

Colonialism engendered a complex new fabric of social hierarchies. The *peninsulares* brought with them the concept of *pureza de sangre*, or blood purity, importing particular ways of conceiving ethnicity and family ties.[69] In Spain, "blood purity" originally was employed by aristocratic Christian families to assert their purported lack of taint by Islamic or Jewish blood. When the concept migrated to the Americas, it was used by settler families to assert themselves as untarnished by Indigenous intermixing. Spanish people born in the Americas came to be known as *Criollo*, "Creole." The term signified proximity to European cultural values and family ties. But this new ethnic term also indicated a relationship to property. The *Criollo* benefited from the system of land tenure and taxation instituted by their European-descended colonial power. *Mestizo* and *Afromestizo* were other hierarchical ethnic terms for people within the colonial contact zone, demarcating family groups seen as tinged with Indigenous or African blood. A new ethnic discourse of Latin America was being engineered in the early 1500s through the *casta* (caste) hierarchy, as *Mestizo* differed from Creole, and Creole from peninsular, in a supposedly upward ascent of blood purity and civility. Latin American cultures developed a large variety of new words and hierarchies with which to classify persons along this blurred spectrum of ethnic bloodlines that spilled from colonial entanglements, including *Mulatto*, *Morisco*, *Chino*, and *Albarazado*.[70] An Atlantic system of colonialism and early capitalism produced new ways of conceiving social difference and human kinship.[71]

Resistance emerged as a permanent feature of the Spanish colonial contact zone. For example, despite the Spanish seizure of power of the Inca empire in the 1530s, armed Indigenous resistance continued for decades afterwards, up until – and beyond – the assassination of the Inca leader Tupác Amaru I in 1572. Resistance also went underground, breaking out again and again over time in pendular cycles of rebellion. In 1772, 200 years after the demise of Tupác Amaru I, in the context of the Spanish Bourbon Reforms that exacerbated the tax and labor burden on Native and *Mestizo* peoples, another great rebellion erupted – this time led by Tupác Amaru II, a distant descendant of the Inca king.[72]

The rebellion of the 1770s and 1780s in Peru took place centuries after the fall of the Inca court. Armed resistance spread to the towns and villages around Cuzco. Rebels executed colonial officials, abandoned Spanish mines, destroyed textile mills, opened jails, tore down gallows, and abolished taxes. This was a reiteration under new circumstances of the rebellious impulse first ignited in the 1530s. In the early twentieth century, the anti-extractivist Zapatista mobilizations in Mexican towns and villages reiterated Indigenous and peasant resistance within the context of nationalist movements of that time.[73] The decolonizing responses to colonial force do not die away – they recur. In this sense, colonialism warps history across decades, generations, and centuries not just because of the colonizers' actions, but also the resilient and irreverent strength of the colonized.

CHAPTER 2

Settlement

I N MARCH 1748, less than two generations after King Philip's War (1675–8), one of the bloodiest settler wars ever in North America, thirteen Native elders wrote to the governor of the English colony of Massachusetts. The petitioners were from Natick, one of the fourteen Praying Towns, or missionary towns, established in the 1600s about 20 miles south and west of Boston. Native Wampanoag peoples established homes in Natick, converted to Christianity, and survived by braiding themselves into and around the settlers' English legal and social regime. The Praying Town of Natick, which in the Wampanoag tongue means "the Place of Searching," was a town where Native peoples survived and endured as cultural and linguistic communities despite the warfare and coercion of Anglo-American settler society. Native peoples in Natick fashioned their survival through settler legal structures and through the settler religion of Puritan Christianity. For example, in the petition of 1748, the thirteen Natick signatories, all converts to Christianity, first identified themselves by their relationship to each other and their lands. They were the "Indian Inhabitants in the Parish of Natick." In the petition, they asked for their fishing rights to the nearby lake to be protected by the Massachusetts state. "Ponds have been a great advantage to us, and supplyed us with Fish of various Sorts, Especially with Ale-wives in plenty, whereby our families have been in a great measure Supported." Fishing, the petitioners said, was an "old and valuable liberty" of their community. The thirteen petitioners explained that this fishing site had been taken into "possession" by an English settler,

Ebenezer Felch, who had arrived in their town in 1723 and had "trespassed upon our said priviledges." They asked that the trespasser and his company "stop their proceeding and resign up to us" all the fishing sites that had been confiscated.[1]

Native peoples had fished on the banks of Lake Cochituate for hundreds and hundreds of years. Fishing for herring had deep cultural significance, and it was a material means for the community to nourish itself. At the time of writing, Natick was almost exclusively inhabited by Indigenous people. There were very few English settlers in the area. Those who arrived set about taking possession of Native lands, often using the apparatus of "legal" property law, but just as often resorting to warfare, trespass, and outright theft. Ongoing unrestricted warfare against Native communities was the condition for settler expansion. In this case, Ebenezer Felch's forceful confiscation of lands around Lake Cochituate and his attempt to exclude all Native peoples from their "old liberty" brought the petitioners to write together to the governor, asserting strength in numbers. Native peoples, confronted with the expansion of "New England," used the social order of settler English society, its language, and its religious systems, in a variety of ways in order to struggle for their own sovereignty and for the endurance of their families, languages, communities, and faiths.[2] Hundreds of Native petitions were written to the Massachusetts general court in the 1600s and 1700s. Natick was an especially active center of petition-writing. As Ojibwe historian Jean O'Brien notes, "Indians selectively adopted particular aspects of English culture in order to resist their complete effacement by an aggressive, expansive English presence."[3] Petitions are not documents of submission and deference, but records of "calculated compliance," and of the selective adaptations that the Indigenous deployed in order to resist the settler push for their eclipse. Resistance is not always armed and confrontational. Sometimes – indeed often – it is "low frequency," submerged, but persistent and permanent nonetheless.[4]

The early map of Natick in Figure 2.1 depicts the boundaries of the Praying Town, representing it as an isolated and abstract enclosure. The map, by Samuel Jones, is from 1716 and shows the parceled and subdivided manner in which English settlers imagined land, with demarcations

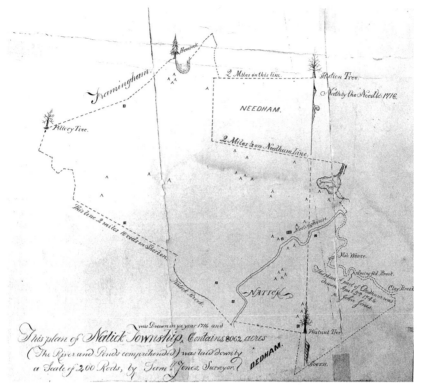

Figure 2.1 1716 Plan of Natick township. Natick Historical Society.

and divisions to specify ownership. The names of neighboring towns were listed on the other side of the dotted boundary lines: Framingham, Needham, Dedham. Certain natural points of orientation were put down by the surveyor: the pillory tree, the walnut tree, the meetinghouse. The enclosed settler colonial imagination of territory depicted in this property map sought to efface the land relations of the majority Native population of the time.

Consider that there is no representation of forests, hills, and places of Native dwelling. And furthermore, no indication is given of the large Lake Cochituate, just north of the "pillory tree." Hundreds of Native petitions focused on Lake Cochituate in order to protect usage rights. The multiple lobes of the lake take up a large portion of the area between the pillory tree and the hemlock tree. But, on this metes-and-bounds map, all that appears is empty space, or *terra nullius*. The claims of the thirteen Natick residents exceeded the terms of the settler map because they argued for durable patterns of Indigenous relations to land that were neither represented on the map nor respected by European settlers on the ground.

The garden-like cultivation of the White settler colonies, with their fenced-in plots and their rotating cropping practices, give the impression that the farm was a kind of moral calling, or a civic mandate, for Anglo-American settlers. Settlers pushed the frontiers of their garden plots deeper and deeper into Native lands across what came to be known as the United States of America and Canada, as well as Australia, southern Africa, New Zealand, and other settler colonies around the world. The demarcated settler plots of land property, with their crops and livestock, and associated with notions of duty and calling, came to characterize the institution of Anglo-Saxon settler colonialism from the 1600s up to our own time.

Settler gardening was reliant on "lawfare," or weaponized forms of legal writing.[5] Writing practices made up settler law: drafting documents, signing deeds, and making probate inventories of ownership to delineate how property would be inherited. This kind of writing worked to commodify lands in a variety of ways – to make land "alienable" and exchangeable on markets. Such writing separated the "ownership" of land from the "usufruct," or the usage, of land. By claiming to own enclosed portions of earth, settlers asserted that they could exclude anyone else from drawing benefit from or coming into any contact with that earth. These cognitive, legal, and ontological impositions on the being of the land had profound consequences for social relations and ecologies.[6]

Already in the 1620s, English settlements on the North American coast introduced general courts of oversight, based on English law, in order to regulate and legislate settler land transactions. The Massachusetts general court created a legal code with a set of statutes based roughly on English common law. English settlers considered land to be the primary source of wealth, as new ideas about the meaning of "property" took shape in the British Isles. Settlers wished to override established Native ways of living with the land on Turtle Island (the Haudenosaunee term for the "American" continent). Despite settler fascination with their own vaunted power to overwrite the sovereignty of Native societies, the fact remains that Native lifeways surpassed the intentions and technologies of colonial rule.

Settler colonial states seek to eliminate Natives through war and through cultural genocide.[7] Settlers imagine Indigenous people as "vanishing," standing on the edge of cultural extinction, and they see themselves as the replacements.[8] Settlers tried to disappear Native peoples from their social ecologies, and to make them into insubstantial apparitions and remnants of the past. We might think here of the prevalence of American sports teams that, even today, "play Indian" with their names and mascots. Or consider the large array of US military machinery that derogatorily carries names of Native nations. Still today, military personnel refer to operational areas, from the Philippines to Iraq, as "Indian Country."[9] As Chickasaw scholar, Jodi Byrd, observes, the US military empire propagates itself through the "production of a paradigmatic Indianness" in its many, and emerging, war frontiers around the world.[10] The visibility of tropes of Indigeneity in settler societies, alongside the compulsive insistence on Indian extinction, suggests, writes historian Patrick Wolfe, that "the native repressed continues to structure settler colonial society."[11]

This settler ambivalence and anxiety about the supposed extinction of Native peoples and cultures, and about the ability of settlers to stand in as "new natives," generates a particular mode of racializing Indigenous persons. I use racialization to name the ways that colonialism creates differential vulnerabilities to premature death among disparate social groups. The racialization of Indigenous communities operates through ongoing settler practices of genocide, and by settler attempts to disguise their genocidal violence as acts of national creation.

As historian Jean O'Brien explains, the coming of settler societies in the Americas went along with the continuous and compulsive reassertion of settler "firsting": compulsive storytelling by Anglo-Saxon settlers about how they were in fact the "first" civilizing inhabitants of the land.[12] Yet, Natives continuously assert themselves beyond and outside this mythic story of settler pioneers. Native peoples stand in the "third space of sovereignty," as historian Kevin Bruyneel puts it, neither "inside" nor "outside" of settler nation-states. Settler law claims to define what exists, including what is *real* estate. Native cultures, on the other hand, continue to assert their authority in time and geography in contradiction to the enclosures of settler writing and settler maps.[13] Seneca scholar Mashuana Goeman has shown the many ways in which Indigenous people today continue to "reclaim" and "remap" their geographies and their bodies in order to sustain vibrant Native futures.[14]

SETTLER ARRIVALS

The Christian Reformation and civil wars swept across European polities in the 1500s and 1600s. The first settler colonial enclaves in North America date to precisely these times. British seafarers set up a colony in 1585 at Roanoke in today's Virginia, and at Jamestown in 1607. There they encountered the polities of the Roanoc and Powhatan peoples. These English settlements aimed to profit from trade with Native communities in coastal north America.

Back in England, the decades at the beginning of the 1600s were marked by intense social strife. As with the preceding "dark" European century of the 1500s, life was mean and often short because of religious wars, pitiable epidemics, and widespread food shortages. The conditions led Thomas Hobbes to publish *Leviathan* in 1651, a book that represented the "natural state" of society as a war of "all against all."[15] Society, seen through Hobbes' jaundiced eye, was a condition of *homo homini lupus* – in which people act as "wolves" to other people. The rule of James I of England and VI of Scotland, beginning in 1603, was marked by simmering instability and disharmony among different religious confessions, Irish Catholic, English Anglican, Puritan, and Scottish Presbyterian, but also by different visions of how a king should rule. James' son, Charles I, confronted the emerging strength of the mercantile and business classes as they opposed the "tyranny" of the court. Charles was eventually deposed from the throne and beheaded in 1649.[16]

It was precisely in these decades of English civil war that the first permanent settler colonies were established in today's Plymouth, Boston, and Baltimore. During the 1630s, English Puritans migrated in great numbers to the North American East Coast, over 21,000 colonists arriving in the bay of the Massachusett people during that decade alone. The spirit of religious dissent, and a desire for space and for respite from political disarray, brought these settler colonists to North America from England and Scotland. The British Isles were resource-limited, disease-ridden, war-torn, and mired in religious strife.[17] The irony was that the pursuit of settler peace required the ongoing waging of colonial war against Natives. This dichotomy is an abiding characteristic of the processes that started to unfold centuries ago, and that still reverberate today.

The Three Fires Confederacy of the Anishinaabe, the Ojibwe, the Chippewa, the Ottawa, and the Potawatomi peoples encountered these arriving settlers on the lands eventually renamed "New England" and "New Netherlands." The colonial motivations of the early English settlers related to the moral and spiritual realms as much as to the political and economic ones. In this view, colonists in New England were refugees from religious persecution in England. Yet, they also set out to impose their own moral and spiritual tenets on the Native polities they encountered.

Settler societies simultaneously sought to vanquish the Natives while also seeking to appropriate and absorb their presence into settler daily life. English settlers inscribed the names of sovereign Native peoples into their own everyday terminologies. Places were named Massachusetts, Ottawa, and Chicago (all words from Indigenous lexicons). Native words for plants and animals, such as *pecan* (pegan), *squash* (isquoutersquash), and caribou, were taken over by settlers and made their own. And Anglo-American settlers in New England would call themselves "Red Men" when they rose up against the British empire during the revolutionary wars of the 1770s.[18]

The lands of Native people were seen by settlers as blank and empty, and waiting to be penetrated and occupied. The colonist and land-grabber John Winthrop, governor of the Colony of Massachusetts for periods between 1630 and 1648, told himself and his settler constituency that he was creating a new outpost for human civilization amidst "waste-lands" and within what he called the *vacuum domicilium*, or the "vacuum of inhabitation."[19] This "vacuum" supposedly awaited the technology, knowledge, science, and pioneering agency of European men and their "incorporated wives."[20]

The societal visions of the New England settlements were thus predicated on extermination. Settler moral and political philosophy had an annihilationist bent. One of the most respected early New England Puritan ministers, Cotton Mather (1663–1728), called all Native peoples "the veriest Ruines of Mankind." Settler language about Indigenous peoples was racial language, reducing Natives to enemy beings that settlers were justified in eliminating. "The New-Englanders are a People of God settled in those, which were once the Devil's Territories," wrote Mather in his *Wonders of the Invisible World* (1693).[21] The settler colonial logic of elimination and replacement encoded Christian theological but also genocidal visions of dispelling demons and establishing the city of God.

LAND AS PROPERTY

For legal experts, the justification for settler colonial elimination was not expressed in terms of demon-slaying, but rather as the taking possession of "vacant" lands. John Locke (1632–1704) was one of the main English theorists of settler colonial political economy and property law. In 1689 he published his *Second Treatise on Government* in London, just a decade after one of the bloodiest settler wars against Native peoples in New England, what Increase Mather had called the "war with the Indians." Locke proposed in his *Treatise* that the purpose of the state is to preserve and protect the "lives, liberties, and estates" of its subjects (paragraph 123). At the core of this pursuit was the logic of possession.[22] And Locke further theorized that European men could claim ownership of the land into which they poured their labor:

> It is labour, then, which puts the greatest part of value upon land, without which it would scarcely be worth anything; it is to that we owe the greatest part of all its useful products; for all that the straw, bran, bread, of that acre of wheat, is more worth than the product of an acre of as good land which lies waste is all the effect of labour. For it is not barely the ploughman's pains, the reaper's and thresher's toil, and the baker's sweat, is to be counted into the bread we eat; the labour of those who broke the oxen,

who digged and wrought the iron and stones, who felled and framed the timber employed about the plough, mill, oven, or any other utensils, which are a vast number, requisite to this corn, from its sowing to its being made bread, must all be charged on the account of labour, and received as an effect of that; Nature and the earth furnished only the almost worthless materials as in themselves.

John Locke, *Second Treatise of Government*, paragraph 43

John Locke, as one of the clearest-voiced English philosophers of his time, captured the moral commitments of his society in this formulation. According to him, the value of land is defined by what it produces for industry through the labor of its cultivator. And the role of the state is to protect the uncontestable rights of those who create marketable profit from the land. We note in Locke's thought how deeply the mercantile principle had penetrated into the realm of productive activity for the English. Value itself was impossible to imagine separate from a long chain of instrumental commodities traded on markets for the benefit of property owners. For the English settlers, the land was an inert object that merely received the labor of the cultivator. It could be commodified by the laws of possession, organized according to the laws of entail, land title, and probate.

This contrasted with Indigenous notions of value, which were rooted in moral commitments to interdependence, shared usage, and the communication between different kinds of living beings. For the Native peoples of Turtle Island, the earth was Mother, and sweet-grass was her hair. The fish and animals were kin, and humans were bound by relationships of reciprocity and inter-species responsibility. The land, for Ojibwe Indigenous peoples, was called Abenaki, "our land," or "the land where the sun was born every day." As Jean O'Brien writes, ideas held by Native people about the social order "were intimately connected to ... working out Indian ways of belonging to the land."[23]

In the commodifying view of Locke, the precinct of human consciousness stood over and above the supposedly inert material world and the subjugated animal world. And humans engaged with the material world instrumentally. This way of thinking of everything that exists as something to be owned, and available for sale and purchase on markets, provided an existential justification for settler colonial war. Settlers claimed they could take over lands and bring them into their market matrix. This justification of the plunder of other peoples' lands, but also other peoples' bodies, through appeals to *industry* would return over and over again in European political economy, from Locke, to Francis Hutcheson, to Adam Smith, to the pages of today's *Wall Street Journal.* Settler colonialism, like the new colonialism more generally, was sparked by what we might call the imperative to commodify the earth.

PITILESS WARS

British settlers waged pitiless wars of extermination against Native communities from the outset. The Pequot War (1636–8) and the massive scale of militia mobilization during King Philip's War (1675–8) meant that Native peoples recognized settler societies as vortexes of unexampled and heretofore unimaginable violence. During the Pequot War, the Connecticut militia unleashed a ruthless and genocidal killing spree against Indigenous peoples. The colonists sent a number of the Native war prisoners to Bermuda plantations to be sold into slavery. Later on, Wampanoag people, captured by the settlers during subsequent colonial wars, were regularly sent by ship to the plantation colonies in Barbados and Jamaica.[24]

In 1675, Wampanoag people under their leader, Metacomet (1638–76), rebelled against the oppressive settler regime of Plymouth Colony. Metacomet came to power in 1662. He grew up in the time of settler consolidation of new colonies and the expansion of the Praying Towns. Metacomet understood the danger posed by the English settlers as they imposed their exclusive systems of law, religion, and society. Settlers responded with extreme punitive force. The Mohigan leader, Owaneko, called it "the war with the general nations of the Indians."

Metacomet planned counterassaults on settler enclosures. English colonists, learning of Metacomet's plans, hanged three of his lieutenants on Boston Commons in 1675. In response, Metacomet and his allies launched an assault on colonial towns across the region. The colonies of Plymouth and Massachusetts combined in maneuvers to "reduce the natives to order." A fourteen-month attack on Native peoples ensued, and the number of Natives in New England decreased from a quarter of total inhabitants to one-tenth. In addition to the acts of killing, colonists honed techniques of detainment and removal. In 1677, in an effort to contain the Native population, the general court of Massachusetts directed all Indians "not owned as a slave by a planter" to be confined to one of four town reservations: Natick, Pancapoag, Wamesit, or Hassa-namasett. This was a genocidal war – a war of extermination – waged by the English settlers against Native combatants and noncombatants alike; even Native children were not spared. The war claimed more casualties per capita than any other direct conflict on American soil over the following 300 years.[25]

LAWFARE

The law itself is a weapon in the hands of the powerful. Native dispossession took place not by weapons alone, but also by the use of courts. Law, with its assertion of jurisdiction and procedure, worked to deceive: to stabilize and legitimize the regime of Native elimination and removal. Warfare went along with "lawfare."[26] Credit and debt relations, and land speculation and mortgaging, became mechanisms of Anglo-American ascendance in the settler colony. The colonial state, as well as individual settler colonists, used land as a commodity that could be used to discharge debt. For example, in 1636 the Confederation Commissioners of Connecticut issued an ultimatum to the Narragansett sachems (or Native chiefs) requiring them to pay a large amount of *wampum* (cylindrical strings of beads, fashioned by Natives, holding ceremonial, cultural, and exchange value), or else to offer a large amount of their lands as security on outstanding loans. If the sachems defaulted on their payments, the Connecticut creditors thus had the right to foreclose on those lands. Settlers created and fomented the conditions of indebtedness in order to dispossess Native peoples from their lands "by degree."[27]

The mortgage was an important new technology used by settlers for appropriation.[28] Mortgages alienated land from Native peoples and placed the title to this land in the hands of settler speculators.[29] The mortgage defined land as a commodity that could be traded on a market, and thus separated it from its cultural meaning and from traditions of shared usage. The mortgage made the titles to enclosed lands into something that could accumulate in the hands of a few capitalists.

Back in England, common law at this time (the mid 1600s) still prevented creditors from taking possession of land in order to recuperate debts. Under English common law, defaulting on a mortgage would *not* lead to losing one's title to land. Creditors could lay claim to the personal property or income of a debtor, or assume tenancy rights, or send debtors to prison – but they could not take away a debtor's property right to their land. Predatory lending developed first in the American colonies, and was tied up with a racializing colonial project that subjected Native people to forced removal and dispossession so that settlers could secure their "life, liberty, and estates."[30]

In western Europe, the enclosure movement began in the sixteenth century, leading eventually to the severe restriction of unenclosed common lands by the nineteenth century. This enclosure of the commons is the story of capitalist principles penetrating into customary land tenure arrangements. Enclosure in England was a long-term project, supported by the state, to curb rentierism and feudal dependency, and to support the interests of the emerging new agricultural capitalists and urban bourgeoisie. In France, by the 1770s, physiocrats such as François Quesnay (1694–1774) promoted ideas about the rationalized and orderly management of privatized land by yeoman capitalists and scientific experts. The project of making agriculture more lucrative went hand in hand with visions of making land more marketable, and landless peasants more industrious and more "civilized." In Europe, it took a long time for the enclosure process to unfold. And the efforts to abolish the decaying feudal tithe and to salvage all land from customary relations continued in western Europe all the way up to the 1930s.[31] Imposing land enclosure in the colonies, by contrast, took place at shotgun speed and on a monstrous scale.

For example, between 1658 and 1660, Humphrey Atherton (1608–61), a member of the Massachusetts militia, foreclosed, along with his syndicate, on the entire Narragansett country (in today's Rhode Island), approximately 37 square miles – more than 1.5 times the size of all of Manhattan Island. Natives were eventually forced to leave the valley, and the remaining lands were claimed by settlers.[32] Meanwhile,

William Pynchon, of Springfield, a fur trader and land speculator, became a creditor to one of the local Indigenous leaders, Umpachela, the sachem of Norwottock. In 1660, Umpachela discharged a debt of £75 to William Pynchon's son, John, by handing over a deed for land. And the predatory lender, John Pynchon, subsequently used the land in order to establish the town of West Hadley. The settlers then pressured Umpachela to sell further lands to settle further debts. He was left with ownership and usage rights to only 5 acres of land in the end. And many other New England towns were formed in precisely the same way, including Northampton, Westfield, Deerfield, Suffield, Brookfield, Enfield, and Northfields, in a process of Native dispossession.

But this does not mean that Native peoples were passive bystanders during the storms of settler land dispossession. Even as colonial lawfare forced Native peoples to surrender their lands to settlers, the very performance of Native land conveyance often re-inscribed Native memory, knowledge, geographies, and sovereign identity onto official English documents. Native peoples preserved and created their own long-lasting oral records of what pre-dated and endured the incisions of colonial law. For example, in 1683, the Wampanoag sachem on the island of current-day Martha's Vineyard, off the coast of Massachusetts, enacted rituals of sovereignty even as she signed lands over to the English settler colonist David Okes in order to settle debts. As Stephanie Fitzgerald's work shows, Queen Wunnatuckquannum is recorded as using "emphaticall speech" while signing the deeds. Furthermore, the documents she signed were not written in English, but in the Massachusett language, alphabetized with English letters. The queen signed the deed, "I am Wunnatuckquannum, this is my hand (X)." We can almost hear her pronouncements as she authenticated the written document. Her action, which resulted in the dispossession of her people on one level, was simultaneously performed as a proud act of personal and community sovereignty on another.

This scene of land conveyance from the Wampanoag queen to David Okes would have included the two signatories, the scribes, and an English magistrate, as well as a group called the "rememberers" – Native witnesses who were responsible for memorizing the agreement and recalling its terms orally. Native rememberers already held a deep oral repository of Wampanoag social memories, and they added records of the queen's actions to their store, passing it down to their kin through generations. Native peoples not only devised performances of sovereignty and continuity within the imposed structures of settler law (such as vernacular writing and speech-making), but also recorded their own oral histories of these events in the living archives of the community rememberers, which are still spoken and remembered today. Indigenous knowledge archives, recorded in Native ritual performances and oral traditions of Martha's Vineyard, are in many ways more alive and more persistent than the dead letters of the settlers' seventeenth-century deeds.[33]

PRAYING TOWNS

New England colonists in the 1600s imposed laws, created courts and jails, and waged wars.[34] And they also missionized. One of the most influential early missionaries was John Eliot of Boston (1604–90). He set up what he called Praying Towns to resettle and sequester Native people, the more successfully to convert them to the religious and moral system of Puritan Christianity.[35] John Eliot was the leading missionary of the interior of Massachusetts, while Experience Mayhew led the missions on the coastal areas. Eliot's Praying Towns for Indians provided the prototype for policies of removal and detention that settler states would reiteratively enact over the course of centuries, in such places as the United States, Canada, Argentina, South Africa, British India, Australia, New Zealand, and Israel–Palestine.[36]

Fourteen Praying Towns were established in New England between 1646 and 1675, initially under the guidance of Eliot. Towns included Natick, Punkapoag, Hassanamessit, and Wamesit in the colony of Massachusetts. These towns represented, as Jean O'Brien notes, a "conjuncture between ideology (English Calvinism) and a particular, mapped, place."[37] Indians were resettled in these towns from surrounding areas, where they engaged in smallhold farming, imbibed "English" ideas about domesticity, orderliness, industriousness, and civility, and listened to recitations from the "Eliot bible" – the first bible printed in colonial America, translated into the Wampanoag language as *Mamusse*

Wunneetupanatamwe Up-Biblum God (1661). Puritans believed themselves to be justified, or even ennobled, by their own virtue and discipline for work. Puritan ministers and missionaries offered Wampanoag, Massachusett, Nipmuc, and Pennacook Indians the legal protections of the settler society, only if they converted to Christianity and accepted their place in the settler colonial world.[38]

Illness and epidemics brought by Europeans decimated Native peoples. In fact, when studying Native grave sites archeologists today use the telltale marks left by syphilis infection on skeletal remains as an indication of contact with European settlers. Many early modern European migrating bodies carried syphilis. And because it took a decade or longer for the syphilitic symptoms of dementia and paralysis to manifest themselves, the disease spread quickly in colonial contact zones. Already by 1619 on Turtle Island, the diseases brought by settlers wrought devastation.[39]

In the context of trying to figure out how to avoid such illnesses as smallpox and syphilis brought by the settlers from England, many Native peoples began to think that praying to the European God alongside their own Indigenous spirits might help stave off killer diseases. Praying Towns also offered physical safety from the rampant warfare wrought by settlers on Native peoples across the region. In other words, conversion to Christianity was more about maintaining and preserving Native kinship ties and lifeways than it was a turn away from a beloved Native community. The Christian religion even became a container to protect Native cultural transmission.

The relationship of settlers to Natives was not just a binary opposition of oppressor to oppressed. The colonial contact zone was marked by internal contestation and interdependence. For example, John Eliot depended on Native experts. The so-called Eliot bible of 1661 was the result of hundreds of hours of translation from English to Wampanoag, and print-setting, by the young Native scholars James Printer and Caleb Cheeshateaumuck at the Harvard Indian College.[40] Native scholars interpreted the biblical text, chose the best way to translate the concepts for their kinfolk, and worked the presses until late at night to produce the massive tomes. And it was through the families of the Natives living in the Praying Towns that these translations were disseminated.

Consider the example of this Natick "Praying Indian" preacher's desk (Figures 2.2–4), created sometime in the late 1600s. This pulpit desk was

Figure 2.2 Natick "Praying Indian" preacher's desk. Late 1600s. Natick Historical Society.

Figure 2.3 Detail of "Praying Indian" preacher's desk. Late 1600s. Natick Historical Society.

Figure 2.4 Detail of "Praying Indian" preacher's desk. Late 1600s. Natick Historical Society.

fashioned for the Reverend Daniel Takawamphait by two Algonquin woodworkers. Takawamphait was the first Native Puritan minister, and headed the Natick church after John Eliot's death. Recall that Natick was almost entirely inhabited by Native people at this time. Notice the many ways that the desk encodes the traditions and lifeways of the Native community. In Native rearticulations of Christianity, we perceive the moral world, the sentiments, and the political strategies of the colonized shining through. The front of the desk follows Early American Style, with its linear grooving, its compact size, its regular, rectangular shape, and its three-part division. Yet, around the side and on the back of the desk – those parts that would be seen by parishioners – the artisans have added unexpected touches that speak to Native heritage and tradition. A deerskin motif surrounds the sides, creating the impression of a desk wrapped in hide. And the feet of the desk are carefully carved to resemble deer hooves, adding an audacious twist of decoration. Soft deerskin was the most common material used for Wampanoag and Nipmuc clothing. And so here Takawamphait's podium is enveloped in Native lifeways.

At another level, this desk, especially as it is mounted on deer legs, suggests something about the living relationship to animal beings and to nature according to the Native community. From this desk, Takawamphait would have read from the Wampanoag bible and delivered sermons to the Native congregants. Indians in Natick preserved their cultural ways through Puritan Christianity itself, but not without friction and the ongoing presence of settler colonial domination equally apparent in this object. Like a palimpsest, the podium serves as a symbol of how church gatherings in Praying Towns betokened both the aggressive attempts to eliminate Native peoples and their cultures, and the means by which colonized peoples insisted on what Anishinaabe author Gerald Vizenor called "survivance," the sharing of community, and the making of futures together. Indigenous people preserve their sense of kinship and belonging, and their connection with their lifeways within the colonial zone. The desk requires us to see with what we defined earlier as parallax, or multiplied vision, not so as to minimize the annihilationist thrust of settler colonialism, but so as to also perceive the structures of decolonial reclamation and resistance that also exist.

REMOVALS

The United States of America was a territorially expansionist entity from its inception. Earlier, we considered the warfare against Native communities during the establishment of the Thirteen Colonies in the 1600s. Another phase of settler war came in the context of the American Revolutionary War in the 1770s. And warfare against Natives would be repeated in the nineteenth century as the USA expanded across the continent and, eventually, across overseas colonial domains. Settler war against Natives was not an occasional recurrence but a permanently pendular condition. Patrick Wolfe famously wrote that settler colonization was a structure, not an event. "Elimination is an organizing principle of settler society, rather than a one-off (and superseded) occurrence."[41]

In the 1760s, as White Americans in New England organized themselves into "Red Men" fraternities in their preparation for insurrection against British rule, Whites in upper New York State simultaneously attacked Haudenosaunee communities, displacing them westward from the Finger Lakes towards Lake Erie. The Sullivan Campaign of 1779, ordered by George Washington, ransacked American Indian settlements in a scorched-earth campaign that forced the migration of Native refugees to Buffalo Creek, a watershed on the edge of Lake Erie. Under the pressure of settler land speculators, the Native community would eventually disperse in the 1840s from Buffalo Creek in different directions – northward to Canada and southwestward to Wisconsin and Oklahoma. The logic of settler colonial racialization is clear: the ongoing settlement of Whites was predicated on the ongoing sequestration, forced migration, and dislocation of Natives.

As Tuscarora historian Alyssa Mt. Pleasant shows, even in this context of disruption and forced displacement, the Haudenosaunee were always "recalling, re-establishing, and maintaining their relationship" of belonging to their lands.[42] Fundamentally, they did this through practices of kinship. Even in diaspora, they maintained extensive affiliations with brothers and sisters, and elders and youths, that went beyond the immediate family. The Haudenosaunee re-established relationships with the land by using place-names with spiritual and historical significance, imbuing their surroundings with layers of storytelling.[43] And Natives also fashioned diplomatic relations among different tribes, creating a multinational political confederation among the various dispossessed and relocated communities of the Onondagas, Mahicans, Delawares and Haudenosaunee. Where settler war sought to break asunder Native peoples' relations to the land and to each other, Native resistance unfolded through the refashioning of relation to kin, earth, and political confederacy.

The Louisiana Purchase of 1803, when the United States of America obtained today's Louisiana and Florida from the French, was a step in what would eventually become the American push westward. This time, President Jefferson, who negotiated the Purchase, combined his expansionist objective with the intention of removing Native nations from their lands to areas west of the Mississippi. The Cherokee, Chickasaw, Choctaw, Creek, and Seminole contended with the "sharp knives" of advancing settlers organized by the US settler state.[44]

The Cherokee homelands lie along the southern Appalachian highlands in today's Georgia. The Cherokee people, historically cultivators, spread their corn fields across the alluvial valleys. They dwelt in small autonomous settlements around the larger mother-town of Kituwah. For a long time leading up to the removals of the early 1800s, the Cherokee people faced pressure to negotiate with settlers. In fact, from the first decades of the 1700s, Cherokees had interacted with the Anglo-American settler migrants, signed treaties with them, and negotiated land settlement arrangements. The Cherokee aided British colonists in their battle with the French during the Seven Years War (1756–63). And it is also important to note that the Cherokee people held enslaved Africans and participated in the British slave trade from the 1700s on. The holding of enslaved Africans was considered a marker of status within the racial order imposed by Anglo-European settlers. But even as wealthy and middle-class Cherokee families asserted their status by the oppression of Blacks, these same Native families were simultaneously held at a distance from White settler society and subordinated within it. Historian Tiya Miles point to the "slanted narratives" of Cherokee slave ownership, characterized by servitude and oppression, on the one hand, but also by the creation of braided Native-Black families and political affiliations, on the other.[45]

Already in the 1770s, settlers, traders, and speculators were forcing Native peoples to cede their lands in order to pay back debts, perpetuating the practice of lawfare that began in the Northern colonies. In the 1790s, the US government sent delegations of missionaries into Cherokee communities to promote Anglo-Saxon cultural norms and so-called "civility." At the turn of the nineteenth century, hundreds of White settlers began pouring into Georgia and westward to the Mississippi River Delta in order to begin cotton plantations. Planters from Georgia, but also from across Alabama, Florida, Mississippi, North Carolina, and Tennessee, formed an alliance for the total removal of the Choctaw and the Cherokee.

Settler Whites confiscated the rich alluvial soil of the Cherokee homelands for industrial cotton cultivation by chain gangs of enslaved Africans. This was the period of the opening up of the plantation economy of the Deep South to feed the hungry textile factories in the Northern states, as well as in Britain.[46] Through Native dispossession, the plantation complex spread into the Southwest – a process that would continue for the duration of the nineteenth century and into the twentieth century. As the scholar Ronald Takaki once observed, "in order to make way for White settlement and the expansion of both cotton cultivation and the market, 70,000 Natives were uprooted and moved from their lands, and 100,000s of Blacks were moved into the Southwest to work the soil as slaves." These displacements were building blocks for the construction of the "Cotton Kingdom" of the nineteenth-century American Deep South.

In 1831, the French political writer Alexis de Tocqueville described a scene from the removals that brings home the level of trauma raining down on the Choctaw people:

> [The Choctaws] left their country, and were endeavoring to gain the right bank of the Mississippi, where they hoped to find an asylum which had been promised them by the American government. It was then the middle of winter, and the cold was unusually severe; the snow had frozen hard upon the ground, and the river was drifting huge masses of ice. The Indians had their families with them; and they brought in their train the wounded and sick, with children newly born, and old men upon the verge of death. . . . The Indians had all stepped into the bark which was to carry them across, but their dogs remained upon the bank. As soon as the animals perceived that their masters were finally leaving the shore, they set up a dismal howl, and, plunging all together into the icy waters of the Mississippi, they swam after the boat.[47]

The plaintive cry of the dogs and their dashing into the icy water provide a powerful trace of the toll of settler warfare at the most intimate level of Native life. American settler colonialism transformed Native peoples into refugees and asylum seekers in Indian Country. In 1831, the Supreme Court's decision in *Cherokee vs. Georgia* codified this racialized condition into American law. Chief Justice John Marshall designated Native communities as "domestic dependent nations." The USA, having violently made Natives into refugees, had no obligation to deal with Native nations according to the precepts of international law, but domestic law. Enacting a kind of settler "God complex," Chief Justice Marshall implied that the US government both giveth and taketh away. Having taken away recognition of the sovereignty of Native nations, the government would give Native communities the status of "wards." "The

[Indians]," Marshall wrote in the decision, "are in a state of pupilage; their relation to the United States resembles that of a ward to his guardian."[48]

And in order to make removals work, the US government made treaties with other Native nations, such as the Osage and other Plains Indians, as settlers sought to re-engineer Indian Country to their own liking and to serve their own ends. Settler expansionary violence swelled up again in the 1860s in Navajo Country, Sioux Country, Cheyenne Country, Ute Country, and, in the 1870s, in Apachee Country and Dine Country during the ongoing Westward Expansion.[49] This amounted to a massive population re-engineering program run by the US government to benefit the needs of White migrants through the widespread exercise of genocidal violence against Natives.

DIVIDING BY BLOOD QUANTUM

The US government adopted new strategies to subdivide and remove Native peoples in the later nineteenth century. The Government policing of the "blood purity" of individuals operated with a different logic from the *pureza de sangre* regime of the Spanish Americas that we encountered in the previous chapter. The Dawes Act of 1887 sought to degrade collective ownership within tribes, breaking up tribal lands into individual units of private property. With the Dawes Act, the US government's Bureau of Indian Affairs began to "scientifically calculate" the quantum, or amount, of Indian blood among members of Native communities, supposedly based on documentation of family relations. A Native person's right to an allotment of land – their parcel of private property – would be determined by the settler colonial state's calculations of Indian blood quanta. This devastating bureaucratic surveillance system atomized Native bodies in the attempt to tear the heart out of Native communities.

In this time of proliferating surveillance, bureaucracies assigned colonial "passports" and "identity tickets" to monitor individuals from racialized communities. Blacks on plantations were issued identity tickets; and Asians entering labor indentureship were given passports, while White Americans received passports only in 1941. Native people, too, were atomized, as they were issued a kind of passport recorded in blood. Dawes Act commissioners claimed to be able to identify Natives as "mixed blood," "full blood," or "half-breed." If "mixed blood," the state said it could determine whether Indigenous persons were "one-quarter blood quantum," "one-eighth blood quantum," or "one-sixteenth blood quantum." Blood quantum determined which Natives could "qualify" as Chippewa, or Cheyenne, or Apache, or Choktaw. The state, run by settler migrants, used the humoral pseudoscience of blood passports to adjudicate which Native individuals could attain entry into their own Native nations. Within three decades of the establishment of the Dawes Rolls, Indians lost half their land, from 155 million acres in 1881 to 80 million acres in 1900.[50] This eliminationist settler arrangement came to an end only with the Indian Reorganization Act (1934), which halted the allotment system.

The allotment system played on the settler fantasy of the permanently vanishing Indian. Native existence was indexed along a blood scale of fractions tending towards disappearance and assimilation. Underlying the pernicious blood quantum laws was this false claim: Indigeneity was disappearing and being absorbed into the settler sea of White society. We shall later see how this particular fantasy about a White settler biofuture contrasted with other settler biofuturistic visions fixated on the "hyperpotency" of African blood. If Whiteness could supposedly erase the Native, it was conversely threatened with pollution by even "one drop" of Black blood. The new colonialism, as we continue to see, is a force field of tensions created by differential logics of racialization – different ways of subjecting oppressed communities to differentiated vulnerabilities of insecurity, displacement, dispossession, and premature death. And this fundamental dynamic of the new colonialism continues to function in our own times.

ECOLOGICAL TANGLES

Settlers brought ecological transformation in their wake. They conveyed laws and guns, but they also arrived with livestock, grasses, vermin, bacteria, and viruses. When settlers traveled, so did their pathogens and their weeds. In New England, biological expansion took place through the spread of cow grass and dock, sow thistle and watercress, white clover, and other grasses and crops. Settler colonists on the pampas and llanos of today's Brazil, Venezuela, and Argentina brought horses, cattle, bacteria, and viruses to the Americas beginning in the early 1600s. Historian Alfred Crosby pointed to New England as the other most active biological contact zone of the 1600s and 1700s, besides the pampas of South America.[51]

The mobile, mixed economy of the Native peoples of Turtle Island involved a well-organized system of seasonally rhythmic fixity and movement across lands. If the spring was a time of fishing, as copious spawning fish came up the rivers, the summer was devoted to gathering fruits and berries. With the fall came the cultivation of crops, including squash and corn. During the winter, villages would split into small groups for hunting and curing, and reunite in the larger village community again in the spring. This ongoing pattern of dispersal and reunion took place within well-established land boundaries among different Native communities, for whom diplomatic political relations were very important.[52]

Settler farming, by contrast, was sedentary and characterized by "mixed husbandry," also known as "high farming." Settlers brought their rye, barley, oats, buckwheat, spelt, hay, and other cultivars, raising them on rotating plots. And they divided their plots to reserve space for livestock. Animals supplied nourishment and many other necessities. Cows, for example, converted grass into milk, meat, and hide. Hence, livestock fed on fodder grasses such as couch grass, crab grass, and dandelion. Homesteads developed when settlers "salted" and "seeded" the land. And through these cultivation practices, settler society said it was "husbanding" the land, improving it, and making it productive.

SETTLER COLONIALISM IN THE PACIFIC

British settler colonial expansion was not exclusive to the Americas. It touched the Indian Ocean and the Pacific Ocean in the late 1700s, just as economic liberalism was beginning to further extend trade and production networks across Asia. These European expansions across other oceans occurred just as American societies started to smolder with revolutionary and Republican fires. The opening up of new White settler frontiers in such places as the Cape Colony (today's South Africa), the Mascarenes, Australia, and New Zealand marked a major political and economic shift in the emerging world colonial capitalist system. Beginning in the 1500s, the Americas, the Caribbean, and islands of the Pacific were targets of the first age of settler colonialism. And a new wave of settler colonialism crashed onto the coasts and interiors of landmasses across the Indian Ocean and the Pacific Ocean beginning in the 1700s.[53]

On the continent known today as Australia more than 500 Indigenous nations engaged in trade, diplomacy, and long-distance sea travel long before the arrival of Commodore Arthur Philips' eleven ships from England in 1787.[54] For centuries previous, the visits of small numbers of Europeans were only a minor subplot in the story of trading networks for foodstuffs, drink, tobacco, pipes, and weapons organized through the trade emporium of Makassar in today's Indonesia. Indigenous Australians also conducted extensive commerce with polities situated across the Pacific Ocean.[55] The Pacific was a sea of interconnected peoples and archipelagoes. With vertebrae of islands stretching across the vast oceanic surface like an articulating spine, Pacific Islanders created vast thalassocracies – sea empires – through their maritime trade and diplomacy.[56]

The English First Fleet's arrival in 1788 foretokened the commodification of Native lands on the coasts and interiors of Australia, and the disruption of Indigenous peoples' place in transoceanic networks of circulation. Settlers arrived with "portmanteau biota," or the host of commensal life-forms, including rabbits, goats, sheep, pigs, cattle, and horses, that comprised the other-than-human passengers on the ships. Over the coming decades, a wholesale transfer of biological material took place to the region soon to be called New South Wales in the southeastern tip of the continent.

Settlers dysfunctionally failed to see themselves as guests arriving into an existing array of land-based and seaborne relations and responsibilities.[57] What exactly did it take for those late-coming European travelers to designate themselves as "first," when there were already 750,000 Indigenous people on the continent, belonging to more than 250 different language groups, and engaged in a variety of prosperous trades and political alliances? The answer, as we have observed thus far, has to do

with both the colonizers' myth of the frontier and *terra nullius*, as well as
the intoxication of settlement. Vanishing the Native in order to "first" the
settler is a specific form of genocidal violence that the Fourth World of
Indigenous groups from different parts of the world continues to contend with today.[58]

Within a few months the colonists put up fences to demarcate space
from the Indigenous communities from whom they stole land. Fencing,
as we have seen, was a crucial technology in settler farming, as it kept
livestock in, but also kept "savages" and vermin out. As fencing expanded
across the settler areas, a new landscape emerged, defined by property
ownership in which even sheep could now be used as security on loans.[59]
The first Anglo-Australian settlers introduced crops into cultivation, such
as corn, potatoes, flax, barley, and rye. Eventually, Australian settler
society would pass over the Blue Mountains into the vast plains beyond.
In the area of Port Jackson and New South Wales, indigenous grasses –
kangaroo grass, white top grass, love grass – attracted the colonists, since
their sheep could feed well on them.[60] Australian sheep wore settler
crops on their backs, and were shorn for their merino wool. Such fine
wool supplied the rapidly growing Yorkshire textile mills in England for
the better part of a century. Even today, Australia produces more than
half of the world supply of merino.[61]

By the 1830s, the great settler colonial transplantation of biological
material and human and animal life accelerated. The British transported
prisoners to their colonies in large numbers for most of the nineteenth
century. Over 160,000 "convicts" were sent from Britain to Australia in
the first half of that century.[62] The White population grew by about
150 percent in the 1830s alone.[63] The British Poor Law Amendment of
1834 reduced the expenditures on poor relief in Britain, raising a major
problem for the state in terms of how it would supply the needs of the
lowest classes. The idea was that, through relocation to the colonies, the
poor could be put to work and made profitable. This policy caused a
great upswing in the number of British migrations to Australia.

The settler narrative refused to recognize their Indigenous hosts.
Rather, colonists pictured themselves as going deep into "the bush," so
that "bush [would give way] to landscape."[64] Settlers sawed, burned,
plowed, and dug themselves across the continent. Land-grabbing

accelerated in the 1850s, in the context of the gold rush. By 1880, New South Wales had a population of nearly 750,000 persons, more than 35,000,000 sheep, 2,500,000 cattle, and 396,000 horses, with 70,000 acres under cultivation.

Along with this came the accelerated extension of cadastral mapping.[65] As Renisa Mawani discusses, cadastral mapping was introduced into British colonial territories in the 1850s, especially in Southern Australia, Canada, Hawaii, Malaya, and the Philippines.[66] A system was put in place to map land as subdivided, enclosed units of private property, and to develop a land registry system to legalize the extension of colonial settlements. A cadastral system, known as the "Torrens system," was named after its legal architect, Robert Richard Torrens (1814–84). He aimed to represent colonial lands as atomized, commodified, resaleable units of White ownership. The cadastral engineer used trigonometric surveying techniques to precisely catalog the dimensions of parcels of land, and to calculate their geographical size and their rental yield. Reiterating the more rudimentary practices we encountered in seventeenth-century colonial North America, the new science of cadastral land surveying imposed abstraction on Native peoples' rich existing relations with their ecologies. Settler abstractions about land served as an essential tool in their endeavor to remake the earth in their own alienated image.[67]

In the twentieth century, settler colonialism would have some of its most virulent new expressions in Africa and the Middle East. The British and French states imposed segregationist tyrannies on the Native Africans in Kenya, Zimbabwe, South Africa, and Algeria. White settlers forcibly acquired African terrains and summarily redefined the Natives as squatters. Black South Africans were displaced to Black townships, had to travel with registration documents, and were subjected to curfews and bans. By the 1950s, settler states in Africa had become totalitarian in character. British settlers met the revolutionary Mau Mau movement in Kenya (1952–60) with emergency laws, mass detentions, genocidal killing campaigns, and the removal and detention of Kikuyu women and children. Meanwhile, the French state's totalitarian impulses became fully manifest with counterinsurgency measures against the Algerian revolutionary movement in the 1950s.[68] And the violent displacement of

Palestinian people accelerated in 1948 in the midst of war with the new state of Israel. Beginning in 1967, the Israeli state further militarized its occupation policy against Indigenous Palestinians.[69]

Settler colonialism, as we have seen, unfolded in a variety of different sites from the Americas to Australia, to the southern tip of Africa. This form of colonialism is distinguished by the compulsive push for the removal, sequestration, and elimination of Natives. Colonists moved to new frontiers and settled there, enclosed land, and claimed ownership. They multiplied their numbers, and the numbers of their livestock, pets, and vermin. High levels of settler migration and many forms of weaponry – from arms to legal codes to bureaucratic surveillance – turn the colonists from numerical minorities into new majorities. The creation of these settler majorities is conditioned on violence and ongoing genocidal campaigns. Ceaseless war consumes the imagination of settler societies as they confront ever more Indian Country. Settler colonists do not recognize the activities, responsibilities, and networks of interchange of the societies in which they arrive. Instead, they see opportunities to commodify: to enclose plots of earth, and on those enclosures to inject the logic of profit-making through a variety of capitalist endeavors. Yet, seen from another angle, settler colonialism is perpetually anxious and fretful about Native insurgency. Native peoples continually reassert their sovereignty in ways that burst out from settler designs.

CHAPTER 3

Plantation

O VER THE COURSE OF THE 1700s, enslaved African people of Haiti (then called Saint Domingue) fled from the plantations to the mountain ranges, to the Massif du North, the Black Mountains, and the Chaîne de la Selle. Across these mountains were caves, ravines, and thick woods where Black Haitian folk hid, formed new revolutionary communities, and emancipated themselves. These escapees from slavery created homes in the mountains, living amidst the thick undergrowth and caverns. These acts of permanent escape were called the *grande marronage.* And they were accompanied in counterpoint by many small *marronages,* as enslaved people temporarily fled from the daily degradations of plantation life and congregated in seclusion in the middle of night for succor and merriment. Both the extraordinary and the everyday modes of resistance, great and small, helped to spark the great Haitian revolution, 1791–1804, as self-emancipating Black communities converged across the mountain passes and descended onto the flat savannahs. Insurrections spread among those incarcerated on the plantations too. By the 1750s, the French colony of Saint Domingue was the largest slave plantation complex on earth, with a population of over 500,000 enslaved Africans and just over 25,000 Whites. The island's sugar, cocoa, and coffee production generated more than one-quarter of the French empire's annual income.[1] Haiti was ground zero for racial slavery.

Saint Domingue swallowed captives from western and central Africa through the Transatlantic slave trade. Transatlantic slavery, from its inception in the early 1500s, was the greatest forced migration process in world history. By the mid eighteenth century, the trade in enslaved African people reached unprecedented levels. The number of people bought into slavery in the Americas tripled between 1700 and 1750, and the number tripled again by 1800. Slaving was a trade of exponential proportions during this period. As a result, in Saint Domingue in the mid 1700s, almost two-thirds of the total enslaved population had been born in Africa.[2] And the enslaved therefore had strong connections with the memories of their homelands, spanning from Guinea to the Congo. By 1750, on Saint Domingue alone, kidnapped Africans working on plantations spoke more than twenty different African native languages, many of which were incomprehensible to each other. And their bodies and minds stored the intense longing for lost loved ones and lost homes. They also stored the skills and knowledge of social organization, political resistance, and spiritual uplift rooted in African heritages. The revolution in Haiti that eventually destroyed the slave system in Saint Domingue was the result of alliances between many insurgent groups, but the memories from Africa supplied the ignition.

For example, the healing spiritual practices of Lemba among the people of the Lower Congo survived the Atlantic Crossing as captives on slave ships headed for the Americas. Peoples from the Congo in Saint Domingue drew on the repertory of Lemba stored in their bodies.[3] Lemba was a healing cult and an institution of social organization, in which members sealed their association together by secret oath, agreeing to put the interests of the group above those of the individual.[4] Practitioners collected together to beat the "drum of sorrow" (the *ngoma*, or *gombeh* drum), sing and pray for salvation, and distribute food, homemade medicines, and care among themselves. Lemba promoted a form of redistributive community justice by which a group of people exercised a strong egalitarian ethic, mutual aid, and a commitment to peaceable interdependence. Lemba in the Caribbean developed in conversation with, and even against, the Lemba traditions in Africa. Haitian Lemba emerged from below and was not dependent upon authorities ruling from above. It fanned the spirit for liberation during the great Haitian revolution beginning in 1791. And the Haitian revolution had ripple effects across the Caribbean and the United States, in Jamaica, Grenada, Cuba, Georgia, and Virginia.[5]

Lemba, from the Congo, alongside Vodun, from the Benin coast, were practices of liberation brought by enslaved Africans to the Caribbean. Even under slavery, the enslaved invented new ways to understand each other, and they molded the French language into a new tongue that was tightly woven with words and phrases from many different African cultures, such as those of the Twi, Kru, Akan, and Ewe. Freedom-minded peoples forged a revolution together based on African religious and political traditions. It rocked the hemispheric colonial world to its core. The Haitian revolution served as an enduring touchstone of the Black Radical Tradition.[6]

DEFINITIONS

The institution of racial slavery maintained that enslaved African people were not human beings but units of property in human form. Saidiya Hartman observes how slavery involved a dual invocation of enslaved people simultaneously as persons and property.[7] The Transatlantic slave trade began with raids and ambushes on African communities and the kidnapping (what British slavers called the "panyarring") of people. Sometimes captives were prisoners of war, sold by west African coastal leaders to waterside European merchants. Captives were marched to the shallow lagoons along the west African coast and forced into massive slave forts. Bound and tortured in the forts, captives waited in dungeons for weeks, and sometime months. Should they survive, they were then funneled through a slit-like door on the fort's coastal wall and pushed onto ships for the long ordeal across the Atlantic. African people became the single most lucrative commodity traded on Atlantic markets from the 1500s to the 1800s. And Atlantic commerce was the most important source of wealth for Western imperial nations during these centuries. Hence, Western wealth is literally built on the trade in millions of enslaved Africans.[8]

Enslaved people were packed into the holds of ships and subjected to unspeakable conditions of squalor and deprivation. Up to 600 people at a time were pushed into the seaborne prison of the slave ship's belly, chained and left without access to fresh air. The manacled and chained captives, generation after generation, bored peepholes and air ducts through the hulls, if not for their benefit then for those who would follow. If they reached the other shore in the Americas – and uncountable numbers of people died or were killed on the way – the enslaved were then subjected to the grotesque procedures of the American slave markets, whereby human beings were appraised, priced, and sold to slave-owners who fed off the life, labor, sex, and intelligence of their living human chattel.[9]

At the beginning of the Transatlantic trade, Nzinga Mbemba, King of the Kongo (1456–1542), sent diplomatic letters to the Portuguese court in 1526 protesting the:

> excessive freedom ... [of] the men and merchants who are allowed to come to this Kingdom. .... The mentioned merchants are taking every day our natives, sons of the land and the sons of our noblemen and vassals and our relatives. Because the thieves and men of bad conscience grab them wishing to have the things and wares of this Kingdom. They grab them and get them to be sold.[10]

Transatlantic slavery was certainly not imposed on the west African coast without a fight. At each step of the trade, at each threshold of captivity, the enslaved responded and resisted in ways that defied the system. Resistance among Africans against the slave raids took many forms, including armed struggle, flight to mountains or to nearby islands, campaigns by African family members to buy relatives out of slavery, and emancipatory suicides.[11] Slave ships, too, were sites of permanent rebellion and resistance. Hunger strikes, riots, coordinated action to commandeer ships, and voluntary jumps overboard were common expressions of agency onboard.[12]

And, as most often was the case, even when ships did not see open insurrection, the succor and tendernesses that enslaved peoples shared with each other constituted a field of resistance that the official historical record can hardly pass on. Captives in the slave-hold became new kin to each other, and some became lovers, or *matis*.[13] In the entrapped space of the slave ship, strange and life-giving human experiences emerged in the midst of unrelenting brutality and deprivation. Although official documents record some 14–20 million Africans eventually put into the holds of ships and sent to the Americas from Africa, the number is much higher and will never be known. Nobel prize-winning author, Toni Morrison, poetically enumerated this uncountable number and the legacies of slavery as the "60 million and more" of those "who didn't make it from there to here and through."[14]

THE NEW WORLD EFFECT

European merchants sent enslaved people across the ocean, a long journey of five to six weeks, to be sold in such places as Jamaica, Berbice, and Brazil. But before the Transatlantic slave trade began, Europeans were already selling enslaved people along the west African coast itself. As early as the 1470s, African businesspeople involved in gold mining or agriculture would purchase people of other ethnic communities from Portuguese and Dutch merchants. European merchants sold African women and children to buyers on the Atlantic islands of Cape Verde, São Miguel, and Madeira, where sugarcane and grapes were cultivated in relatively small amounts.[15]

So the Transatlantic slave trade, with the earliest shipments of enslaved people to Cartagena, Salvador na Bahia, and Veracruz in the early 1500s, extended from the slave-trading economies that were already at work on the west African coast. At first, the European involvement with slavery was characterized by an expansion of routes and markets, and not the invention of a wholly new form of human bondage. In fact, commanding labor from slaves was a common practice across African societies, and was also a feature of European, Asian, and some Indigenous American societies. Servitude and bondage were not new, but old dynamics.

However, the European involvement in slave-trading in the 1500s transformed its scale, the intensity and forms of brutality exacted upon the enslaved, and ultimately the meaning of slave bondage. As Stephanie Smallwood explains, slavery became "saltwater slavery," or a new form of slavery involving the permanent removal of captives from their native cultures and their families. The natal alienation and the "social death" it involved were unique characteristics of Transatlantic slavery.[16] Europeans thought of themselves and their role in the Atlantic trading economies in new ways because of their access to the colonial Americas.

This informed the emergence of a new, monstrous form of slavery. Beginning in 1500, for the first time in history, peoples on the west coast of Africa were encountering Europeans who believed themselves to be from cultures that conquered and settled a New World.

The new infectious mentality of the *conquistadores* and settlers combined with the long-standing mercantile mindset of the slave-trader. The effect was an intensification of violence and a new drive to make enslaved people into commodities within a network of accelerating New World trade in human beings for gold, sugar, weapons, textiles, rubber, and tobacco. In other words, the rise of racial slavery came through a change in the intensity, scale, and speed of pre-existing dynamics. The change was so extreme that it actually generated a wholly new institution, fundamentally unlike the slavery customarily existing in other parts of the world. The process of commodification transformed social and economic relations between people and things in the way that leaven transforms dough: irrevocably and from within.

The leavening power of New World colonialism affected European traders everywhere they were involved in other peoples' economies across the African and Asian coasts. As slave-trading changed by degree, and eventually changed in kind, it had an impact on the development of west African statecraft. The most powerful polities of the Denkyira, Akwamu, and Asante, for example, consolidated themselves through their participation in the trade in captive persons and gold for weapons, textiles, and other goods from the Americas and Asia. The Atlantic slave economy was not foreign to early modern African coastal societies, but contributed towards their very rise and consolidation. Slavery was simultaneously an enemy to vulnerable African peoples, especially women, children, and subordinated ethnic groups, and one of the most important sources of wealth and political strength for the African elites who held local power in slave-trading states.[17]

RACIAL COLONIAL CAPITALISM

How did the emerging web of racial capitalism, tethered to the frontiers of conquest and settlement in the New World, transform the pre-existing institution of slavery? The historian Stephanie Smallwood captures the answer succinctly: "[the enslaved] inhabited a new category of marginalization, one not of extreme alienation *within* the community, but rather of absolute exclusion from *any* community."[18] The new slavery involved forced migration across 3,700 miles of ocean, to a strange society run by settler colonists and focused on extracting commodities from out of the bowels of the earth using coerced labor. For the enslaved, this meant the obliteration of family ties, and the stripping away of all cultural bonds of obligation and protection. It was not oppression alone, but the unparalleled degree and kind of oppression that made this new slavery distinctive in history. Sylvia Wynter discusses the unprecedented transformation taking place in striking and precise language:

> The "slave mode of production" on the plantation was to be a mode of production quite different from the slave mode of production in the non-market economies of Africa. The word "negro" which the slave traffickers – Portuguese, Dutch, English, and other Christian, civilized European nations – applied to the multitribal African took on a specific meaning. The "negro" was no longer a slave as in the African tribal context. He was now essentially a form of labor power calculated in terms of his exchange value, bought and sold not as a slave, but as a commodity. He was "labor power" in the economic system, which produced goods for the world market, not on the basis of fulfilling relatively constant needs, but on the basis of maximizing profit, which was limitless.[19]

Racial slavery sought the total commodification of human beings. Human beings were treated as units of currency. Slaves were referred to as "pieces," or *pieza* or *peça da India*. Able-bodied men were priced as one piece, or one unit, of human property. Enslaved women and children – who constituted the majority of those shipped across the Atlantic to the plantations – were priced as two-thirds of the value of a full unit price.[20] These categories and calibrations of early capitalist enterprise were imposed upon vulnerable and unprotected African peoples.

The Black abolitionist writer Olaudah Equiano recalled that when he was incarcerated on the plantations he saw slaves "put into scales and weighed; and then sold from three pence to six or nine pence a pound."[21] European institutions of slave-trading reduced Africans to a denigrating set of valuations.[22] Slave-traders and slave-owners, and the anti-Black racial order that worked through them, accorded prices to slaves based on their "physiognomy, the regularity of their looks, their capacity of rapid movement, their ability to converse, the size of their genital organs, the texture of their muscles, the quality of their skin, the traces of past whippings on their back, their height and their size."[23]

Considering the Transatlantic trade triangle, we recall that such commodities as salt, ivory, textiles, and guns were traded for enslaved Africans on the African west and east coasts. Human commodities were then transported to the Americas and traded against commodities desired in Europe, such as sugar, cotton, and tobacco. Slave ships would offload their cargoes of enslaved human beings at various ports in the Americas, making stops across the rimland of Brazil, Jamaica, Barbados, Carolina, and Massachusetts. They sold their human cargoes for an array of commodities that would earn lucrative profits when the fattened ships returned to European ports. These same ships, once emptied again of their cargoes, would be ladened up once more with guns and finished textiles from European factories and from the Asian trade, along with silver from South American mines. And then they would chart their course back to the African coasts to buy human beings in exchange for their mineral, metal, and fabric freight. The commodity cycle continued its widening spiral for centuries, engulfing millions of lives.[24]

FORTS

By the late 1600s, slave-trading had become a predominant European economic activity. The Portuguese, followed by the Spanish, the Dutch, and the English, set up forts (*feitorias*) or castles (*castelos*) on the west African coast. The Portuguese established Castelo de São Jorge da Mina in 1482, eventually known by its nickname, Elmina, or "the mine." On the Gold Coast of today's Ghana, and on the Bight of Benin of today's southwest Nigeria and Benin, other forts were quickly established. More than seventy slave forts rose up over the course of the 1600s on fore-shores from Senegal and Senegambia all the way down to Angola.

Slave forts were economic zones, with many different kinds of trades and different people, European, African, Asian, women and men, caught up in tangled relations. Around the slave forts, artisans fashioned chains and bolts from the bronze manilla bars that also served as currency along the coast. Others were involved in manufacturing armaments and building ships.[25] Some merchants offered insurance and financing for the trade. Slave forts housed administrators and record-keepers who managed flows of slaves, gold, ivory, and raw materials, and manipulated local political relationships to their advantage. African women of different social stations labored in the shadow of the forts in providing sexual recreation for licentious European and African men, and then also doing the care work of rearing the children that resulted. In fact, right next to Elmina fort was the nursery for babies born from the sexual predation of the Portuguese, Spanish, Dutch, British, and French, as well as the men of mixed European and African ancestry, who worked in and around the slave fort as administrators, soldiers, merchants, and wardens. Slave forts produced new ethnic communities from their tangled relations, a mixed group called *Mulatto*.

This tangling of social relations created the conditions for the complicity of many Africans within the slave fort system. But, on the other hand, this same knotting of trades and sexual relations also meant that the seams of resistance and insurgency were exposed. Slave forts were constructed with moats, ramparts, and battlements because of the continual threat of massive uprisings and raids. And the threat of conspiracies and coups from within the thick walls of these forts explains the need to construct special fortified dungeons, reserved for the high crimes of betrayal and insubordination. Embossed into the very architecture of the slave fort is evidence not of its effective control, but of the lack of control it exercised over the consequences of industrial slaving.

By the end of the 1600s, the Portuguese, Dutch, French, Latvians, Swedes, Danes, Germans, and English had all established fortified outposts in west Africa, with varying degrees of success. Slaving was a lucrative business, and served as one of the most important inputs in the long production chain that permitted the industrial revolutions of Europe and North America by the mid 1700s. Slave-traders exhibited their own gruesome forms of industriousness in order to make enslavement more economically efficient. European slave-traders developed a whole range of methods for reducing their risk, including using faster ships, forming merchant partnerships, and spreading their shipments of slaves over many voyages to mitigate the hazards of the seas.

Many of the most important forts were run by European joint stock companies. These new forms of enterprise served the profiteering interests of stockholders, as well as the mercantilist interests of early modern European states. In coastal Ghana, the Dutch West India Company occupied the former Portuguese ports of Elmina and Schama in 1639. Just two miles away, the British Royal Africa Company established its fort at Cape Coast Castle in 1672. Between the late seventeenth and mid nineteenth centuries, British companies occupied more than fifty forts and outposts in west Africa, stretching from James Island on the Gambia River to Ouidah on the Benin coast.[26] The French Senegal Company ran the huge slave fort on Gorée Island, just off the coast of Dakar. And Luanda, the major city on the Angolan coast, was a center for Portuguese slaving. Luanda also later served as the bridgehead for Portuguese attempts to expand plantation production into Angola itself, during the rapid expansion of Portuguese plantation slavery.[27] By the end of the eighteenth century, all the main European forts in Africa had been established, including centers on the east African coast, especially on the island of Zanzibar and in coastal Mozambique.[28]

Slave-trading companies cultivated relations with the heads of African kingdoms. They intervened in the processes of royal succession and supported African contenders who were compliant with their aims. European slave fort governors by the 1700s sowed discord between local states through their alliances. European chartered companies became so politically dominant that they took possession of the royal stools of west African kings, examples of which are today on display in museums in London and Leiden.[29] Slave forts acted as nerve centers for persistently interfering with, undermining, and reconfiguring the sovereignty of African states, disrupting their sovereign development.

For centuries, the forts encouraged an atmosphere of industrial-strength treachery and mistrust within coastal Africa that permeated hinterland polities too. European slave markets created opportunities whereby people could sell enemies, or the vulnerable and unprotected, in ways that severely depleted the communal life of the society that remained.[30] European slave forts latched onto the African coasts, feeding on the flesh and blood of African peoples and societies, and leaving pockmarks of discord and social disfigurement behind. The forts also pumped in guns and gunpowder, as well as luxury commodities from Asia and the Americas.[31] All this unfolded as African kingdoms continued their economic concourse with the "men from the sea."[32]

JAN NIESER: A CASE STUDY

Jan Nieser was a *Mulatto* African. He was born in 1756 in Accoda (Akwidaa), in today's Ghana. His father was a German medical assistant and his mother an African woman, possibly enslaved. As early as the 1500s, there are reports of large numbers of people of mixed ethnicity living in fort areas.[33] Nieser grew up in the shadow of Fort Dorothea, a German slaving site administered by the Brandenburg Company. When Nieser was 8 years old, his father left with him for Europe, taking him from his mother and leaving her behind. We do not know what happened to her. Perhaps, her child abducted, and left without protector or patron, she was forced through the door of no return and onto a slave ship. Or perhaps she formed a new family, grew older, and tended the memory of her child until his return.

Young Nieser obtained six years of education in the Netherlands. He returned to the Gold Coast in 1770, now a young man, and began working for the Dutch West India Company, some 70 miles down the coast at the Elmina slave fort. By 1790, Nieser was one of the most prosperous private traders at Elmina. He moved to Accra in 1793 to carry on his business, becoming a trafficker in enslaved people from the Ashanti hinterlands. Returning to Elmina in 1806, Nieser conspired with Ashanti leaders against the Fanti state that held control of the town and surrounding areas. He was also closely aligned with the Dutch who administered the shipment of enslaved people into Atlantic networks from Elmina fort. Nieser thus played the role as a fulcrum for political maneuvering and mercantile bargaining between Ashanti leaders and European merchants.[34]

Jan Nieser's letters from Elmina show how human beings were reduced to mere commodities through the operation of slavery capitalism. In a letter to his business partners in Liverpool (Figure 3.1), dated 1803, Nieser organized a trade in African captives in exchange for weapons and luxury goods from Europe and Asia. He promised "5 to 6 slaves per Danish gun." He itemized a full list of commodities that would earn an outgoing consignment of "400 slaves." Along with Danish guns, powder kegs, and West Indian rum, Nieser asked for a large number of specialty commodities from the India trade in exchange for the hundreds of captives. The textiles he desired were many and diverse. As part of the bargain for the 400 slaves, he requested specific amounts of Indian textiles: "200 Chellos, 200 new Neganipattis, 300 Castracundies (Manchester and Indian), 400 Chintz, 100 Cottoneese, 100 Policatts, 100 Blue bandanas, 150 Abanga Romalls, etc."[35] Note the price mechanism at work in this letter. Nieser priced out human beings in terms of pieces of specialty fabric. The British and Dutch trading empire, stretching from the Americas, to coastal Africa, to the Indian Ocean, made these awful equivalences and this total evacuation of human value possible. Human value was replaced with abstract ratios of price-based exchange.

In order to enforce the abstract equivalence between "pieces" of human beings and pieces of things, permanent overwhelming violence was required. The "door of no return" best captures the obliteration experienced by those forced into racial slavery. This door was the passageway in the dungeons of slave forts through which captives were marched in order to pack them into ships for the transit across the Atlantic Ocean. As the door of no return connected land to water, the people who passed through that door experienced the liquidation of their existing family and social networks. The Atlantic Crossing put the sea into the blood of the enslaved and all their descendants. Guyanese-Canadian poet Dionne Brand writes, "water is the first thing in my memory. ... The sea sounded like a thousand secrets, all whispered at the same time."[36] People did not return to their villages and homes after passing through this door. They entered a system of commodification, carceral enclosure, and punishment known as the plantation system. From the time they were forced into the pens of the slave fort and then

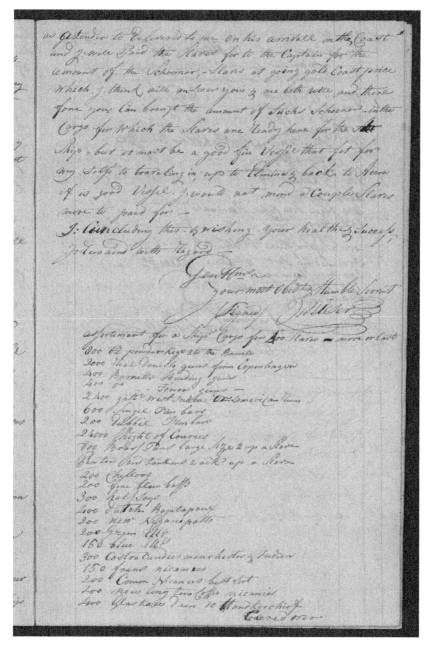

Figure 3.1 Jan Nieser. Letter to Liverpool. Accra, June 2, 1803, Nationaal Archief, Nederlandse Blok Nr: 158, Bezittingen op de Kust van Guinea, 1133. Used with permission of the Netherlands National Archives, The Hague.

through the door of no return, the experience of slavery called forth new modes of being human in and through the cultures, identities, and intimacies that erupted out of the hold.

PLANTATION COMPLEX

Plantations were nerve centers of racial capitalism. From the 1500s to the 1800s, across the circum-Caribbean region, tens of thousands of separate slave plantations innervated a giant and world-spanning trading network. Each plantation enclosure was divided up in ways that reflected the logic of racial slavery. There was a Great House, often situated in a clearing and overlooking the plantation fields (see Figure 3.2). Here lived the planta-tion owner and his family. In cases in which the owner was an absentee, an attorney took up residence. A portion of the surrounding land was gener-ally reserved for year-round cash crop cultivation. Another portion was set aside for feeding and sheltering draught animals used in plantation production, with a portion left over for the plantation's expansion. And a section was reserved for private cultivation by the enslaved. The "slave yard" could be a set of small, thatched, one-room dwellings, built in barrack-style rows or cramped together in tattered shanties. This spatial

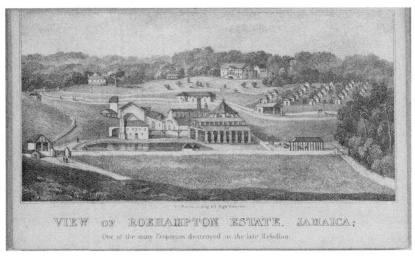

Figure 3.2 View of Roehampton Estate, 1833. Schomburg Center for Research in Black Culture, Manuscripts. Sc Rare 326.972-G. The image is in the public domain.

organization of the plantation suggests something about the forms of subjection, interdependence, intimacy, and abuse that abounded, as people lived not just next to each other, but in and through each other in the daily reproduction of racial violence.

Black women and men labored in the fields cultivating crops, and worked as engineers and skilled craftsmen in all aspects of plantation production. Under racial slavery, labor was commanded through brutal violence, punishment, torture, humiliation, starvation, and death. Workers lived in sheds, barracks, or "lines" on the very fields they tilled. A small, coercive managerial class of drivers and overseers stood over laborers as they worked in "chain gangs" in the fields. Laborers were registered (often branded) and strictly policed, and unregistered movements off the plantations were prohibited. Most of all, plantations punished. As Sidney Mintz famously argued, the long chains of violently supervised gang work, intensive daily labor, and servitude made the plantation into a heinous early form of the industrial factory.[37]

Plantations were a factory system in the bush. These factories specialized in intensified extraction: labor was extracted from enslaved workers; juice squelched from cane; cotton bolls plucked from the bush; oil pressed from fruit. Plantation owners shipped these products to other ports in the Americas or across the seas to Europe, to yet other factories where they were again processed in the production of industrial consumer goods. To be clear, plantation agriculture was itself a capital-intensive, industrializing endeavor. Sugar production, for example, was not like the settler farming of grains, such as wheat, for subsistence use and local trade. Plantations required not just agricultural cultivation, but highly technical and high-intensity labor that grooved into an international schedule of consumer demand and the ecological rhythms of crop production. The first crop of sugar took fifteen to eighteen months to grow. Thereafter, sugar fields could yield a harvest every nine months. Sugar had to be processed at the point of origin. It required a large amount of expertise and capital: coopers, masons, keepers of livestock, mill technicians, insurance brokers. Merchants sought increasing control over all aspects of sugar production, and found ways to engineer their sugarcane and their fertilizers to optimize yield. Plantation owners wrote and exchanged cultivation manuals to share their views about how best to optimize their yield, but also how best to control and punish their slaves.[38] On the plantations of the settler Americas, Black slaves were expected to work in particular ways: long hours from sunup to sundown, without days off, and often without any consideration for childcare or illness. The enslaved were terrorized in daily life and subjected to the worst abuses that the powerful could visit upon the unprotected, since the enslaved were given no protection under White settler law.

New kinds of labor usage were developed to take advantage of the harvest cycle pre-dating the rise of factory discipline in Atlantic Europe later on. Chain gangs, labor clocks, and 24-hour-shift labor were all innovated on plantations. And when it came to the shipment of plantation commodities overseas, new ways of loading ships were engineered that allowed ships to ply more journeys per year. Slaves worked on fields, but they also worked in planters' homes. They cooked meals, cleaned bathrooms, combed slave-owners' hair in the morning, and put their children to bed at night. The enslaved also designed and constructed buildings, engineered waterways, and navigated ships.

In some respects, enslaved Africans were the first proletariat of the Americas, although they earned no wages and were "paid" only with allowances for bare subsistence, and with merciless, bitter punishments for their persistent and unconquerable assertion of human needs, desires, and intellect.[39] In plantation colonies, the Black proletariat outnumbered Whites and slave-owners by factors of five or more. For example, in Saint Domingue, there were ten enslaved people to every one White person. In 1870, at the peak of the Mississippi Delta plantation complex, there were 130,117 African Americans in a population of 193,797 persons.[40] The scale of racial slavery meant that the Black experience, alongside the experiences of Native and Indigenous peoples, is not one of historical "minorities" – these are actually majority histories. Centuries of colonial violence and ongoing colonial disguise conspire to make the big stories seem like footnotes.

CONSUMING THE SLAVE HARVEST

The historians Fernando Ortiz and Sidney Mintz observed that the coming of large amounts of tobacco, chocolate, tea, and, especially, sugar to Europe from the 1600s onwards coincided with a revolution in European consumption patterns, as well as radical transformations in collective nervous responses across western European societies. Consumer tastes were changing, as refined sugar came to be accessible for the first time to the European masses, generating a revolution in European cooking and baking at this time.[41] In the 1650s, sugar was no longer a rare "spice," but a common staple. The quintessential English table of tea, jam, biscuits, and sweet cakes dates to this time, and is predicated on racial slavery.

The unprecedented availability of new stimulants, with their intense effects on the mind and nervous system, actually transformed European culture in a drastic way. It would be too reductive to claim a causal relationship between the coming of plantation-processed stimulants pouring onto European markets and the dawning of Europe's early modern acceleration of industrial and cultural production in the 1600s. Yet still, we can observe how the European Renaissance and the Enlightenment were strongly conditioned by recombinations of land, labor, and botanicals in the colonies. Plantation products had significant physiological and psychological effects on consumers in Europe and its settler colonies. The plantation production of nutrients (e.g. sucrose) and intoxicants (e.g. nicotine and caffeine), clothing fiber (e.g. cotton), and fats and saps (e.g. palm oil and rubber) would drastically transform European societies' tastes, and European bodies. The labor of enslaved Black folk was condensed into all of these products.

In one of his poems, Derek Walcott envisions "provinces, protectorates, colonies, dominions, governors-general, knights, ostrich-plumed Viceroys, deserts, jungles, hill-stations, all empire's zones" spilling from the "small tea-chest" of polite imperial society.[42] Indeed, a relay of commodity exchange emerged that transformed African people into slaves, and slave labor into cotton and cane, and cotton and cane into yarn and sugar, and yarn and sugar into clothing and food, and then into money profit for capitalists. This chain of commodification was a manifestation of the mercantile principle penetrating deeper and deeper into the realm of life, increasingly fusing together processes of production, distribution, exchange, and consumption. This new slavery under the conditions of colonial capitalism was racial slavery.[43]

The regime of racial slavery really attained its first peak in the British slave colonies of Barbados, the Carolinas, and Virginia in the mid 1600s. This was followed by a second peak from the mid 1700s onwards, as the British, French, Spanish, Portuguese, and Americans consolidated the plantation colonies of Jamaica, Saint Domingue, Brazil, Cuba, and the Mississippi Delta – the five great centers of plantation slavery on earth.[44] And the final stage of the slave plantations expanded across Cuba, Brazil, and the US American South in the period from the 1830s to the 1880s. But, as we continue to see, the legacies continued much after, and are alive today.

RACIAL SLAVERY AND GENDER

Historian Jennifer Morgan's work shows the particular devastation of the economic and legal systems penetrating into the intimacies of enslaved families.[45] The slave market split families apart, as mothers were sold to different buyers from their children's. Moreover, probate law, or the English laws of inheritance, also introduced insecurity into the families of the enslaved. The enslaved were treated as movable property to be redistributed along with the division of estates. After a slave-owner died, Black families were often broken apart, as children were cleaved from their parents and sent to heirs and beneficiaries, according to the wishes of the testator, or will-writer. Yet, historian Tera Hunter has shown how antebellum Black families stayed together despite slave laws. Enslaved people married each other in spite of legal interference. In the case of mixed-status unions, free Black women and men worked to manumit, or purchase the freedom of, their partners and relatives.[46]

In the United States context, even after the official end of slavery at the conclusion of the Civil War, the "one-drop rule" prevailed as a legal apparatus to impose subordination and unequal treatment on Blacks across the USA, from North to South. The "*partus sequitur ventrem*" (or, "that which is brought forth follows the womb"), codes of inheritance enshrined in English colonial slave laws, stipulated that the children of enslaved women would also be slaves.[47] Children were thus born into the world in bondage. White supremacy invented ways to reproduce the institution of slavery through biological increase. The legal disempowerment that came with the North American racial order was extended to anyone who was seen to have even a drop of African blood. Across the United States' South, even after final emancipation in 1865, Blacks continued to be incarcerated on plantations and in mass prisons through the sharecropping and convict leasing systems. The unequal access to property ownership and to other social goods – healthcare, education, government services – imposes a living racial colonial legacy of injustice and disposession on Blacks in the United States.[48]

In contrast to the Anglo-American one-drop rule, the "Black Codes" in the French and Spanish empires provided residual or limited rights to families with mixed European and African ancestry. And yet, persons considered to be insufficiently mixed with Whiteness – an arbitrary estimation based on malleable cultural constructs of *Mulatto* or Creole ethnicity – were still relegated to the lowest rung in the caste system of racial slavery. The *Code Noire* in French colonies and the *Cedula* in the Spanish provided nominal legal rights to the enslaved and gave them a route to legal recourse in the case of abuse by slave-owners. In practice, however, these nominal protections were largely ignored. The experience of the enslaved in the Spanish and French colonies remained different in degree, but not in kind, from the depredations suffered by the enslaved in the British, American, and Dutch colonies. The *Code Noire*, which remained in place in French plantation colonies until 1848, permitted slave-owners to enslave children they had had with enslaved women. Any semblance of slave "rights" was warped and grossly disfigured by the racial logic that human beings could be owned by other human beings on the basis of birth. The enslaved were not treated as legal persons, but as living, commodified flesh.[49]

SURVIVAL AMONG THE ENSLAVED

Yet, human life under slavery was defined by the indomitability of life itself, even as it was transformed by racial capitalism. The artifacts in Figure 3.3 are from the quarters of enslaved people on the Ten Hills Farm Estate in Medford, Massachusetts. The estate was owned by Isaac Royall Jr. His family made immense amounts of money in Antigua as plantation owners. The Royalls eventually moved to the Boston area and purchased a 5,000-acre plantation on the banks of the Mystic River, along with other properties in surrounding towns. With their wealth from

Figure 3.3 "Gaming pieces," Royall House and Slave Quarters, Medford, Massachusetts. c. 1750s. Photograph by Alexandra Chan. Used with permission of the Royall House & Slave Quarters, Medford, Massachusetts.

slavery they acquired enough land within the interior of the Massachusetts colony to incorporate a new town, naming it Royalston.[50]

This wealthy, slave-owning family owned at least sixty enslaved people at the Ten Hills Farm Estate in Medford. Records show that about thirty-two of those enslaved were women. The practice of bringing Africans to New England as house slaves, or to be "let out," or rented, for agricultural labor on farming plots, commenced with the earliest days of the settlement. The first enslaved persons from Africa arrived in shackles in Boston and New York in the 1620s. The institution was more than a hundred years old in New England by the time the Royalls arrived from Antigua.

Sparse records from the estate show that the Royalls ruled with terror. In 1737, enslaved people organized an armed revolt against their enslavers. As a result, White judges subjected two enslaved men to heinous and extreme punishment. One of them, Hector, who was also an overseer, was "burned alive for conspiracy to revolt." And his collaborator, Quaco, was "banished to Hispaniola" (today's Haiti). The Royall household, which performed respectability and opulence in New

England White society, was founded on racial terror and abomination at home.

A woman named Belinda, originally from Ghana, served the Royalls for eleven years before the family fled to England during the Revolutionary Wars. Belinda, along with Stephy and Mira, who were incarcerated in the Royalls' house for twenty-three years, were all involved in the most intimate aspects of the Royalls' life. Racial slavery was about generationally reproduced forms of intimate interdependence operating under conditions of brutal violence and social codes of racial separation. So, some of the enslaved on the Royall estate lived in the "slave quarters," but others slept in the kitchen, while others still stayed in rooms next to the bedrooms of the members of the Royall family. The enslaved fed, clothed, and entertained the Royalls. Isaac Royall would not even put his own shoes or wig on; nor would he ever shave himself.

In 1783, eight years after the loyalist Royall family relocated to Britain, Belinda dictated a petition demanding payment from the Royall estate as reparations for slavery. Belinda had cooked for the Royall family and attended to their daily chores. She cured meats, washed laundry, made candles and soaps, carded and spun wool, waited on tables, washed and ironed, lifted barrels and huge steaming pots, made preserves, dusted furniture, and scrubbed the wooden floorboards. In her petition, Belinda mentions that she still recalled the experience of being kidnapped from her home on the banks of the Volta River, in today's Ghana. She remembered the door of no return. Her whole family was taken into captivity, and she was subsequently separated from her mother and father either on the slave ship or in the slave market. In her petition to the Massachusetts legislature for reparations, Belinda proudly stated that now she finally stood in the state "the Almighty Father intended for all the human Race."

The gaming pieces shown in Figure 3.3 were possibly used by Belinda, her child, and the other enslaved people on the Royall estate. We see two marbles and three diamond-shaped tiles that were used by enslaved folk for recreation. Enslaved parents made marbles for their children, forming perfect spheres from clay and firing them in the kitchen oven. Meanwhile, plates were procured from the china closet, broken into pieces, and recreated as gaming tokens for adults. The enslaved men and women on the estate may have used these diamond pieces to play games originating in Africa, such as *mancala* or *wari*.

The enslaved fashioned games from everyday objects associated with their labors. African people on the Royall estate created their own secret time to laze, laugh, and find merriment together. One of the greatest expressions of the human spirit, crafted so poignantly by the enslaved in the Royall House, is the capacity to recreate. Recreation involved stealing time from the slave-owner's clock in order to rest and play. But that very stealing away also transformed everyday objects of racial subjection and industrial slavery into equipment for pleasure, and social connection. In their practices of leisure, late at night or on Saturdays, the enslaved stole sugar, and stole themselves away from the conditions of their denigrating oppression while still physically existing within its system. They resisted through revelry, friendship, and relaxation, too. These were small acts of "testing the chains": small, everyday trumpets of humanity from inside. They also suggest very modern modes of release and recuperation from the increasingly mechanized and regimented labor that the enslaved experienced long before the dawning of the nineteenth-century industrial age.[51]

PLANTATION RESISTANCE

The plantation complex was not a monolithic space of dread and domination. The enslaved also created and sustained their networks of commerce and of trade. They grew and cultivated their own crops and made decisions about what to sell on the Sunday markets. Plantations, as agricultural plots, were divided between land for the cultivation of cash crops (such as cane, cocoa, coffee, and cotton), land for pasturage for animals, and land that was left in reserve or used for timber. The huts of the enslaved were built either in straight rows or in clusters, and were often located near a village or stream for the procurement of water. The enslaved were afforded small portions of land called their "provision grounds," or "plots." The labor on the provision grounds was performed by close friends, and most often by women. Here they would plant their own subsistence crops, roots and tubers, grains and greens, that they used for sustenance, but also for trade in the extensive informal and underground economy that linked the enslaved and free Black people. Provision grounds were of great cultural significance. Produce such as yams, eddoes, calabash squash, African rice, and callaloo (a kind of spinach) were part of a genealogy of cultivation and sovereignty that tethered enslaved people back to their African ancestors. The very word "yam" is of west African origin and means "eat."[52] These roots and grains were brought on ships with the captives, and they gave new life to the diasporic African communities under slavery.

The provision-ground system was first instituted in Jamaica in 1696 and spread to other plantation islands soon afterwards. The enslaved were granted Saturday afternoons and Sundays to cultivate their own plots. The Sunday markets in Barbados and Jamaica were very large, and provided occasions to exchange goods and participate in the local cash economy. Markets were established in towns and in small villages, and internal distribution networks emerged, again organized largely by women. Internal banking systems developed among the enslaved. They repurposed African community-banking techniques, such as the *asue* system, in order to support short-term saving. In the rotating credit system of *asue*, a group of friends formed an association and regularly put money into a common purse. After a certain amount of time, the sum of the money was disbursed to one of the group members. Saving recommenced and was similarly periodically disbursed in rotation to each member in the association. Plantation society was thus not deter-mined and controlled by the structures imposed by the slave-owners: the enslaved created their own social institutions and peasantry-like social formation, even in the absence of a wage and in the face of everyday forms of racial terrorization and brute force.[53] The rebellious proletariat, or the underclass of industrial laborers, was one of the by-products of industrialization in Europe. The rebelliousness and ingenuity of the enslaved provide a different perspective on the contradictions of capital-ism. Enslaved African peoples practiced labor politics in ingenious ways, often by withdrawing their labor or fleeing from the plantations. Work was slowed down, feet dragged, and strikes were called. When they were questioned by the slave-owners, the enslaved responded with evasiveness and satire.

The desire for autonomy and for freedom was no abstract wish, but filtered into the very depths of Black culture and materialized there. The Black church became a central site of resistance. Christianity, as itself a collection of teachings and cultural traditions from different cultures syncretized over time, was re-formed and re-shaped by Black preachers and practitioners into something new. They incorporated African spirituality, as well as Native spiritual and medicinal practices of remedy and cure, in the songs and rituals of the Black church. Spiritual practices and religious rituals, especially in the observation of birth, death, and rebirth, emerged as sources of social and personal energy.[54]

When free from the gaze of the slave-owners, their attorneys, and the plantation overseers, the enslaved participated in "unlicensed movement, collective assembly . . . [and] acts as simple as sneaking off to laugh and talk with friends or making nocturnal visits to loved ones."[55] And when they were together, perhaps rubbing shoulders in the fields, walking together at the Sunday market, or enjoying the refuge that came with the night, enslaved people enacted and embodied community by performing repertoires of music and dance, such as juba, or gumbe. These repertoires, as Hartman observes, "[used] the body for pleasure and [protested] the conditions of enslavement."[56]

The work songs, spirituals, and ballads that Black people sang, which became the basis for the blues, jazz, reggae, hip hop, and rap, expressed deep philosophical reflections on the kinds of injustices that slavery involved, as well as the kind of radical freedom that Black folk insisted on. Out of the Mississippi Delta, for example, arose what Clyde Woods has called the Blues mode of "social explanation." Blues music is filled with lyrics that reflect on racial slavery, and provide emotional and conceptual categories for Blacks to contain and entertain the psychic and spiritual burdens with which they were forced to reckon.

Blues songs often described the terror of racial slavery with a note of wry humor:

> In the South, when you do anything that's wrong
> They'll sho put you down on the county farm
> They'll put you under a man called Captain Jack,
> Who'll write his name upon and down your back.[57]

Blues lyrics captured the scope of ongoing epic catastrophe and devastation, while also evoking a disposition of musical equanimity and coolness, tinged with bitter recognition. And this mental tone nurtured the capacity to reflect on present catastrophes without being overwhelmed by them:

> The whole round country, Lord, river has overflowed
> Lord, the whole round country, man, is overflowed
> I would go to the hill country, but they got be barred
> ... So high the water risin', I been sinkin' down
> Then the water was risin', at places all around
> It was fifty men an chillum, come sink and drown.[58]

The Blues also called for celestial and divine justice as a way of examining the ongoing lack of social justice for the enslaved, their ancestors, and their descendants:

> Oh, Mary, don't you weep, don't you mourn
> Oh, Mary, don't you weep, don't you mourn
> Didn't Pharaoh's army get drowned?
> Oh, Mary, don't you weep[59]

Toni Morrison reflected on the significance of Black music traditions that developed under slavery:

Black Americans were sustained and healed and nurtured by the translation of their experience into art above all in the music. ... My parallel is always the music because all of the strategies of the art are there. All of the intricacy, all of the discipline. All the work that must go into improvisation so that it appears that you've never touched it.[60]

Morrison conveys the music and magic of Black experience in her novels, including *Song of Solomon*, in which some of the characters even have the power to fly home, across the chasms and divides created by slavery:

> Sugarman done fly away
> Sugarman done gone
> Sugarman cut across the sky
> Sugarman gone home.[61]

And as cultural studies critic Paul Gilroy observed, one of the main social tenets that comes from the Black arts movements under slavery is the insistence that "ordinary people do not need an intellectual vanguard to help them speak or to tell them what to say."[62] Social explanation, moral reflection, and the route to the divine was not the possession of the Man, but belonged to everybody.

ABOLITION

Forms of resistance and creativity disrupted the plantation complex from within, even as large-scale political forces were dismantling the institution of slavery from within and without. The Age of Revolutions that erupted across the Americas from the 1770s went hand in hand with abolitionist movements across the hemispheric Americas over the coming decades. Abolition was tied up with Republicanism, especially among those groups calling for radical democracy, equitable representation, and the liberation of all peoples from tyranny. An age of abolitionism stretched from the 1770s through the 1880s, as grassroots groups mobilized, and rebelled, to declare the rights of Blacks, the Indigenous, and women.[63] Some 500,000 slaves freed themselves in Saint Domingue in 1804. One million enslaved people across the Caribbean Sea and Indian Ocean attained their freedom between 1833 and 1839. And 4 million African people rose out of slavery in the United States in 1865.

White abolitionists in such cities as London, Boston, and Paris – especially the Quakers, Methodists, and Nonconformists – certainly played an important role in the abolitionist cause. By 1775, anti-slavery societies were formed in Pennsylvania, Massachusetts, and Vermont. A committee for the abolition of the slave trade was established in London in 1787. In 1788, activists in Paris formed an anti-slavery society. But the political movement to destroy slavery relied on slave rebels, maroons, Black authors, and community mobilizers more than anyone else. The end of slavery was activated from the roots.[64]

In the 1770s, across the plantation colonies of the Caribbean – Saint Domingue, Jamaica, Dominica, Tobago, St. Vincent, and Grenada – African people tested the chains in massive slave revolts.[65] This era saw an increasing number of mass rebellions against plantation slavery because levels of exploitation had grown so extreme. The exploitative conditions of the enslaved were exacerbated after the Seven Years War, as its aftermath led to heightened imperial competition between Britain and France for the economic superiority of their respective plantation colonies, especially Saint Domingue and Jamaica. This was a time of great capitalist greed, especially as the consumer demand for sugar sky-rocketed. British workers demanded more and more cheap calories to survive the intensifying factory labor regimes of the first industrial revolution.

Levels of plantation production reached unprecedented heights in the 1770s, as did the number of enslaved people being consigned to plantations. By this decade, the number of Blacks in Jamaica outnumbered the number of Whites ten to one. In Saint Domingue, there were almost twenty Black people to each slave-owning White person.[66] And with the need to organize vast numbers of plantation laborers more efficiently, and also to secure the interests and safety of the small minority of White planters, racial hierarchies became more rigid and the exercise of violence gruesomely more extreme.

The rise of the French and British plantation complexes, with their industrial rates of whippings, dismemberments, lynchings, rakings, rapes, and other monstrous acts, met with widespread and growing insurrection among the enslaved. In Jamaica, the Coromantee Wars broke out from the 1760s to the 1780s, named after enslaved military leaders from the Gold Coast. This was followed by the Second Maroon Wars in 1795. In Haiti, rebellion turned into revolution during the period from 1791 to 1804. In nearby Grenada, Féydon's uprising against British racial slavery erupted in 1795, directly inspired by revolutionary Haiti. Leaders such as Toussaint L'Ouverture coordinated a variety of mass actions, including: general strikes; the destruction of property; solidarity-building between enslaved Blacks, free Blacks, and *Mulattoes*; mass exodus; and revolutionary warfare.[67]

Once Black folk were freed from slavery, either through flight or fight, or through their manumission, many redoubled their efforts to tear down the system of oppression. Powerful freed Black authors published their treatises. In 1773, Phillis Wheatley, an emancipated Black woman in Massachusetts, published her book of poems, defiantly asserting the dignity of African humanity within a racial order that reduced African people to the status of things. Ottobah Cugoano penned *Thoughts and Sentiments on the Evil and Wicked Traffic of Slavery* in 1787. Olaudah Equiano published his famous *Interesting Narrative* in 1789, hailed as a masterpiece.

Black abolitionist writing and visual culture emerged in the nineteenth century, linking authors across the United States, the Caribbean, Britain, and Africa.[68] This was the era of Black revolutionary activists Sam Sharpe, Nat Turner, Harriet Tubman, Mary Prince, Harriet Jacobs, and Sojourner Truth. Sojourner Truth (1797–1883), born Isabella, was enslaved for forty years in New York before she attained her freedom. The Black abolitionists, much as they put experience into words and created representations of slavery through their print and art, also continually pointed to the unrepresentable and unspeakable that lurked in the experience of slavery. Sojourner Truth wrote, "were she to tell all that happened to her as a slave … it would seem to others, especially the uninitiated, so unaccountable, so unreasonable, and what is usually called so unnatural (though it may be questioned whether people do not always act naturally), they would not easily believe it."[69] Harriet Jacobs (1813–97), who lived thirty years under slavery before her escape, insisted that the pen could never articulate the experience of servitude: "O virtuous reader! You never knew what it was to be a slave." Slavery, these writers repeated, involved the experience of the "unspeakable."[70] Black abolitionists, when they pointed to the unspeakable, were not gesturing to acts or events considered to be profane or indecent, since indecency defined the whole institution of slavery from the start. Rather, they pointed to a social condition that was outside the framework of feeling and representation of the established racial order. They pointed to the experience of Black being under slavery, which refused translation and assimilation within a White racial order that could not reflect on or interrogate its own deep-seated disrepair.[71] Black abolitionists continually toggled between public representation of the experience of slavery and a refusal to give an account.

When we study slavery and plantation histories we embark on an exploration of particular forms of colonial violence that are different from but interlock with the violence of Native elimination and replacement, as we explored in the previous chapters. Colonial capitalism transformed African bodies into an unprecedented kind of commodity. Slaves were commodified as chattel property, while also being forced to expend their intelligence, sensibilities, and their spirit for the benefit of European and European-American capitailst consumption.[72] The figure of the "slave" was paradoxical. Slave-owning societies conceived of Black "slaves" as rent-bearing assets (as commodified human flesh) and *simultaneously* as suppliers of the most intensive and intimate forms of modern human labor. Furthermore, this paradox of the "slave" refracted the paradox of the "master." Racialized White society came to cultivate a form of being human that was grotesquely inhuman in its conceptions of currency and value, conditioned upon the compulsive degradation and destruction of Black and Indigenous life.

White racialization insisted on its own autonomy and incomparability. Whiteness, we might say, is characterized by disguise: inhumane practices of alienation, instrumentalization, consumption, and self-isolation masquerading as modes of human interrelation. Whiteness insisted on denying interdependence with other human communities, while growing actively parasitic upon those same communities. This form of racialization has prevented responsible interdependence with other peoples who practice different kinds of humanity. Through racial slavery, one definition of the human was elevated above all others. The practice of racial slavery took White society out of proper relation with other human groups, and therefore, we might observe, out of proper relation with its own humanity. In this way, reckoning with the legacies of racial slavery must not be the work of Black communities only. Black communities have long confronted the horizon of social death and found ways to endure and to create new kinds of human possibility and human recognition. Reckoning with slavery also calls for racial, capitalist White society to reflect upon its ongoing distorted relationship to other varieties of humanity.[73]

CHAPTER 4

Port

I N 1859, fourteen weary Chinese indentured laborers on sugar plantations in Cuba sent a petition to a British Commission of Inquiry. The petitioners requested relief from the terms of their employment. They had all signed agreements and taken on debt to travel overseas and work as agricultural laborers in the Caribbean. However, even though they had agreed to the terms of employment, their "free labor" felt more like bondage. The fourteen workers described their vulnerability to arbitrary reprisals from employers. Castaways on the shores of Havana and Manzanillo, they detailed their administrative entrapment in a maze of permits, fines, and penalties. They worked without respite to pay off their debts and were subjected to surveillance and regular abuse. In fact, around the world, from Cuba to Mauritius, captains of capitalism recruited Asian migrant laborers to service the second industrial revolution fueled by railroad construction, steel machinery, steamships, and big agriculture. Giant sugar, coffee, cotton, indigo, rice, fruit, and rubber plantations arose across the temperate Americas, while "bonanza farms" of wheat and corn cultivation spread in the American North. Some call this emerging international labor regime the Second Slavery, as new coercive strategies pressed Asian, Afro-Caribbean, and Latino migrant laborers to serve the giants of industry.[1]

The petition by the Chinese workers in Cuba provides an insider's description of labor under the Second Slavery:

> If a Chinese [person] did not have the "Proof" issued from the owner, he
> could not apply for a "Freedom Paper" from the official. If he did not have

the "Freedom Paper," the patrol could force him into the official workshop whenever they wanted to. In Cuba, the official workshop is no different from prison. They just make a conspiracy to trap the Chinese workers to work at the official workshop forever since they do not need to pay us anything and also they can skim profits by binding us. Apart from the "Freedom Paper," there is the "Walking Paper," which requires a fee to renew every year. Without that paper, one could not walk on the street. If one wanted to travel to another town, one would have to ask the local officials for a "Traveling Paper"; otherwise, one could be put in prison.[2]

Contract papers stipulated the length of time Asian contract workers would have to serve their employer. Oftentimes, after contracts ran out, laborers were compulsorily re-indentured against their will. "Freedom papers" allowed Chinese workers to take extended periods of time away from their jobs, often six months to a year, to take up temporary employment. Once the period indicated on these papers ran out, employers compelled workers to return to the fields, under penalty of imprisonment. "Walking papers" permitted laborers to move about outside the confines of their plantations or work sites. Without them, indentured laborers could again be imprisoned and whipped. For indentured laborers, even walking around had to be licensed. Asian laborers, by a variety of paper-based technologies, experienced lock-up in a system of mobile incapacitation.

The forces of the new colonialism had long used travel licenses and passports to command movement, including the *cartaz* and *asiento* systems discussed earlier. Ever since the 1500s, enslaved Africans had to wear metal "tickets" when they left the boundaries of their assigned plantations. Yet, when, in the 1830s, the formal institution of racial slavery began to crumble around the world, colonial power developed new technologies to register, surveil, and engineer large-scale labor mobility at the bodily frontiers of migrating and seafaring peoples. Colonialism functions not only by incapacitating people and things in a particular place, but also by regulating and restricting people's movements.

COLONIAL PORTS

Chinese workers in colonial Cuba feared traveling to other towns, or departing from the workshops, or even walking the streets. Yet, in order for workers from China to be indentured in Cuba in the first place, colonialism's drive to commandeer and control movement had to function not only through plantation and township patrols on the island, but also across rimlands and ports spanning global expanses. A port is a political and economic domain where mobility over land connects to mobility over seas. As conduits allowing ocean trades to debouch onto land, ports are also governmental apparatuses for the command of movement across land and sea, and between societies. Yet, ports are also anarchical locations of smuggling, contraband, vice, and piracy; they simultaneously serve as sites for the exercise of colonial command, and for the contestation and breach of it.[3]

Human mobility is movement, often circulatory in nature, away from local or native environments. For millennia, and long before the dawn of the new colonialism, high levels of human mobility ranged across ports along the rimlands of the Indian Ocean and the South China Sea, enabling large-scale transoceanic trade.[4] As much as Asia is a region of landmasses – continents, peninsulas, and archipelagoes – it is also a constellation of ports connecting the vast thoroughfares of Asian seas. And so, when Europeans started their entry into Asia in the 1500s, they were entering the big leagues of seaborne trade. Europeans who first began participating in Asian trades sought to mimic the trading cultures of Asia, as much as they also attempted to assert their mercenary dominance.[5]

In the early Dutch *periplus* map, or "voyage" map, of Asia from 1754 shown in Figure 4.1, note how your eye comes to focus primarily on the expanse of sea and not the landmass. Informed by pre-existing Islamic Asian maps, in which seawater takes center stage, this early Dutch depiction highlights the importance of port cities along the Indian Ocean rim, designating them in red ink.[6] From the 1500s onwards, as the new colonialism developed, European colonial forces increasingly sought to commandeer these ports at such places as Manila, Malacca, Bombay, and Kochi in order to control their associated mobilities. Beginning in the 1750s, permanent European factories, or trading posts, were established on the Chinese coasts at Guangzhou, Xiamen, Songliang, and Ningpo.

Asian and African port cities eventually played an important role in the expansion of western colonial power. Already by the late 1600s, the

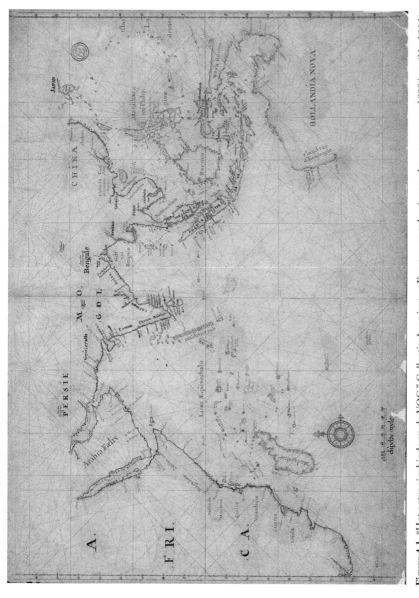

Figure 4.1 "Het octrooigebied van de VOC." Collectie Aanwinsten Kaarten en tekeningen. Anonymous. c. 1600 inv. (Nr. 16A1). Used with permission of the Netherlands National Archives, The Hague.

Cape of Good Hope (today's Cape Town), Colombo (in Sri Lanka), Batavia (today's Jakarta), and Dejima (a part of today's Nagasaki, Japan) were major hubs of Dutch trade. Eventually, during the 1700s, these port towns and their networks were woven together by the spindles of British and French imperial oceanic trading. The new port centers of Bombay, Madras, Calcutta, Singapore, and Hong Kong also arose, oftentimes based on or near pre-existing Asian trading marts.[7] Dutch, British, and French port colonialism overwrote, but did not supplant, the pre-existing networks of maritime connection across Asian shores. Major ports of Asia, such as Canton, Hormuz, Mombasa, and Calicut, continued to be important centers of inter-Asian trade even after the deep political and military incisions of European and American power in the nineteenth century, discussed below. The history of maritime trade in Asia and the Pacific is a palimpsest of sea routes and port towns, in which the European presence is a relatively recent overlay. Even today, dhow ships manned by Indian, Chinese, Arab, and Southeast Asian captains and crews continue to ply ancient sea routes between Asian ports, carrying out their conveyance with relative independence from European shipping capital.[8]

Due to an innovation in international business practice, the joint-stock company, European colonial power took on an increasingly *imperial*, or inter-regionally coordinated, formation across Asia by the 1600s. Ports played a central role in facilitating this imperial turn. Joint-stock companies, based in such cities as Amsterdam, London, Edinburgh, and Paris, coordinated a myriad coercive colonial acts across Asian seas for the benefit of their stockholders.[9] During the 1600s, joint-stock companies emerged as "incorporated" firms, owned by stockholders. To a much greater extent than the fledgling Portuguese empire in Asia in the 1500s, joint-stocks received sanction from their respective European governments to create trade monopolies in their regions of operation. The British imperial state, for example, granted the East India Company a monopoly on all British trade with India, and the Royal West African Company received exclusive rights to British trade on the west African Coast. The Dutch empire granted the Dutch East India Company a trade monopoly over the Dutch East Indies. And the infamous French Mississippi Company held a state-sanctioned business monopoly over the

French colonies in North America and the West Indies before its collapse in 1719. As monopolies, these firms were also military organizations outfitted to forcibly impose their trading privileges on distant lands and seas.

The distinguishing feature of the joint-stock company is its responsibility to its shareholders. This joint ownership structure meant that capital for new ventures could be raised much faster than ever before. And the granting of monopolies sanctioned violence on a higher order. With the coming of joint-stock companies into Asian trade in the 1600s, European investors introduced unprecedented war-making machinery in their attempts to command the pre-existing high levels of industry. These entities were not just private businesses, but satellite European states acting in other peoples' sovereign domains. Historian Philip Stern explored the imperial state-like character of the East India Company, which had its own army, coinage, flotilla, and diplomatic corps. Eventually, the Company actually became the permanent colonial state in such port cities as Calcutta, Bombay, and Madras.[10]

From their perches in port cities, these large-scale enterprises coordinated plunder, slave-trading, diplomacy, administration, shipping, and production across oceans.[11] By the 1760s, European joint-stock companies were heavily involved in carving out new industries in their colonies, such as in cotton from Charleston, Carolina; furs from Charlesfort, Nova Scotia; sugar from George Town, Guyana; and coffee from George Town, Penang.[12] The era of joint-stocks also saw the rise of what some historians call the "blue-water strategy" of British imperial expansion.[13] Inaugurated by the Navigation Laws passed by the British Parliament in 1650, England began creating "wooden walls" at sea – that is, territorializing the oceans through the sheer dominance of its naval ships.[14] By the end of the 1700s, Britain was the dominant naval power on the high seas. By the mid nineteenth century, this would eventually lead to the "All-Red Route," connecting different British imperial holdings across the globe's oceans.

The imperial drive to maximize profits for shareholders on a large and coordinated scale compelled colonial incisions into the economies of other sovereign groups on earth. The Dutch East India Company forcibly imposed indigo cultivation on peasants in Java. Indigo produced a blue dye widely used in textile production, especially in the manufacture of Dutch English, and North American military uniforms. The British and Dutch empires battled to gain control over spice-producing zones across the Indian Ocean: cloves from Zanzibar, cinnamon and nutmeg from Sri Lanka, and black pepper from Malabar and Malacca. In each of these areas, European militaries intervened in local sovereignties in order to modify labor regimes and production schedules to better appease European markets.[15]

Over the course of the 1700s, the transformation in capitalist development revolutionized the colonial port.[16] The British East India Company dredged watercourses and reclaimed land from the sea in Calcutta and Madras in order to support the shipping trade. At Madras, Bombay, Calcutta, and Jakarta, we see the erection of customs houses; "writers' buildings" for company clerks; banking and insurance "agency houses"; military encampments; and jails. Grand residences for European governors soon appeared. By the late 1700s, imperial architectures of transport and transaction became the symbols of the new age of racial capitalism.[17] European imperial powers used guerilla diplomacy and warmongering to coordinate colonial expansion from these administrative ports.[18]

CAPITALIST WAR AT SEA

Capitalist war involves the use of violence against sovereign peoples for the furtherance and intensification of commercial exploitation. And one particular form of capitalist war targets the sea. This mode of war developed through settler colonialism, the creation of "closed seas," and racial slavery in the 300 years leading up to the nineteenth century. Especially from the late 1700s onwards, capitalist war expanded through European empires across Asia. Ports became gateways through which emerging European and American imperial powers commanded the liquid commodities of moving people and mobile things.

No exceptional kind of rationality distinguished European economic development from that of societies in China, Japan, and India in the centuries leading up to the 1800s. No "European miracle" or "industrial revolution" in the eighteenth and nineteenth centuries set western Europe apart from all other groups on earth. These are myths. In fact, for centuries leading up to the 1800s, Asian ports visited by Asian dhow and junk ships constituted the preeminent world center of merchant enterprises. Asian capitalists started plantations, sought to innovate crops, lent money, diversified capitalist portfolios, traded in commodities, sold slaves, and practiced different forms of colonialism long before Europeans arrived in Asian waters. Banking instruments in Asia were highly developed, with *hundis*, or bills of exchange, securing trade over long distances. Many different kinds of moneylenders, such as the *sarraf* or *sahukar*, provided credit lines to support the long-distance Indian Ocean trade.[19] Furthermore, many powerful empires, with their own long-standing colonial pursuits, ruled over polities in Asia in the 1600s, including the Ottoman and Mughal empires, as well as the Safavid and Qing courts.

What made the expansion of European empires across Asia so distinctive was the combination of capitalist trade with unprecedented levels of racialized warfare. Europeans innovated the use of brutal forms of warfare, disguised under the dogma of civility and freedom, in order to intensify levels of social oppression and extractive activity.[20] Through the onslaught of capitalist war, ports became the apertures through which colonial interests injected themselves into sovereign Asian lands, while also sucking the productive forces from those societies into the circulatory system of oceanic trading networks. Conversely, these same conditions of capitalist warfare across Asia generated new possibilities and imperatives of response and contestation. Asian histories were activated in new ways and to unforeseeable outcomes by the winds of colonial capitalism in a myriad small Asian odysseys at sea.

European proponents of economic liberalism and free trade, emboldened by the economic ideology expressed in the writings of Adam Smith, called for the deregulation of the seas, the reduction of custom duties, and the end of mercantilism. And one of Adam Smith's main considerations in his foundational treatise, *An Inquiry into the Wealth of Nations* (1776), related to European seaborne trade with Asia. Shipping, Smith observed, allowed the conveyance of goods between different distant marts, or economic centers. Smith correctly saw Asia as a teeming arena of maritime trade activity. He marveled at the level of commerce "carried on by the native Indians; and vessels navigated by the inhabitants of China and Japan, of Tonquin, Malacca, Cochin China, and the island of the Celebes."[21] For Adam Smith, modern capitalism had to devise the best way to connect these different trade centers. Only this would allow for what Smith called "the natural progress of opulence." According to his theory, the "intercourse" between different marts, each specializing in their particular kinds of goods and services, would lead to the advantage of all parties involved. "As long as the one country has those advantages, and the other wants them, it will always be more advantageous for the latter rather to buy of the former than to make."[22]

Adam Smith envisioned free intercourse and communication between different centers of production and trade. Yet, he ignored the many forms of plunder and conquest that were the condition for European involvement in Asia in the first place. For the European philosophers of economic liberalism who followed after Adam Smith, colonial violence was not an enduring structure, but merely an intermittent event. That is, liberal theorists of the nineteenth century insisted that colonial violence was episodic and occasional. They denied the ways in which colonial warfare was actually symptomatic of imperial liberalism itself.[23]

The coming of liberalism and "free trade" actually coincided with the more extensive exercise of European military violence across regions of Asia. By the 1820s, European warships in Asia, the Middle East, Africa, and the Caribbean used the threat of gunboat firepower in order to extract financial, economic, and legal privileges and concessions from other peoples.[24] In 1825, French gunboat diplomacy forced the Haitian government to begin paying a huge indemnity to the imperial French state for the successful Haitian democratic revolution. In 1838, European gunboats imposed the Anglo-Ottoman Commercial Convention, which opened Ottoman Turkish markets to British traders. The concessions that European "free traders" garnered from other sovereign powers were often compelled at the barrel of a gun.[25]

In the midst of the abolition of slavery in the mid nineteenth century, European capitalist warfare pressed into new colonial frontiers. For example, even as the British Slavery Abolition Act was signed in 1833, bringing emancipation to more than 800,000 people of African descent, British-owned firms obtained new licenses to directly exploit peoples and economies in British India, Sri Lanka, and Malaya. Dutch and French Abolition in 1848 also coincided with the expansion of their colonization in Asia. And in 1838, European and American colonial powers combined to wage war on the Chinese empire in order to maintain the lucrative, and illegal, European opium trade in China.

By the 1830s, European capitalist war in Asia was a war of ports. It was waged by official navies, and by informal bands of privateers and mercenaries. Seaborne bands of men with guns and weapons did their masters' bidding, sailing across oceans and bays, and traveling upcountry via riverways. Free-trading capitalists hired ruthless mercenaries for the job. In Assam, for example, European planters who moved onto alluvial valleys to start tea plantations in the 1830s hired strongmen to force peasants, landless laborers, and Indigenous communities to work the fields. Indian moneylenders also played a crucial and complicit role in European colonial designs as the *asámi* land tenancy system emerged. Indebted peasants could be compelled to give up more of their land for the cultivation of agricultural commodities, or could be coerced to work longer hours on plantation fields. And if the impoverished and indebted workers refused, they were physically threatened or punished by hired

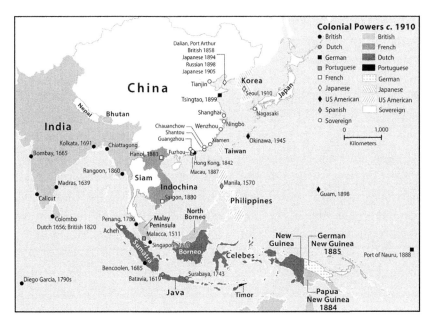

Figure 4.2 New colonialism in Asia, c. 1910. Created by the Tufts Data Lab: Carolyn Talmadge, Deirdre Schiff, Patrick Florance.

strongmen and overseers, or taken to court and harassed by government administrators.[26]

Similarly, across the Kandyan provinces of Ceylon (today's Sri Lanka), European tea entrepreneurs hired mercenaries to drive peasants from the land after the British passed the "Wastelands Ordinance" in 1830.[27] Mercenaries were simultaneously employed in the Tamil Nadu country-side to round up impoverished laborers and ship them across the Palk Strait onto Sri Lankan plantations. In India, during the early nineteenth century, the alchemy of brute force and debt forced the expansion of indigo and opium cultivation across the hinterlands of Bihar and Orissa. And in the 1830s, the Dutch imposed the *cultuurstelsel* (cultivation) system on Indonesian indebted peasants, forcing them to grow coffee for international markets.[28] Forcing "free trade" and liberal empire on other peoples' societies took place through the brandishing of guns. The rise of European "free trading" in the 1800s brought about the expansive militarization of the seas and colonization of Asian lands (see Figure 4.2).

NARCO WARS

During the long century of the 1750s–1880s, European imperial powers waged a long century of permanent drug wars across Asian seas and landmasses. Ports across Africa and Asia served not just for official trades, but also for all manner of private exchange in goods and people that developed outside the official control of Western imperial states. Traf-ficking in people and in drugs enriched the coffers of European "men on the spot," the representatives of European power in Asia.[29] The East India Company facilitated the private deals of its employees and mercenaries. Most of the increase in opium trading to China, for example, came after 1773 as the British East India Company began to support private enterprise.[30] After 1781, the East India Company took over the purchase of all the opium produced in its territory and created a government drug monopoly. But even then, up until the end of the eighteenth century the East India Company placed few restrictions on the private activities of its servants, allowing them to profiteer from the "country trade." In response, the Qing dynasty developed the "one-port" system during the latter 1700s to more effectively control unregulated

European drug-trafficking alongside the legal trades. The Chinese government designated Guangzhou as the only bridgehead for maritime trade with Europeans. A sliver along the coast became the center for European traders in the region, known as the Thirteen Factories.[31] British opium sales in China helped make up for the immense British trade debt to China. The East India Company exchanged chests of opium for teas, silks, porcelains, and lacquered goods from Chinese traders. It then sold these goods on European markets for pounds sterling. This narcotics-laced triangle of exchange was an important aspect of the "Asia trade."

The British increasingly used opium instead of silver coin as the means of payment for Asian goods, causing alarm among Chinese authorities. By the 1820s and 1830s, opium was the largest single commodity exported by the British empire to China.[32] British merchants, operating in ports across Asia, trafficked in drugs as a way of facilitating their vast lucrative business with Chinese merchants, eventually earning the wrath of Qing imperial rulers. Asia became a major theater of war across which Europeans promoted "free trade," as they sought to transform the South China Sea into their own proprietary lake. The first Anglo-Chinese War (also known as the First Opium War), 1839–42, provides a clear example of this militarization at sea, as European powers contravened the sovereignty of the Chinese state.

In 1838, the Qing imperial state again took decisive measures to close down the European narco trade, given its detrimental implications for Chinese merchants and its deleterious effects on the health of Chinese people. Qing restrictions on the European drug trade were enough to prompt a declaration of war by European free traders. In 1839, the East Indian Company sent more than forty warships to Guangzhou to crush the defenses put up by the Qing state. The Anglo-Chinese War lasted for three years, as the British and their European allies sought to exercise dominion over Asian seas.

During the hostilities of the war, more than 20,000 Chinese persons were killed, contrasted with only 69 British. This was asymmetrical warfare on a vast scale. During the nineteenth century, European capitalist colonizers, backed by state power, unleashed many such belligerencies. Free trade required its servants to conquer and command new areas for

Figure 4.3 New colonialism across the Pacific, c. 1910. Created by the Tufts Data Lab: Carolyn Talmadge, Deirdre Schiff, Patrick Florance.

industrious activity, using gunboats and heavy artillery to get their way.[33] The 1842 Treaty of Nanjing established British trade privileges in Mofuchou, Ningbo, Fuchow, Amoy, and Shanghai, and the Crown Colony of Hong Kong. Opium was conditionally legalized as an import, and China received no concessions in return. This "unequal treaty" imposed European liberties and curtailed Chinese sovereignty. The establishment of Hong Kong as a British colony, along with other treaty ports, at the conclusion of the Anglo-Chinese War in 1842, led to renewed attempts to penetrate into the hinterlands of mainland China to supply the growing international demand for Chinese indentured labor. As Europeans expanded trafficking in drugs across the South China Sea, markets for cheap Chinese labor also opened up in North and South America, southern Africa, Australia, and New Zealand, and across the plantation archipelagoes of the Pacific Ocean, such as Fiji and Samoa.[34]

The British instigated a Second Anglo-Chinese War (the Second Opium War), 1857–60, after Chinese officials seized a British ship on suspicion of piracy. In order to break the back of Chinese imperial resistance to British trade objectives, 7,000 British Indian troops landed at Hong Kong and captured Guangzhou and Tianjin. The colony of Hong Kong was extended to include the Kowloon Peninsula. Ultimately, the unequal Treaty of Tianjin was signed, announcing British maritime supremacy over the South China Sea. Ports such as Hong Kong and Singapore played an important role in the expansion of the "Crown Colony" system that spread protectorate colonialism across Asia during the reign of Queen Victoria (r. 1837–1901).

European empires created port enclaves, and established their own courts and legal systems so that "islands of Europe" could arise out of Asian seas (see Figure 4.3). Naval or "admiralty" law emerged to adjudicate the contested domains of the sea. As European imperial states set up their trade centers in other peoples' seas in the nineteenth century, they increasingly imposed their ideas of freedom, and law and order over sovereign seafaring peoples. In the so-called "free ports," European law claimed to supersede the existing Asian legal systems.[35] British extraterritoriality in Asia, or the creation of special zones in which British law prevailed, first sprouted up in the British Indian presidencies of Bombay, Madras, and Calcutta. The system spread to the port of Singapore in 1819, and after the First Anglo-Burmese War (1824–6), British imperial law was imposed on Burma. After the First Opium War, extraterritorial treaty ports were created along the coast of southern China. American and French imperial states also created "free ports" in coastal China in the 1840s. With the Treaty of Wuanghia in 1844, US citizens claimed protection by American law while in China.[36] A decade later, in 1855, Americans and Europeans began asserting extraterritorial rights in Japan. Meanwhile, in 1895, Japan responded to this context by undertaking the colonization of Taiwan, and then of Korea in 1910. The competitive pillaging of Asian archipelagoes and coasts drew imperial nation-states to the verge of the First World War.

INDENTURED LABOR

Large mobile workforces were necessary for the extractive industries that had exploded across the planet by the mid nineteenth century. From the 1820s onwards, the expansion of imperial liberalism and free-trade capitalism went along with renewed efforts to command the mobilities of Asian migrants for the ultimate benefit of Western business interests. The expanding trade in drugs was accompanied by a huge expansion in the trafficking of racialized laboring people. Ultimately, some 12,000,000 Asian bonded laborers, most of whom were from India and China, traveled the oceans to distant worksites under a variety of coercive contract arrangements. Chinese migrant workers especially came from the countrysides of Shandong, Jiangsu, Zhejiang, Fujian, and Guangdong. Meanwhile, Indian workers left from the regions of Bihar, the Punjab, and Tamil Nadu.

The islands of Réunion and Mauritius in the Indian Ocean were the first destinations for bonded or indentured laborer flows. By 1830, some 3,000 Indian toilers had arrived in Mauritius from the French Indian colonies of Pondicherry and Karikal to work on sugar plantations.[37] The number of indentured workers rose to 25,000 by the end of the decade. Working people also came from the hinterlands of Bengal and Bihar in northeast India, funneled through the port of Calcutta.[38]

The main feature of the "indentured labor system" was that those who entered it had to agree to commit themselves in advance to a fixed term of labor. Over time, the system became highly regulated. It involved five-year contracts and an elaborate system of limits imposed on workers (including criminal sanctions against such infractions as "absenteeism," "desertion," "improper performance," "idling," and "vagrancy"). Workers would indicate consent by either signing or applying their fingerprint to the contract. Indian laborers, by agreeing to the contract, became *girmitiyas*. Oftentimes, *girmitiyas* did not even know the details of the agreements they had signed, since they could neither understand nor read English. Nevertheless, indentured contracts were often renewed, sometimes with consent and sometimes without. For many indentured workers, a long-term work contract turned into a permanently new life. In the Indian case, only about one-third of the laborers who left for distant climes in the Americas would return to India.

The indentured labor system depended on coercive contract relationships, or civil relationships that were enforceable through criminal
law. The threat of incarceration in jails and "workshops" created the
characteristic coercion of the system.[39] Indenture relied on close col-
laboration between government and enterprise. The state remained
active in all aspects of the system, from recruitment, to transportation,
to oversight. As Walter Look Lai points out, this apparent system of
rationality and control was riddled with contradictions: arbitrary wages,
rampant abuses and intimidation, the habitual resort to extreme punishments and fines for minor "offenses," extrajudicial punishments,
and the racialized biases of the colonial justice system that favored
the interests of Whites.

Indentured laborers were often referred to by the racial term "coolie."
The term originally came from the precolonial Indian context, where it
designated menial servants employed to bear loads and transport goods.
But "coolie" was appropriated and repurposed by British colonial authorities in the early nineteenth century to refer specifically to indentured
or contract laborers for extractive capitalist industries working on plantations, in mines, and on railroads. "Coolie" soon became a term of racial
identification, adopted for Indian and Chinese workers entering overseas labor diasporas.

Although borrowing aspects of the slave-labor regime, the system of
indenture marked a new development. Guyanese historian Walter
Rodney once pointed out that capitalist plantations required a particular
type of labor: "Labor must be cheap and plentiful, and, even more
important, the labor must be easily controlled. Unless labor can be
provided under conditions that maximize the industrial control, you
cannot have a functioning plantation system."[40] In order to create a
cheap labor supply, British, French, and Dutch mercantile interests
penetrated into the pre-existing markets for human trafficking across
Asia, including the *adikari*, *kangany*, and *maistry* systems of India, and the
khe-tau system of the Chinese coast. Contracts, kinship ties, and debt
relations were employed in order to gather up impoverished and vulnerable workers, and to control them as they traveled. And once they
reached their labor sites, technologies of incarceration, registration,
and physical deprivation, along with chain-gang labor, were used to

command the labor of indentured workers, as was the case under slavery. Even as plantation slavery came to an end across the British, Dutch, and French empires from 1833 to 1848, Asian laborers were barracked on the old slave yards. The poison of coercion was fatefully blended with free will in the emerging system of labor servitude.

Regular flows of indentured labor from China commenced after 1847, after the end of the First Opium War (1839–42). The narco war of European imperial powers against the Qing state was an effort to lay claim not only to Chinese territory, but also to mobile Chinese laboring bodies that were funneled through them. By the 1850s, the majority of Chinese immigrants to the Americas came from an area of no more than 7,000 square miles, including Macao, Canton, and Hong Kong on the Pearl River Delta.[41] However, India sent the greatest number of indentured migrants into the world, to such destinations as British Guyana, Trinidad, the French Caribbean, Suriname, Réunion, East Africa, Natal, Fiji, Burma, Ceylon, and Malaya. By the end of the nineteenth century, more than 425,000 people were emigrating from India annually to the magnetic centers of capitalist extraction.[42]

The 1840s and 1850s saw a spike in Chinese port revolts among indentured people shoved into the bowels of ships, such as the Canton riots of 1846 and the Amoy riots of 1852.[43] These same decades also witnessed a number of revolts against imperial hydrarchy and mutinies at sea, such as when Chinese laborers mutinied on the American ship *Robert Browne*, killing the captain and crew. And in 1857, revolutionary war broke out across British-ruled India, engulfing ports and hinterlands.

RELATIONAL MOBILITIES

The racial category of the "Oriental" was used by European empires in Asia in order to coordinate oppression. Edward Said observed in *Orientalism* (1982) that European ways of representing Asian cultures from the Arab World to South Asia to East Asia were shaped by the myth of Western imperialist exceptionalism. The "Orient" was constructed in European minds so as to affirm the "West" as the realm of freedom, progress, and rationality. The Orient, by contrast, was imagined as the place of backwardness, despotism, and irrationality.[44]

Orientalist fantasies and fears were projected onto the bodies of Asian migrant workers. Using the depersonalized racial language of large numbers to speak about diverse groups of people, Asians were collectively dehumanized with such labels as the "yellow peril" and the "mongol horde." Asian workers were enveloped in the web of Western capitalism, only to then be perceived as contagious threats. In the era of expanding free trade, Asian workers were simultaneously viewed as model migrant laborers and as swarm-like security risks to White nations.

Colonial capitalists in the Americas fantasized about the possibilities of mass labor mobilization from Asia in ways that interlock with histories of both racial slavery and Native genocide. In ports, Orientalist racism interlocked with other logics of oppression, especially the anti-Native "firsting" of settlers and the anti-Black legacies of racial slavery. Racial capitalism worked to position Asian laborers over against Native populations, who were said to be vanishing from the land, on the one hand, and over against Black populations, denigrated as indolent and lazy "property," on the other. Asian populations were introduced into this racial matrix of colonial White supremacy, creating a new tangled weave of colonialism's matting.[45]

In 1848, Leonard Wray, a Scottish Jamaican plantation owner in Sri Lanka, known as the "father of the Sri Lankan coffee industry," announced his comprehensive vision for Chinese laborers in the expanding European colonial global economy. He proposed that the "intelligent, enterprising and industrious Chinese [are] the best emigrants under heaven." Chinese workers, Wray wrote, were "like the negroes," in that they could "withstand the effect of the West India climate." But, unlike Blacks, they were supposedly industrious and obedient, not "indolent." He even foresaw the eventual replacement of Black laboring peoples of the Caribbean with an industrious Chinese race. The Caribbean isles of the future, wrote Wray, would be peopled by the "enterprising, [cheerful], and prudent" Chinese. According to his Orientalist fantasy, "obedient" and "industrious" Asian laborers would contribute their efforts willingly to White capitalist societies.

Wray, who had grown up in Jamaica, called for the shipment of 300,000 Chinese indentured servants to the Caribbean, doubling the island's population.[46] This was not a mere figment of the imagination, even though it was science fiction. By the 1870s, already more than

500,000 Chinese contract laborers had been sent to the Caribbean and South America alone. In Wray's racial imagination, Chinese workers would serve as the perfect labor replacements in the supposed transition from the system of slavery to the emerging system of free markets. Asian workers toiled on the expanding plantation frontiers, they constructed tunnels and laid railroad lines across expanding settler colonies, and they excavated minerals from mines.

Historian Manu Karuka shows how the construction of the Central Pacific Railroad from California to Nebraska involved both the elimination of Native communities and the importation of Chinese contract labor. With the Pacific Railroad Act of 1862, the government confiscated lands of the Lakota and Pawnee peoples of the Midwest, violently recategorizing Native sovereign land as belonging to American federal "land grants." Large companies soon became involved in the construction of transcontinental railway lines and the exploitation of subterranean minerals on Native lands.[47]

Thousands of Chinese laborers were employed to lay the railroad. And the railroad planners, unsurprisingly, maintained that Chinese workers would be more industrious and dependable than "idle" Black workers. Chinese workers were paid roughly one-half the wages of White workers, and were forced to work longer daily hours than Whites. A whopping 90 percent of laborers employed to build the Central Pacific Railroad were Asian "coolies."[48] They blasted tunnels out of rock and worked through snow and frigid cold. Hundreds of Chinese workers died during the first five years of construction due to the extreme conditions.[49]

On June 25, 1867, some 3,000 Chinese workers went on strike to protest the deplorable work conditions and the unequal standards.[50] The strikers asked for the working day to be reduced to eight to ten hours, instead of the stipulated fourteen hours for Asians. And they also demanded the end of the use of the whip. Charles Crocker, the general superintendent of railroad construction, refused to grant even a 25-cent increase to the striking Chinese laborers' wages. The strike was broken after two months of bitter anti-labor intransigency. Ironically, two years later, as the railroad construction was coming to a close, 300 unionized White workers marched to eject Chinese folk from the labor force. White unionists demanded that agreements be signed to prohibit Chinese workers from employment on the nearly completed tracks. And in these racist demands, the White workers were successful.

The instrumentalizing of Asian migrants under colonialism operated in relation to other histories of oppression. Asian indentured laborers were used to define and stabilize the categories of White, Black, and Native in a period after the abolition of slavery, when labor relations were in flux.[51] The construct of the Oriental as "servile" and "hardworking" served to reaffirm for Whites the supposed laziness and irresponsibility of post-emancipation free Black people. And the fantasy of the industrious Oriental worker was also used by Whites to bolster their ideology of dispossessing Native peoples from their territories in order to supposedly establish more industrious and productive economies. Asian workers were simultaneously treated as permanent foreigners, people of toil, and tokens of settler myth.

Beginning in the 1880s, exclusion laws against Chinese workers were introduced in different settler colonies. An international legal regime developed at the end of the nineteenth century to keep Chinese workers, subjected to political and social villainization, on the margins. They were allocated liminal status in the settler colonial states of the USA, Canada, and Australia, and assigned the condition of eternal outsiders. Settler epithets for Asian migrants, such as "yellow peril," conspired to disguise the infiltration of vast numbers from Europe. More than 10 million Europeans migrated to the USA between 1880 and 1900.[52] In 1882, at the onset of the European population deluge, the US Congress passed the Chinese Exclusion Act, suspending the legal migration of Chinese workers. Capitalist elites pitted Chinese immigrant workers against supposedly vulnerable migrant working-class Whites.[53]

Asian exclusion laws were in full force in the period from the 1880s through to the Second World War across different imperial and colonial formations. White settler states such as Canada, the USA, Australia, and New Zealand were among the first, along with Mexico, to establish anti-Asian legal regimes. Beginning at the turn of the century, Asian immigrants were for the first time subjected to a set of "sanitizing" practices meant to demarcate them as a cultural and racial threat to the bodies of White American citizens.[54] Their hair was shorn, their clothing fumigated, and they were subjected to bathing, delousing, interrogation, and inspection by medical examiners.[55] These approaches to racial population control prefigured the border security measures enacted on national boundaries in the later twentieth century and in our own time.

VISIONS OF RESISTANCE

A Chinese indentured laborer in Georgetown, Guyana, made this wood-cut depicting the life of the coolies on a sugar plantation. It was repro-duced in an 1871 book by Edward Jenkins: *The Coolie: His Rights and Wrongs* (Figure 4.4). Beyond its literal representation, we can read the depiction for its metaphors. Different experiences of diaspora are "thrown together," to use the language of Trinidadian writer Earl Lovelace.[56] The scene gestures to the different and uneven mindsets, cultures, and relationships woven into each other through the tangled histories of slavery and indenture. The image is a condensation of different temporalities, different experiences of time and meaning. Notice the Chinese worker apprehended by the stairs of the Great House, and how a thought bubble opens up to signify his ongoing psychic and emotional connection to his family back in China. As he is thinking of his family, his blood is being symbolically drawn, as a small boy captures it in a cup. The same bloodletting occurs in the foreground with an Indian indentured subject, whose heart has been punctured, again with a boy collecting the flowing blood. Colonial extraction bene-fits not only the colonizers, but also their children and descendants. It pays compound interest across generations, just as it also unleashes compound harm.

During the bloodletting, the plantation driver seems to hold the coolie's head as if to try to control his thoughts. The metaphor for the extraction of labor could not be clearer. The planters divide and separ-ate their workers by ethnicity, a common strategy of labor control. Indians, with their arms bound, are kept on the left and Chinese coolies on the right. And yet, the workers share solidarity in their experience of bloodletting. Notice how the blood from laborers is carried up the stairs by a boy. In the Great House we see what looks like European attorneys engaged in their own reverie – one is thinking about his mistress, it

8   THE COOLIE.

Figure 4.4 From Edward Jenkins, *The Coolie: His Rights and Wrongs* (New York: Routledge, 1871), p. 8. The image is in the public domain.

121

seems, as another group of overseers pores over account books while possibly enjoying a meal. Meanwhile, the women and children of the house remain enclosed inside, sequestered in the domestic space, peering out onto the violence below. This is a picture of multiple kinds of social worlds and oppression living next to each other, on top of each other, even *through* each other, with the foundation provided by the extraction of life energy from the bound workers.

Yet, the coolies resist the multiple strategies of control and of resistance, physical and mental. In the bottom right, a Chinese laborer runs away – one of the most common forms of resistance. Notice, too, among the Indians, two of the bound laborers face the group to offer entertainment, perhaps telling a story or performing a play. The scene is one of oppression, but also one of survival: the coolie dreaming of his family, the indentured workers huddling together to find strength in numbers, the make-believe of storytelling and plays, the courageous act of flight. Another form of survival appears in the foreground, as an Indian worker tends his cows and goes about his own business with a certain equanimity. The forms of creative, intellectual, and performative resistance among the laborers contrast with the contained, alienated lives of those living in the Great House. The author of this image critically reimagined human freedom amid the conditions of colonial oppression. Indentured laborers created unexpected histories through the experiences of the ship, the port, and diaspora.

WRECKAGE OF HISTORY

Colonial diasporas emerged as living legacies spun through ports by imperial infrastructures and warfare. Diasporas are the dispersal of a people caused by the exercise of colonial violence in ways that transform the traveling people and their cultures into something new. The cultures that emerge in diasporas bear the distinctive mark of their particular global histories of survival and resilience. The novel *Sea of Poppies* by Amitav Ghosh, set in 1838, tells the story of diasporic Asian seafarers navigating the turbulent winds of capitalist war across Asian waters. References to war are frequent in the novel, and they take many forms. At the center of the novel is a ship called the *Ibis*. A decommissioned slave ship plying across the Atlantic, the ship, we learn, will soon be refitted and recommissioned as a gunboat on the South China Sea to promote British narco wars. The ship thus sails across interlocking global histories of European imperialism and colonial violence, connecting ventures in racial slavery and drug-trafficking. But before going further East, the *Ibis* also carries a contingent of indentured laborers and convicts from Calcutta to Mauritius, to the plantations and prisons of the "pepper island." Sailing between multiple histories of violence, the ship carries their tangled burdens within its hull.

Yet, through the novel, we also recognize the *Ibis* not only as a vessel of conveyance, but also of transformation. The coolie ship becomes a metaphor for not just the wreckage, but also the creative reshaping, of people and cultures that result from capitalist warfare. The *Ibis*, as seaborne debris, also kindles unintended consequences and unexpected futures. The first time we encounter the ship, it seems to sail to us from the future. Appearing first in a dream, the ship sails towards the main character, Deeti, a poor Brahmin woman in the small opium-manufacturing village of Ghazipur, some 500 kilometers from the port city of Calcutta. In her dream, Deeti foresees the *Ibis* bringing wreckage to her life, but also transformation. Because of the *Ibis*, a free Black man from Baltimore named Zachariah Reid, and a group of Indian women fleeing the gender and caste constraints of patriarchal families, and a host of other partly free and partly bonded people, crash into Deeti's life and change its course.

As the *Ibis*, with its Black second officer, Zachary, departs from the port of Calcutta to journey to Port Louis, Mauritius, the ship disrupts the societies left behind. Some of the indentured women on board, including Deeti, flee into indenture in order to wreck the oppression they experience back home, including the patriarchal institutions of child marriage and sanctioned family rape. Others on board the *Ibis* experience wreckage in other ways. A wealthy Calcutta landlord is reduced to the status of a chained criminal after falling into a debt trap to an English businessman. Meanwhile, a Dalit man, from an untouchable caste in Indian society, abandons his caste identity as he enters indentureship and takes on a new name. And yet, his journey on the *Ibis* almost capsizes when an Indian police officer on the ship tries to reimpose the social imprisonment of caste.

These small wreckages on the *Ibis* are not the result of choice and freedom. The constraints are clear: manacled prisoners, the indentured labor regime, caste hierarchies, and racial tropes. And yet, within these constraints, the novel is interested in the twists of contestation and the new life that irreverently foams up over the tides, churned by the winds of capitalist war and imperialism. *Sea of Poppies* is a novel of shared and tangled lives battered by the sea, punctuated by the journey through ports. It provides a study of the unexpected outcomes of wreckage, as materials and lives are thrown together to recognize new relations that arise from interlocking contexts.

Relocated to archipelagoes, deltas, and the shores of snaking rivers around the world, Asian laborers generated new diasporic cultures that were different from the world they left behind. Asian migrants wove themselves into new societies and cultures that were not totally unfamiliar, even as they were foreign. Shipwrecked histories of colonial force, empire, and capitalist war made for uncanny acquaintances among distant colonized folk. In the Caribbean, South Asian cultural practices commingled with musical traditions from the African diaspora to create new genres, such as *chutney soca*. Coolies brought their food ways, which tangled with the Indigenous and African culinary cultures, yielding new kinds of home cooking, such as goat curries, bussup shats, and dal puris. Chinatowns arose across all the cities and towns of the Chinese diaspora. These became centers for political and cultural autonomy and association. Indian rituals and festivals, such as Muharram and Diwali, were practiced in the diaspora, but with twists. In the Caribbean, Indian religious festivals came to mix with the style of the great Black cultural fêtes, such as Junkanoo and Carnival.[57] Diasporic cultures of renewal continually survive the weather of colonial violence.[58]

PART II

ELEMENTARY ASPECTS OF COLONIAL POWER

CHAPTER 5

Science

F OR MANY EUROPEAN TRAVELERS from the 1700s onwards, the earth came to appear as a great repository of objects and entities just waiting for their collection and classification. So much had changed in the realm of economics, politics, and society in and through the preceding 200 years of colonialism, trade, warfare, and racialization. It became possible for groups at the center of imperial networks to conceive of the world as a research laboratory opened for their study. By the 1700s, the Swedes had a sprawling overseas empire. In 1735, the Swedish medical doctor and botanist Carl Linnaeus (1707–78) published his classification system of plants, animals, and minerals, which he called the "General System of Nature." The text proposed a new system for naming and cataloguing all entities that naturally exist, as well as their relation to one another. It was an endeavor to map and describe ecological existence within a total cosmological order. Linnaeus developed an open-ended naming system, using numerous diminutive and compound words from Latin and Greek. His method was meant to index the finest differences among naturally occurring entities and to organize these entities according to "classes, orders, genera, and species. All natural existence could thus be seen as related within great proliferating families, marked by continuities and gradations, and by an exquisite elaboration of life's plenitude over the course of geological time."[1] At the core of Linnaean science was not just the imperative to catalog and arrange, but also to attain a single viewpoint that could see all the planet's biodiversity from a universal perspective. In fact, Linnaeus saw his method of describing the natural world as a mode of divine worship.[2] Taxonomy was a means of reading out, and revealing, the orderly plans of God in what Linneaus believed to be the Maker's creation.

> If therefore the Maker of all things, who has done nothing without design, has furnished this earthly globe, like a museum, with the most admirable proofs of his wisdom and power … and if he has placed in it Man, the chief and most perfect of all his works, who is alone capable of duly considering the wonderful economy of the whole; it follows, that Man is made for the purpose of studying the Creator's works, that he may observe in them the evident marks of divine wisdom.[3]

Linnaeus developed and promulgated a method of thinking about the arrangement and order of things that existed. He taught his method to his students at the University of Uppsala.[4] A group of young Swedish naturalists emerged, soon to be nicknamed the "Apostles of Linnaeus." In the later 1700s, this group of students went on overseas travels to the settler colonies of North America and South America, and to parts of Asia, Africa, Australia, and the Middle East. They were on missions to read the signs of nature, and to name and describe the order and arrangement of natural life across the seven seas.

Swedish seaborne scientists made use of the extensive trading and naval networks of European joint-stock companies and oceanic militaries. Aboard the ships of the Swedish East India Company, the Dutch East India Company, and the British Royal Navy, these mercenary scientists eagerly incorporated more and more of the world's flora and fauna into Linnaeus' general system of nomenclature. They also wrote descriptions of the different human societies they encountered, arranging them in a hierarchy from those supposedly most closely adjacent to apes, to those closest to the angels. Africans were identified as among the "lowest savage races," according to European Afrophobic descriptions going all the way back to the time of Aristotle. Meanwhile, Europeans saw themselves as the best exemplars of *homo sapiens*, and closest to the gods.[5]

The European practitioners of natural history in the 1700s believed that they could categorize human beings just as well as they could categorize trees, birds, or insects. Linneaus' apostles applied his taxonomical method on whichever shore they reached. Pehr Kalm, in his

Travels into North America (1770), gives us a sense of how the Linnaean method was practiced.[6] Encountering the heavily forested area outside Philadelphia, Pennsylvania, Kalm explained that he had a "first opportunity of getting an exact knowledge of the state of the country, which was a plain covered with all kinds of trees with deciduous leaves." Kalm then made an annotated list – a catalog – of the trees of the woods "closest to Philadelphia." "I shall put that tree first in order, which is most plentiful, and so on with the rest, and therefore trees which I have found but single, though near the town, will be last." Based on the shape, color, size, and texture of their leaves and bark, Kalm enumerated a list of fifty-eight trees, labeled with the Latinate denominations of the Linnaean method:

1. Quercus alba, the white oak, in good ground.
2. Quercus rubra, or the black oak.
3. Quercus Hispanica, the Spanish oak, a variety of the preceding.
4. Juglans alba, hickory, a kind of walnut tree, of which three or four varieties are to be met with.
5. Rubus occidentalis, or American blackberry shrub.
6. Acer rubrum, the maple tree with red flowers, in swamps
7. Rhus Glabra, the smooth leaved Sumach, in the woods, on high glades, and old corn-fields

    . . .

35. Kalmia latifolia, the American dwarf laurel, on the northern side of mountains
36. Morus rubra, the mulberry tree, on fields, hills, and near the houses
37. Rhus vernix, the poisonous Sumach, in wet places[7]

Notice Pehr Kalm's use of the Linnaean binomial matrix of genus and species. Notice, too, Kalm's enumerated list, providing a scientific inventory of the Philadelphia woodland on that autumn day of September 8, 1768. Kalm himself shows up in the taxonomy in entry 35: "Kalmia" was the name of a genus of evergreen shrub. Linnaeus authorized this name in honor of his student, Pehr Kalm. In fact, many of Linnaeus' students ended up with their names given to living things. Ternstroemia, designating a genus of Asian evergreen, was named for Christoph Tärnström. Pehr Osbeck's name was applied to the Asian herb that Linnaeus called Osbeckia. Daniel Rolander's name was bestowed upon a beetle (*Aphanus rolandri*). Rothmannia, an African flower, was named after Göran

Rothmann. And Afzelia came to designate a tree found in Africa and India, named after Adam Afzelius. All of them were Linnaeus' early students, and, of course, today scientists still emblazon their names on taxonomies of newly discovered forms of life.

These scientists were not just seeking to put names to their new discoveries. They were also seeking to memorialize themselves in and through their descriptions. Of course, each of these plants had names before the coming of European scientists: they fit within existing ontologies (i.e. systems of describing the arrangement of what exists) of other societies, long pre-dating the coming of Linnaean compound names. Consider this list:

Linnaean name	Native name	Native use
Kalmia latifolia	*ulvta* (Cherokee)	a liniment, a salve for skin
Rothmannia	*mutamba webungu* (Shona, Zimbabwe)	a cure for sores and eczema
Afzelia	*munyama* (Swahili)	a prized hardwood, used to make boats
Osbeckia	*heen bovitiya* (Sinhalese)	a medication for jaundice and diabetes

As the Linnaean botanists traveled and described, they engaged in an expansive translation project. And they depended on the knowledge of many local and native collaborators to make the "discoveries" to which they put their names. In fact, these traveling European scientists did not "discover" new plants and animals at all. Rather, they translated plant and animal life from native systems into what they viewed as the general and universal system of "Man."

Linnaean cataloguing was the endeavor of a relatively few humans on earth who claimed to speak in the name of "Man," and to articulate a system of relation in which they stood at the center. This use of Linnaean scientific methodology changed the world it labeled. Like a hammer or a hoe, this scientific methodology itself was a kind of tool that could dig things up and put them into new arrangements. This emerging discipline of natural history would become an important tool in colonizing acts around the globe. Plants, animals, and minerals already woven into the lifeworlds of other human communities were assimilated into the system that Linneaus described as "Man entering the theater of the world."[8]

UNIVERSALIZATION

"Science," as a method of inquiry, is constructed, molded, and utilized by groups of people for underlying, and often unstated, political ends. Modern scientists like Linnaeus and the Linnaeans pursued what was called "the study of Natural History." This endeavor arose during Europe's long Enlightenment, c. 1650–1815, and became the template for almost all other modern academic disciplines, from biology to philology, sociology, and art history. One imperative of science during the Enlightenment was to assign, classify, and compare; to rank, order, and place all the differences on earth into a comprehensive schema, enabling a supposedly universal perspective on existence. Philologists would soon start developing catalogs of the world's language families and their histories; meanwhile, ethnologists claimed to catalog the earth's racial families and arrange them in a hierarchy ascending from the savage to the civilized.

Sciences of comparison and calculation allowed imperial states to forcibly and militarily place their colonies and subject peoples in measurable relation to other colonies and subject peoples, and to ports, hinterlands, and metropolises around the world. Colonial power used practices of cataloguing, measuring, auditing, and containerizing in order to transfer laborers and commodities between colonial locations, and across cultural and political borders.[9] Military operations, seaway engineering, railroad and river canal construction, environmental sciences, and ethnographic surveillance – what we might call the applied sciences of the Enlightenment – were some of the most important professions of the globalizing capitalist economy.[10]

By the second half of the eighteenth century, European governments were promoting scientific institutions and expeditions. Expeditions served to display imperial prestige, but also to define new frontiers for colonial extraction. In the late 1700s, the Spanish, British, Swedish, French, and Russian crowns, and the king of Brandenburg, were all funding colonial scientific expeditions as a matter of priority. This was an age of botanical gardens, curiosity cabinets, and museums, such as the British Museum. The first colonial botanical garden was established on the French colony of Île Bourbon (today's Réunion) by Pierre Poivre (1719–86) in the 1760s. In the 1770s, Kew Gardens, a research garden for colonial plants, was established in London by Joseph Banks.[11]

Napoleon Bonaparte's Egypt expedition of 1798–1801 provides one of the boldest expressions of the nexus between science and colonialism. As an army general during the French Revolution, Napoleon propelled his Egyptian campaign with the ethos of scientific fervor. He summoned some 167 French mineralogists, engineers, philologists, linguists, biologists, and other scholars to participate in his invasion of Egypt. The Napoleonic forces in Egypt and Syria had the largest complement of scientists, or *savants*, ever deployed in a European military campaign. Napoleon intended to conquer not only by armed might, but also by the muscularity of universalistic Western science. As the postcolonial scholar Edward Said observed, "[Napoleon's] idea was to build a sort of living archive for the expedition" that would help lay the groundwork for French domination of the whole "Orient," outstripping their British imperial competitor.[12] Said argued that European ways of representing Asian cultures, from the Arab world to South Asia to East Asia, were shaped by a metanarrative of Western imperialism. The "Orient" was constructed, even caricatured, in the minds of Europeans in contrast to "the West," which was presented as the realm of the "rational, developed, humane [and] superior." At the core of Orientalism is the assertion "that the Orient is at the bottom something either to be feared ... or to be controlled."[13]

Legions of European imperial forces mobilized at the turn of the 1800s to control fantasized Others, especially found in the "Orient." Science was weaponized in a variety of new ways. Scores of French knowledge professionals worked together to collect and categorize zoological, ethnographic, architectural, and literary artifacts, and these were collated and published in twenty-three enormous volumes between 1809 and 1828, in the encyclopedic *Description de l'Égypte*. The massive scale of such weaponized cataloguing was matched by the "information empire" of British India around this same time.[14] During this period, the East India Company hired science professionals to survey the flora, fauna, mineralia, topography, and the plethora of ethnic groups and cultures of South Asia. But these journeys by European knowledge consultants were made possible only by an unnamed and unacknow-ledged entourage of translators, local experts, porters, and assistants. For example, in 1854, the directors of the East India Company con-tracted three German explorers, the brothers Robert, Hermann, and Adolf Schlagintweit, to map the topological, magnetic, barometric, and ethnographic contours of the Indian subcontinent. They employed more than a hundred local assistants in their entourage, including *dubhashes* (translators), *dhobis* (for washing), *chaprassis* (for procuring supplies), *chaudedars* (for guarding the camp), *bhistis* (for fetching water), *ghasvalas* (for cutting grass), *saises* (for attending horses), *kalassis* (for pitching tents), and many local guides.[15] As colonial projects became increasingly hungry for knowledge on ever greater scales, the practice of colonial science relied on huge amounts of the physical and intellectual labor of the colonized themselves.

COLONIAL INSTITUTIONS OF SCIENCE

European museums became the repositories for many of these pilfered goods. The British Museum, established in 1753, witnessed the rapid expansion of its collections in the nineteenth century. Many of the acquisitions were derived directly from wars waged by the British mili-tary against colonized peoples. For example, Hans Sloane brought back the earliest geological, botanical, and anthropological objects of the British Museum's collection from the British slave colonies of Jamaica and Virginia, including torture devices used on the enslaved.[16] The pilfered Rosetta Stone and other Egyptian artifacts arrived in 1802 after the Treaty of Alexandria and the defeat of the Napoleonic expedition. The Parthenon Marbles were looted from Ottoman Greece in the same year. Soon came statues and jewels from India; Buddhist *stupas* from Sri Lanka; and bronzes from Benin.[17] European museums proliferated in the nineteenth century. This was the direct outcome of colonialism and militarism, as European scientists "primitively accumulated" – that is, plundered and stole – large numbers of cultural objects from the lands they colonized. An 1880 report on acquisitions by the British Museum celebrated new friezes from Amravati, India and statues from Ottoman Egypt. A decade later, artifacts came pouring in from colonized Africa.[18]

Propelled by the amassing of new cultural artifacts, empires went on public display.[19] The Crystal Palace Exhibition of 1851 set the precedent, envisioned as a great public museum of the British empire. A British natural philosopher, William Whewell, said the exhibition "[annihilated] the space which separates different nations, [and] annihilated the time which separates one stage of a nation's progress from another."[20] Exhibitions were "visual encyclopedias," and they aimed to collate a general system of all human difference from the singular perspective of European observers who considered themselves to be at the pinnacle of civilization.[21] The late nineteenth and early twentieth centuries saw a succession of colonial fairs: the Paris Exposition Universelle of 1889, the Chicago World Exhibition of 1893, and the Berlin Colonial Exhibition of 1896, to name a few. Ornamentalism and the museum display of "exotic" life in European colonies provided dumbfounding expressions of imperial power.[22]

ORIENTALIST ACTS

As much as it found expression through material objects, Oriental science was a technology of the mind – a toolkit of concepts and methods to generate useful representations of Asia to bolster the imperial European personality. By the late eighteenth century, new academic institutions emerged increasingly as researching bodies charged with producing knowledge to prepare prospective terrains for imperial conquest and appropriation, and to manage and contain the messy outcomes resulting from colonial conquest.[23] For example, the Geographical Society was founded in London in 1788 under the title of "the African Association for promoting the Discovery of the interior parts of Africa." Meanwhile, in Paris in 1795, Sylvester de Sacy at the School for Living Eastern Languages created an international center for Orientalist scholarship. French militaries were competing against the British for control over ports and territories across the Indian Ocean at this very time. Not only did the Orientalist study of living Asian languages and cultures help to facilitate conquest, but Orientalism also digested and stored artifacts, including books, statues, cultural objects, and bones, pilfered from the colonies.

During the nineteenth century, German scholarly academic institutions especially were receptive to new Orientalist approaches, appropriating vast amounts of cultural objects from the East.[24] The full institutionalization of Orientalism came to German universities early on, for example at Berlin University in the 1810s. Although German states mostly did not have direct access to overseas colonization before Unification in 1871, Germans nevertheless fantasized about colonial pursuits, and they eagerly participated as professionals in the empires of other European powers.[25] Max Müller (1823–1900), for example, studied Oriental languages at Berlin University before traveling to Britain to become the most eminent Orientalist scholar at Oxford University. And Müller cultivated a whole group of German-speaking scholars who went to work in India as philologists, paleographers, bibliographers, and archeologists. These scientists were the intentional or inadvertent scouts for coming colonial wars, as their research into texts and cultures provided reconnaissance for mercenary campaigns.

European empires, as they expanded into Asia in the eighteenth and nineteenth centuries, confronted and undermined the sovereignty of many Islamic states. In India, the British gradually plotted the dismantling of the Mughal empire – and Orientalist scholarship aided and abetted this plan. Victory over the Mughal empire finally occurred with the great Indian war of 1857. However, already in 1841, Orientalist scholars were preparing the groundwork. Mountstuart Elphinstone, British colonial administrator in India and governor of Bombay (1819–27), placed the centuries-long history of Muslims in South Asia on the margins of his rendition of Indian history in his *History of India* (1841). He celebrated, instead, what he claimed to be India's authentic, ancient Hindu origins. Meanwhile, British imperialists developed plans to undermine Ottoman, Safavid, and Qajjar sovereignty. Islamic sovereignty across Asia represented a different universalism that Western empires set out to destroy and replace.

Muslims, with their different practices of self and sovereignty, were presented in British fantasy as fanatics and terrorists.[26] In 1871,

William Wilson Hunter, a member of the Indian Civil Service, published his treatise, *The Indian Musalmans.*[27] His was a work of imperial panic and domination writ large. Hunter envisioned Muslim society as a reservoir of "fanaticism" and "sedition" infecting British rule in India.[28] For instance, the Wahhabi Trials (1865–71), a series of raids, litigations, and detentions targetting insurgent Islamic revivalist groups across the northwestern frontiers of modern-day Afghanistan, Pakistan, and India, served as a spectacular display of British Orientalist anxiety.[29]

In language that resonates all too well with 9/11 rhetoric and the most recent war in Iraq, Hunter warned of a "standing rebel camp" of Muslim fanatics on the northwest frontier of India and of a "chronic conspiracy within [the] territory." Not coincidentally, in the late nineteenth century British imperial warlords identified the northwest borderlands abutting Afghan territory as the next frontier for colonial conquest. Hunter's treatise was a racial screed in which Muslims were cast as "traitors" and practitioners of violent jihad.[30] Hunter envisioned South Asian Muslims as belonging to a network of rebellious tribes stretching from Afghanistan all the way to Bengal. "The bleak mountains which rise beyond the Punjab are united by a chain of treason depots with the tropical swamps through which the Ganges merges into the sea."[31] Unsurprisingly, no mention is made by Hunter of the British Indian government as a war-making state. By the 1870s, the East India Company, followed by the British crown, had continuously waged wars large and small against Muslim, Hindu, Buddhist, and Sikh polities for more than 120 years.[32]

The rise of Hindutva, or Hindu majoritarian nationalism, in India today draws on the taproot of anti-Muslim British colonial Orientalism, along with other historical strands of Islamophobia. The Rashtriya Swayamsevak Sangh (RSS), a powerful Hindu cultural guild and political organization, siphons inspiration from the fascist Orientalist sciences of the 1920s and 1930s that proclaimed the greatness of ancient "Aryan civilizations."[33] Today's Hindu majoritarianism is the result of many other factors, too, including the worldwide early twenty-first-century crisis of neoliberalism, and the recurring compulsions of capitalist war and colonial command by postcolonial nation-states. Old mental technologies of anti-Muslim Orientalism return today in new ventures in colonial penetration, conquest, and violence.[34]

SCIENCE AND DEATH IN THE COLONIES

Sometimes scientists also acted as cleaning crews after colonial wars. They carried out the gruesome task of sweeping up the devastation caused by colonial warfare and cataloguing it away in the vaults of empire.[35] The history of colonial bone-collecting in European imperial museums is a case in point. Before the First World War, the German empire com-manded more than 14,000,000 subject colonial people. These colonies became centers for industry, but also for the production of German science. The partitioning of Africa went along with vast amounts of dislocation, disruption, and sheer genocidal violence that came to a head in the period from 1905 to 1908. German West Africa and German East Africa saw two events that pre-dated the racialized genocide carried out against the Jews of Europe in the 1930s and 1940s, and that provided an important template for that later holocaust.[36]

Over the course of the nineteenth century, the practice of colonial science rendered sovereign groups on earth more vulnerable to early death. Science conspired to make the very death of colonized subjects "valuable" in unexpected ways. For example, the rise of eugenic biomed-ical science in the late nineteenth century was premised on using and destroying the bodies of "undesirables" – the colonized, the poor, and the disabled – for the supposed greater good of the imperial "noble race" (*eu-genos*). Black and Brown colonized societies in India, in the Caribbean, and in the American South became giant laboratories for scientists to make medical observations, and to collect ethnographic and craniological measurements.[37]

Colonial science could create scientific value from the incarceration, and even the murder and genocidal elimination, of colonized peoples. The German genocide of west African people at the turn of the twentieth century provides a clear example.[38] In 1905, German Schutztruppe (the colonial defense force) punished the Ovambo, Herero, and Nama peoples of today's Namibia for rising up against German rule. The German military officers on site unleashed a *Vernichtungskrieg*, a war of annihilation, against belligerents and civilians alike, killing more than 100,000 people in Germany's first genocide of the twentieth century, whether through direct extermination campaigns, or displacement into squalid concentration camps.[39] At the same time, in German East Africa (today's Tanzania), German colonial troops unleashed a second genocide, in response to the Maji Maji rebellion of 1905–7: Tanzanians had risen up against the imposition of German economic exploitation, especially the plantation economy. Here, German warfare led to mass killings and famine. Some 300,000 Ngoni people perished.

Yet, there is also a hidden story within this history of genocide. In the case of the German genocide in Namibia (1903–7), a large number of detainees were taken to death camps on the Shark Island peninsula. Eyewitness reports document the murder of the male detainees and the swift harvesting of their body parts for the pursuit of German scientific investigation.[40] Skulls, bones, brains, and skin – thousands of "specimens" in total – were gruesomely accumulated from murdered Africans. The body parts were then packaged in jars and crates and shipped off to Berlin. The remains of the Ovaherero people were parceled out among a variety of German biomedical and ethnographic institutions for their research and display: brains were sent to the Berlin Pathological Institute; skulls and skin samples were sent to the Berlin Institute of Natural History and to the Ethnographical Institute in Berlin. These sacred remnants of dead human beings, now severed and preserved in the coldrooms of German science in Berlin, Jena, Vienna, and elsewhere, were used to develop and "prove" eugenic theories of race.[41]

Felix von Luschan (1854–1924), medical doctor and ethnographer, played a prime role in coordinating this grotesque trade. As curator for the African collection of the Berlin Museum, and a professor at Berlin University, von Luschan was Germany's leading physical anthropologist in the early twentieth century. He widely advertised to German colonial officials and travelers his wish to obtain harvested bodies from the colonies. Von Luschan sharpened his god-complex and his predilection for collecting human beings by organizing the Berlin Colonial Exhibition of 1896. The event took place in a large open expanse in southeast Berlin, Treptower Park. Von Luschan and the other organizers put on display groups of living people from German East Africa, German

West Africa, Togo, Cameroon, German Papua New Guinea, and the Tsingtao Protectorate. They were placed in pavilions in the Treptower grounds, and made to wear "native dress" and perform "native culture" for the German public amidst parades, bands, and fair concessions.

Von Luschan saw the living exhibition as a means of public education. And he also saw an opportunity to advance his research. He measured the skull sizes and catalogued the skin tones of many of the African people in the show. It was this comparative research, begun in 1896 in Berlin, that informed von Luschan's decision to pursue the collection of thousands of murdered African bodies from German West Africa a decade later. By the time of his death in 1924, von Luschan amassed a personal necropolis. He possessed more than 7,000 skulls of Ovaherero people in his personal collection, besides the thousands of other skulls he acquired for scientific institutions in Berlin. Von Luschan's sordid private collection was eventually sold to the American Natural History Museum in New York in 1910, where it still resides today.

Von Luschan came to the United States in 1914 to study the "American Negro Problem," as he called it. From Europe, he journeyed eastward by ship, first to Australia, then to Hawaii, and onward to San Francisco. Along the way, he carried out his particular brand of racial research at every stop. Von Luschan's trademark racial science techniques were widespread among eugenics researchers and included taking measurements of skin color, head length, head width, nose height, nose width, upper facial height, ear height, ear width, thickness of the lips, and body size.

Von Luschan also developed his own scientific tool to aid his manipulations of humans – a panel of colored tiles he named after himself: the "Luschan skin color scale" (Figures 5.1 and 5.2). Each colored glass tile had a calibrated number. Von Luschan used his tool to "measure" the skin tone of individuals who belonged to designated "racial groups," averaging his measurements to establish the "mean shade." Luschan's scientific tool was invasively applied, as described in this report about how he treated the people he studied:

He made him [his ethnographic subject] take off his shirt ... and lift his arm, because he wanted a patch of where the sun had never shone. He ran

Figure 5.1 Felix von Luschan "Hautfarbentafel" case. Museum Collection. © President and Fellows of Harvard College, Peabody Museum of Archaeology and Ethnology, PM 2005.1.168.

Figure 5.2 Felix von Luschan "Hautfarbentafel" scale. Museum Collection. © President and Fellows of Harvard College, Peabody Museum of Archaeology and Ethnology, PM 2005.1.168.

the cards along the patch of skin until the match – when the color of the skin through the quarter-sized hole was the same as the printed card surrounding it. That gave him a number that he wrote down. He got all the subjects measured, he added up the numbers, divided by the number of subjects, and got what can only be called a "mean shade."[42]

Now, he intended to apply his research methods to the extensive study of living Black people in the United States. European and White American anthropologists of von Luschan's day hotly debated whether human beings belonged to a single family of genetic relation, or to multiple unrelated families. Von Luschan, believing that human beings constituted a single extended genetic family, was nonetheless interested in the outcomes of the so-called "mixing of races." He received the assistance of anthropologists, plantation owners, and government officials for his research, in Louisiana, Tennessee, Missouri, Alabama, and South Carolina for his researches. Wielding his skin color scale, he also took body measurements of and administered questionnaires to more than 350 African Americans on plantations, in public schools, and in segregated Black neighborhoods across the Jim Crow South. At the conclusion of his research, von Luschan determined that a large proportion of African Americans had mixed racial ancestry. His conclusion, to be fair, conflicted with the thrust of widespread American White supremacist and segregationist discourse that claimed Whites and Blacks to be unrelated racial groups.[43] On the other hand, von Luschan's research ignored the experiential, direct knowledge about the regime of slavery: Black and White families in America were woven together through centuries of intimate violence, the "one-drop rule," and reproductive exploitation.[44] And while he claimed to "discover" rampant mixing between Blacks and Whites, he also believed that Blacks were an "inferior" racial group, and Whites a "superior" one.

Felix von Luschan's investigations, rooted in German colonial extermination and racist categories of eugenic science, bore their own kind of strange fruit. Von Luschan concluded that "most African Americans could be educated and would become useful citizens"; and that a "sky-rocketing mulatto population" posed no danger to American society, since "negroes are largely content with their conditions."[45] Later on, von Luschan complained to his friend, Frantz Boas, the most eminent American anthropologist in the United States, that his research was being ignored by the American anthropological establishment because it was too "pro-Negro."[46]

However, African American scholars such as W. E. B. Du Bois rejected von Luschan's interpretations, while also enlisting his research against the White supremacist establishment. In 1911, in a letter to von Luschan, Du Bois reiterated his own commitment to social critique and societal transformation in the United States. He wrote:

> I am afraid that you are getting a one-sided view of the Negro problem. You must remember that in America it is arranged that foreigners should see the American side of the race difficulties. I can supply you with a good many figures and can also disabuse your mind of the assumptions that American Negroes are content.[47]

Du Bois insisted that race, including von Luschan's concession to the biological superiority of Whites, was fundamentally a mechanism of social oppression: a strategy to curtail the fair redistribution of social goods, including civil rights, wealth, and education.[48]

Much later, Du Bois would strategically repurpose von Luschan's claims to his own ends. In 1946, thirty years after his correspondence with the German anthropologist and two decades after the latter's death, Du Bois recalled a lecture by Felix von Luschan at the 1911 Universal Race Congress in London. In *The World and Africa* Du Bois wrote:

> I remember with what puzzled attention we heard Felix von Luschan, the great anthropologist from the University of Berlin, annihilate the thesis of race inferiority and then in the same breath end his paper with these words: "Nations will come and go, but racial and national antagonism will remain. . . . [A nation] has to respect the right of other nations as well as to defend her own, and her vital interests she will, if necessary, defend with blood and iron.[49]

Du Bois used the reference to von Luschan not to dwell on the limitations of German race science, which were obvious, but to criticize militarism and the central role of European imperial competition in disrupting the sovereignty of Africans.[50] Du Bois remembered von Luschan's research as an expression of militarism and racism. Science did not produce timeless "truths" for Du Bois, but political *claims* about truth. Racist and colonial claims of science had to be recalled, criticized, and put into question for the irreverent purposes of cognitive justice and societal equity. If colonial science compulsively sought to catalog, arrange, and assign the colonized, then a decolonizing approach to science should tirelessly question these categories of containment.

We might understand the pursuit of science, growing out of the Enlightenment and the experience of colonialism, as a product of the imperial modes of arrangement and organization. Yet, there is another way to think about the meaning of "enlightenment." In 1784, the German philosopher Immanuel Kant published his essay, "What Is Enlightenment?" Kant proposed that "Enlightenment is ~~man's~~ emergence from ~~his~~ self-imposed immaturity" [my strikes]. This involved the use of what Kant termed "public reason," or the human capacity for critical thinking, argument, and reflection independent of any governmental, religious, or corporate entity.[51]

Enlightenment, Kant proposed, was not a Linnaean project of universal description, but rather a project of total questioning – of exercising freedom to put everything up for scrutiny. For Kant, enlightenment named an ongoing process of reflection and self-critique. Enlightenment did not require cataloguing, but the unfolding urgency to query. If we take this definition seriously, then we recognize the resistances and questions that poured in from among the colonized as major currents of enlightenment's unfinished process.

School

I N SIXTEENTH-CENTURY MEXICO, Spanish missionaries taught
Indigenous people stories from the bible and instructed them in
epic tales about Europe. The new colonialism, from its earliest
moments, involved practices of teaching and pedagogy. Teaching was
not only a practice of imparting knowledge, but also of creating scenes
in the minds of the colonized – scenes full of moral meaning about
who was supposedly good, virtuous, and strong. Colonizers hoped that
the mental replay of these scenes would keep the colonized in place
and in thrall. Spanish missionaries, like most colonial missionaries
until the nineteenth century, taught not primarily through the dissem-
ination of written texts, but through the use of storytelling and
performance.[1]

For example, as Performance Studies scholar Diana Taylor shows us, a
popular scenario staged in colonial Mexico in the 1500s was a mock battle
between Moors and Christians.[2] These performances served to commemorate an epic, although recent, story from Europe: the "reconquest" of
Spain after the expulsion of Muslims and Jews in 1492. In the 1500s,
European states reckoned with the Islamic Ottoman empire under Suleiman I. Ottoman troops on the eastern edge of Hapsburg lands besieged
Vienna in 1529. The conversion play in the Spanish colonies, then,
encoded ongoing Christian anxiety about Islamic incursion into central
Europe. This Christian-versus-Moor drama was meant to communicate
the virtue of the Christian polity and the righteousness of its conquests. In
Mexico, these performances ended with the defeat of the make-believe

Moors and a mass baptism of the Indigenous. This was a morality play and history lesson all in one. Missionaries sought to inculcate in Indigenous people a scheme for evaluating ideas of good and bad according to the colonizer's worldview, in order to solidify an understanding among the colonized of how they fit into the colonizer's myths.

And yet, the performance of these scenarios by the colonized generated tensions between the actors and the roles they performed, as Native Mexica people were enlisted to play both the Spaniards and the Moors. As the Indigenous performed these roles, they acted out their own repertoires of storytelling, refracting their tense social relationship with the colonizing missionaries through the play itself. Sometimes, the scenario was re-enacted to humorous effect, such as one particular performance in which the character of the "doomed Muslim king surprisingly turned into that of the conqueror Cortés." Indigenous performers acted out their wish to be rid of the treacherous Cortés and to reclaim their lands. They both followed the script and parodied it. The colonized restaged, rearranged, and reinterpreted the mythic forms of the colonizers. The resistance by the colonized counteracts the attempted indoctrination by colonial power.

The "bad education" of the colonized – their ongoing reclamation of their own memories and knowledge – is strikingly manifest in the cultural gestures and performative practices of colonized societies. These practices include storytellings, writings, spectacles, music-making, re-enactments, dance, and song. These are all ways of apprehending reality within a community of shared historical experience. In the first century of Spanish colonialism in the Americas, this profane repertory of performance among colonized peoples began to grow. It continues today, despite the efforts of colonial force to stamp it out.

The Indigenous made their own meaning in defiance of colonizers' intentions, and despite the laws and edicts against "heathenism" and "demonic practices" (promulgated, for example, in 1539, 1544, and 1555). In Mexico, the sacred observations of Indigenous cultures were woven into colonial Christianity. Even today, Mexica people call Our Lady of Guadeloupe (Mary, whom Catholics revere as the Mother of God) by the name of Tonantzin, the mother of their Indigenous gods. And native, local deities are associated with Catholic ones. The outcomes of missionization and colonial schooling are not straightforward. Indigenous converts to Christianity fused the stories, scenarios, and myths of European colonial powers within their own repertoires.[3] Yes, the relationship between missionary instructors and pupils served as a means of colonial expansion, but also as a way to challenge colonial force.

MISSIONARIES

From the beginning of the new colonialism in the Spanish Americas, missionaries fought among themselves about what colonial education should mean for Native peoples. Bartolomé de las Casas (1484–1566) was a Spanish Dominican friar and colonist in New Spain, today's Mexico. While he pursued the conversion of Mexica people around Chiapas, teaching them through stories from the bible and Spanish myth, he also grew increasingly critical of the *encomíenda* labor system that Spanish settlers imposed on Native peoples. He wrote his first treatise of protest in 1516, *Memorial de Remedios para las Indias* (*Memorial on the Remedies for the Indies*). His "remedies" included dismantling the *encomíenda* system, which made Indians the bonded laborers of Spanish landlords.

However, de las Casas' writings and agitations were opposed by other religious leaders. In the Castilian capital of Valladolid, in Spain, a debate between de las Casas and Juan Ginés de Sepúlveda took place in 1550, staging a central tension within colonial missionary ranks and within the Spanish administration. While Sepúlveda viewed the Indigenous as feckless savages, de las Casas argued that Indians were "barbarians" who nonetheless exercised reason and had an understanding of law and justice. In an archetypical disputation that would bedevil discussions among colonizers for centuries, Sepúlveda insisted that Natives ought to be enslaved because of their baseness, while de las Casas maintained that Natives required colonization in order to be improved. One view insisted on colonialism through coercion, and the other on colonialism through persuasion. Already in the Valladolid Debate of 1550, in which he described colonialism not as theft, but as a gift, Bartolomé de las Casas offered an early expression of the civilizing mission.[4]

Missiology is the branch of Christian theology seeking to spread Christian salvation to non-Christian peoples. In the 1500s, Catholic orders such as the Dominicans, Augustinians, and Jesuits prioritized the study of missiology as they endeavored to make their mark across Spanish America and Asia. In the 1600s, Puritan missionaries from England such as John Eliot and Thomas Mayhew were busy at work in North America. By the 1700s, Protestant religious organizations had begun extensive overseas missionary endeavors. A great increase in international missionization came with the activities of nonconformist missionary groups, especially the Methodists and the Moravians. These groups differed from establishment Anglicans in their support for Christian baptism for all. Evangelical Christians believed that all "heathen" and "pagan" peoples around the world could convert to Christianity through an instantaneous change of heart. These proselytizing missions quickly spread across the slave colonies and the settler colonial Americas, and across European colonies in Asia.[5] Missionaries were abettors of European colonial conquest.[6] But missionization also created openings and opportunities for the colonized to work out their own ideas of freedom to disrupt colonial oppression from within.

In the Caribbean and North America, for example, the African diaspora had formed its own Methodist and Baptist churches by the 1770s. Consider the account of Mary Prince, a woman born into slavery in Bermuda in 1788. Her mother was enslaved in the home of a harsh and abusive slave-owner. Mary Prince was sold a number of times to various violent slave-owners between Bermuda and Antigua. Eventually, in Antigua, Prince attended a Moravian meeting with other enslaved women on the Winthrop plantation. "I went; and they were the first prayers I ever understood. ... One woman prayed; and then they all sung a hymn; then there was another prayer and another hymn; and then they all spoke by turns of their own griefs."

The Christian community that Mary Prince joined was an underground Black Church associated with the Moravian confession. Life in this community led Prince to "have [her] name put down in the Missionaries' book." Prince married a free Black man from the local church. And later, when forcibly separated from her husband and brought to London by the slave-owner, she fled from her captor and found amnesty with the Moravians and the Anti-Slavery Society.[7] Prince's conversion involved repeated fugitive acts: discovering the underground Black church; marrying her husband despite the violent opposition of the slave-owner; fleeing from the slave-owner's home. For Mary Prince, Black Christianity offered a passageway for an irreverent escape into freedom.

So many of the intellectuals, philosophers, and revolutionary activists of Black communities in the era of slavery came out of Black churches. Sojourner Truth (1797–1883), an evangelist, abolitionist, and feminist, was born in slavery in Swartekill, New York. She delivered herself to freedom at age 30 and marked the occasion by taking on a new name. Sojourner Truth became an anti-slavery activist and preacher. Her words instructed fellow Black people in the fuller meaning of freedom, including the need to free their consciousness from the effects of racial aggression. During her itinerant speeches across the East Coast and Midwest of the USA, Black and White audiences "drank in all she said." Song was an essential part of her preaching, and the hymns she sang were said to send an "electric shock" through her listeners. She famously confided to a friend, "what a beautiful world this would be, when we should see everything right side up. Now, we see everything topsy-turvy, and all is confusion." For Sojourner Truth, a change of optics was necessary to see social problems clearly. Her practice of "ardent piety" was a way of "awaking from a mortifying delusion" of racial inferiority, and she inspired her listeners to do the same.[8] Sojourner Truth's example shows that as much as religion could be the drug of the masses, it could also bring sobriety, inspiration, and clarity of vision to the oppressed, all depending on who was using its power, and to what end.[9]

FROM SALVATION TO IMPROVEMENT

By the late 1700s, colonialism increasingly presented itself not as an endeavor in conquest and conversion, but as a humanitarian pursuit of improvement. For example, under Governor General Cornwallis (1786–93), the British in India turned to an "improving" form of colonialism, beginning in the late eighteenth century. Cornwallis oversaw administrative endeavors in regulation, urban planning, public education, and public health. Improvement relied on public reform, schooling, and the instruction of colonial pupils. For example, as a public health measure, residents of Calcutta were required to dig ponds close to their dwellings in order to improve the level of hygiene and reduce "miasma" in the city. (It later turned out that this very practice encouraged the spread of cholera.) Under Cornwallis, the British also introduced the "permanent settlement" that aimed to rationalize the structure of landholding among Bengali landed elites (*zamindars*), and to streamline the collection of land rents. The effect of this endeavor was to cause decades of widespread confusion.[10]

Under the regime of Cornwallis' successor, Richard Wellesley (1798–1805), colonial administrators presented themselves as protectors of the colonized. At this time, the Utilitarian Movement in Britain and India was developing, anchored in a political philosophy of the supposed greatest good for the greatest number. For Utilitarians, the ends justified the means, and large-scale government-led social intervention was the name of the game. Utilitarians preached the gospel of improving colonial society through the use of European Enlightenment science: measuring the land's productivity, organizing its social groups, and civilizing its population through educational initiatives. The aim was to exercise command not just by the sword, but also through the arts of persuasion. British colonizers wished to convince Indians they were better off colonized and under Albion's "protection" than free.[11]

Some of the earliest missionaries in British India, such as William Carey, took this charge seriously. In 1792, Carey, a Baptist pastor, along with colleagues, founded the British Missionary Society in Kettering, England. He left for Calcutta in 1793 and over the coming four decades devoted himself to the "improvement" of Indians. Carey went about what he saw as an heroic calling: establishing a printing press, a school, and a research garden for his missionary group at Serampore, Bengal. The work of the Serampore missionaries dovetailed with the improvement work of the secular English Utilitarians in Britain. A cohort of high-caste young Bengali writers and reformers emerged around Carey, contributing to the Young Bengal Movement. They absorbed British styles of dress, writing, and reasoning, but also struggled in order to assert their cultural difference and distinctiveness in contradistinction to their colonizers.[12]

One of the characteristics that distinguished the emerging colonial statecraft of the 1820s and 1830s from what preceded it was the deployment of the state apparatus to oversee and administer education programs. Thomas Macaulay, a high-ranking colonial official in British India, argued in his public memorandum of 1834 for the need to cultivate cadres of English-educated Indian elites who would help maintain a stable civic and administrative colonial order. Education, for Macaulay, was a major means of assimilating a colonized people into the culture of the colonizers. Macaulayan reforms were implemented in India over the coming decades, including the creation of British-style universities and high schools, and the cultivation of Indian representatives within the ranks of the Indian civil service and the Indian courts.[13] Yet, brutal invasion provided the underlying machinery for the British civilizing mission. The British army in India planned frequent maneuvers against Indian polities across the Gangetic plains and the Indus Valley. The army fought against Indigenous tribal groups, such as the Santhals and Kols, in the 1830s. And a decade later, colonial forces warred against Indian sovereign states, including those of the Marathas and the Sikhs.[14]

In the 1830s, the French also invaded Algeria using violent methods, including bloody attacks on villages. The French resorted to *razzia*, a form of unconventional warfare that targeted Algerian civilians. Alexis de Tocqueville, a great supporter of the French civilizing mission in Africa, regretted the "unfortunate necessities ... which any people who want to wage war on the Arabs are obliged to submit."[15] The French colonial state in Algeria, after its bloody conquest, imposed its command over the colony using cultural institutions. Combining endeavors in coercion and persuasion, the French established a *lyçée*, or high school, for Algerian youth in Algiers, just one year after the *razzia* attacks.[16] De Tocqueville, like many members of French society, saw the French colonization of Algeria as a humanitarian, republican project. Colonialism was an opportunity to translate "European civilization" into terms comprehensible to "backward" Arabs. The British in India, like Thomas Macaulay, agreed with this view.[17]

COLONIAL SCHOOLING

By the later nineteenth century, settler states such as the United States, Canada, Australia, and New Zealand began formulating ideas about their respective "Indian Problem." Schooling programs played an important role in settler colonial attempts at cultural elimination, especially in the form of residential schools for Indigenous peoples. These "re-education" institutes forcibly took children from their parents and placed them into boarding schools or with White foster families. These institutions represented huge operations in social disruption, and were notorious for separating children from families, for endemic abuse, and even for murder.[18] In both Canada and Australia, such residential schools remained in operation until the late 1960s.[19]

In the case of the United States, the Carlisle Indian Industrial School in Pennsylvania emerged as one of the central technologies for instruction and forced assimilation from 1879 to 1918. The school sought to incorporate Native youth into Anglo-Saxon settler cultural norms. Set up by government authority in an old army barracks, the school offered a curriculum that practiced cultural genocide as it set out to "kill the Indian to save the man."[20] An Anglo-Saxon dress code was imposed, and corporal punishment was meted out against students who spoke their Native tongue or who refused to cut their hair.[21] The procedures of colonial education targeted the body of the colonized as much as their minds.

Assimilation was the main objective at Carlisle. The assimilation program included the "outing" system, whereby thousands of Indian children would spend their summers with local White families and be precluded from returning to their own homes.[22] Native girls were forced to cook, babysit, and clean for Whites in the name of training them in domestic ideals of "refinement." Students were also instructed on farms in agricultural skills. When they went to work on the farms, they were restricted from traveling outside the plots' boundaries without a chaperone under a regime of functional incarceration.

Sundays came with mandatory "Sabbath school." And all Indigenous forms of recreation were prohibited. Students were taught settler narratives of history, intended to supplant and erase the storytelling traditions of their own people. They were forced to internalize White people's views about Indians, and were groomed to convert to Christianity. Pedagogical methods for teaching history included theatrical performances, including stagings of encounters between "civilizing" White settlers and "savage" Natives. Native children had to dress up in pilgrim hats, or in buckskins and war paint to "play Indian." Often, students who graduated from Carlisle, having been educated to suppress or reject their people's histories, would never return home. For all intents and purposes, many of these children were stolen from their cultures just as their cultures were stolen from them.[23]

CONFLICT AND THE CLASSROOM

The French Third Republic, which began in 1870 after the collapse of the regime of Napoleon III, redoubled French policies of assimilation in ways that contrasted with settler colonial states in North America, South Africa, Australia, and New Zealand. Settler colonialism, with its logic of Native removal and replacement, generated forms of instruction that differed from what emerged under European empires in such places as India or Vietnam in the era of empire and liberalism.[24] Imperial rule in Asia differed from settler colonialism for a number of reasons. In Asia, European colonists were fewer in number with respect to the overall population as compared with the settler colonies, and they were thus unable to "first" themselves as they had in the Americas or the Pacific. In addition, Europeans tended to recognize Asian systems of society and governance as counterparts, although "backward" and "degenerate." Meanwhile, Native systems, especially in the English-speaking settler colonies, were not seen as counterparts, but as "savage" predecessors vanishing on "empty" frontiers.

French imperial education policy in Vietnam in the late 1800s gives us an example of colonial schooling that contrasts sharply with the contemporaneous curriculum at the Carlisle School of Pennsylvania. The French conquest of Northern Vietnam, which took place in 1884, used deadly force, but it also emerged as a persuasive endeavor, deploying schools, churches, and cultural institutions to win hearts and minds. An echelon of the established Vietnamese elite had long bristled against the political and cultural dominance of the Mandarin-speaking Qing empire. French colonialism in Vietnam, while introducing French-language institutions and Western ideas about the meaning of progress, also promised to cultivate the Vietnamese vernacular language and culture and to protect it from Chinese cultural domination. As with British imperialism in Asia around the same time, the French conquerors made a bid not just for domination, but also for hegemony, or, the acceptance by Indigenous cultural groups of European rule.

European imperial colonizers of Asia received some acquiescence from Asian social elites; but explosive contradictions and resistances are the larger story.[25] In fact, we observe a wave of protest and resistance – of anti-colonialism – developing in and through the very systems that were intended to create hegemony. French policies of tutelage in Vietnam created a turbine for one of the greatest and longest anti-colonial wars of the twentieth century: the Vietnam War, which began with French mobilizations in 1945 against the Viet Minh, and continued from 1955 to 1975 under American imperialist forces.

In fact, the turbine of anti-colonial radicalism began in 1887, when the French established Hanoi in Tonkin province as their imperial capital. A governor general's palace was constructed in the Ba Dinh district, which became the center for official French buildings and monuments, with rectilinear roads and electricity grids. At the turn of the century, Governor General Paul Doumer focused on developing the city into a fitting symbolic center for "civilizing" French colonial rule. Major public works were erected in the neoclassical European style, including the major institutions of knowledge and power, such as hospitals, schools, courts, and municipal theaters. At the *École Française D'Extrême Orient*, French researchers collected, categorized, and studied aspects of local Vietnamese culture. And the Interpreters College opened, to train a group of Vietnamese translators and scribes in support of French proconsular command. In 1806, the British had already established Halibury College in Hertford, UK, and in London the School of Oriental and African Studies opened in 1916. The Dutch and Germans created new institutions for Orientalist scholarship in the 1890s, such as at Leiden University and at the Berlin Seminar.[26]

In 1917, the French imperial state in Vietnam inaugurated a sweeping set of educational reforms. Under the direction of Governor General Albert Sarraut (in office 1912–14 and 1917–19), hundreds of traditional Chinese schools were closed down. The Confucian exams, a long-standing aspect of Vietnamese education based on the traditions of the

Qing empire, were abolished. The French University at Hanoi was revamped, and, in addition to French, began offering advanced courses in Vietnamese, as opposed to Mandarin. In 1919, more than 1,100 Confucian schools in Tonkin were converted into Franco-Vietnamese schools. School curricula were standardized throughout all Vietnam, with a cadre of French inspectors traveling to all French schools across the country to ensure uniformity.[27]

The French imperial state styled itself as a protector of Vietnamese culture and language.[28] French Vietnamese schools taught *Quoc ngu*, the Vietnamese writing system in Romanized script. This opened the door to an expansion of the Vietnamese vernacular literary world. Note the difference between this approach and the rabid assimilationism at work in many settler colonial contexts at the time. In fact, the French imperialists in Vietnam promulgated a policy of "association" instead of "assimilation." In a proclamation of multicultural imperialism, French administrators said they wished for Vietnamese cultural practices to coexist alongside French. Such a multiculturalist educational policy was itself a strategy of rule, and an attempt at achieving hegemony.[29]

By 1918, between 10 and 20 percent of public expenditure in French Vietnam went to financing the school system.[30] All of this, Governor General Albert Sarraut insisted, was necessary in order to bring the Vietnamese people out of their dependence on old traditionalism, out of the shadow of Chinese imperial despotism, and into the modern times promised by French protection. Under the new curriculum, French teachers represented Chinese suzerainty over Vietnam as the cause of social decadence and decay. Colonial officials contrasted French education with the bugbear of Chinese Oriental corruption. Geography was now taught in terms of French Indochinese geography. And legislation in 1924 made it impossible for the Vietnamese to open or run anything except government-approved schools with the assigned curriculum or "moral education."[31]

In his liberal philosophy of assimilation, Sarraut said he wanted to make Frenchmen of the Vietnamese. In *La mise en valeurs des colonies françaises* (*The Value of the French Colonies*, 1923), written during his tenure as Minister of Colonies of France (1920–24), Sarraut contrasted the crude, outdated, and coercive "colonial pact" of the past that sought the exploitation of colonial subjects with a new liberal *doctrine française*. This new doctrine, he insisted, "[would] focus upon and seek to augment the human wealth, the moral and social values, and the principles of humanity, among the protected races (*races protégées*)."[32]

Vietnamese students, for their part, used French colonial institutions for their own diverse ends. Pham Quynh (1892–1945), born close to the northern Vietnamese capital of Hanoi to an elite family with prestige and pedigree, was 25 years old at the time of the 1917 reforms introduced by Sarraut. He graduated from the French School of Interpreters. Quynh worked closely with the Sarraut administration in disseminating, through journalism, the vision of liberal French Vietnam. He wrote in Vietnamese, not Mandarin, and made an important contribution to the cultivation of Vietnamese letters. His newspaper, *Southern Wind,* represented French official views. All of Quynh's articles had to pass censorship review before publication. Quynh, like a large number of participants in the Reform Movement, celebrated the Vietnamese engagement with France as an opportunity for cultural modernization and for the preservation of Vietnamese tradition.[33] He believed that Vietnam could thrive as a culturally distinct compartment of the larger multicultural French overseas empire. He eventually served as a government minister during Emperor Bao Dai's administration sponsored by the French imperial state.

Another young Vietnamese intellectual, Nguyễn Sinh Cung (1890–1969), took a much different path as he pulsated through the circulatory channels of the rising French empire. About the same age as Quynh, he was also born close to Hanoi. Unlike Quynh, however, Cung was from a peasant family. His father became a clerk at the Ministry of Rites, and served in the extant traditional Confucian bureaucracy that presided over parts of Vietnamese small towns. But the son, graduating from a French-Vietnamese *lycée* in Hué, rebelled against the village. He first went to Saigon and from there traveled on French shipping vessels across the Indian Ocean and around the African Cape to Marseilles, arriving in 1911. Cung, who by now had taken the name Nguyễn Tat Thành, did odd jobs, working as a gardener and as a cook. And for two more years he traveled.

From Marseilles, he went to Le Havre, and then Dunkirk, Lisbon, Tunis, and Dakar. He found his way to the shores of the United States, and to the archipelagoes of the Caribbean, and on to Mexico and South America. Through this mobility, he noticed the continuities of colonial oppression, as well as the differential experiences among Arabs, Africans, African Americans, and Indigenous and Black peasantries in South America. By 1917, he had returned to France, submerging himself in diasporic radical Vietnamese nationalist politics in Paris. The emergence of Vietnamese anti-colonial nationalism in French Indochina and among the Vietnamese diaspora corresponded with the rise of the French African and African Diasporic Négritude movement of the 1920s and 1930s, and the rise of Arab nationalism under French rule.

Having traveled a very different route from that of Pham Quynh, but deeply ensconced nonetheless in French imperial networks in his own way, Cung (a.k.a. Thành) eventually changed his name one final time, to Ho Chi Minh. In 1954, Ho proclaimed the founding of the Democratic Republic of Vietnam, also known as North Vietnam, in opposition to European and American imperial forces. Back in 1919, Ho believed that the liberal reforms of Governor General Sarraut were a fig-leaf over the indecency of French colonial oppression. The *lycée*, for Ho, was not a space of cultural incorporation, but a hotbed for radical politicization.[34]

As would be the case across every single colonial society in which imperial liberal reforms were carried out in the nineteenth and twentieth centuries, the responses and contradictions among the colonized were multiple, and they disrupted colonizers' intentions. Colonized societies at the turn of the twentieth century, faced with policies and technologies of "protection," "improvement," and tutelage, were overwhelmed by the ensuing social frictions. Colonial subjects like Pham Quynh and Ho Chi Minh found themselves grappling with the contradictions of colonial tutelage, but worked out solutions in very different ways.[35]

The prestigious Albert Sarraut *lycée* in Hanoi, named after the erstwhile governor general, was opened in 1923. French colonial administrators fretted over assimilating the Vietnamese youth too effectively, as this could give way to possibilities of sabotage from within. Albert Sarraut himself warned that colonial education would create "a dreadful dilemma." French officials found themselves in a double bind of restricting education and risking popular protest, or expanding education and hazarding the unintended consequences of growing criticism and unrest among educated colonial elites. Sarraut sought to reconcile these parallel dangers by recommending that higher education only be available to "a strictly chosen elite," and that diplomas should be carefully correlated with the number of available administrative jobs. The French colonial *lycées* developed an "adaptation model," whereby students were to be taught curricula tailored to local customs, but curtailed so as not to overly agitate the minds of Vietnamese youth, and possibly stir up resistance. The Lycée Albert-Sarraut, in particular, became a major center for training literary and political leaders and elites, but also future leaders of anti-colonial revolution. Alumni included the mathematician Hoàng Xuân Hãn, the writer and diplomat Pham Duy Khiêm, and the ethnologist Nguyên Van Huyên.[36] The latter served as the minister of education in Ho Chi Minh's government after the August Revolution of 1945.

This high school, the *lycée* Sarraut, carrying the name of one of the most influential French colonial officials of the time, became a fertile recruiting ground for young Vietnamese radicals.[37] In the 1920s, Vietnamese teachers in the *lycées* often departed from the curriculum in significant ways, undermining the official script of the state. And even though students had to pledge allegiance to France at the beginning of every day, and even as the *lycées'* curriculum focused on subjects that were normed to Parisian standards, Vietnamese students matured into political actors by contesting the given terms. One student wrote in 1937: "the organization of the university here is clearly anti-democratic. ... The atmosphere of oppression in the schools derives from the atmosphere of oppression in the society, and it is worse than that."[38] The Vietnamese *lycée* was a political space mediated by vigorous contestations of power.

The actual architecture of the Lycée Albert-Sarraut tells us something about its objectives. Its campus was constructed in 1919. Note, in Figure 6.1, the rectangular structure of the school and the vast compound, at least six city blocks in area. The school had large modern buildings with state-of-the-art laboratories, libraries, and sports facilities. In the photograph, notice the two large quadrangles planted with rows of trees. Like so much French architectural construction in imperial Hanoi, the scale was opulent, and the style was intended to showcase the blending of French classicism and Vietnamese traditional design.

Figure 6.1 Aerial view of the Lycée Albert-Sarraut. Agence économique de la France d'Outre-Mer. 1931. FR ANOM 30Fi119/45. Used with permission of Archives Nationales d'Outre-Mer, Aix-en-Provence, France.

Consider the cantilevered roofs of the first row of buildings in the bottom right of the image. Constructed in what the French called the "Indochinese style," the edifice sits alongside buildings with conventional French colonial roof design in the second and third rows. The school was coeducational, and open to all European students and to select Asian students. By 1935, 39 percent of the study body was Asian. Here, written into the built environment, was a message of French imperialism: association, not assimilation.

But what must it have been like for students to attend this school in the 1920s or 1930s, as anti-colonial resistance to French rule began to spring the lock? A speech given by Pham Due Kim, a Vietnamese teacher and alumnus of the school in 1937, gives a clue. The occasion for the speech was the Prize Distribution Day at the end of the school year, during which French books were given to Vietnamese students to acknowledge accomplishments and to reaffirm their allegiance to the French imperial state. The Vietnamese teacher stood on stage alongside senior French officials and thanked them for their guidance. It was a performance of colonial obedience and of calculated compliance, but the counterpoint was at work, too. In the commencement speech to the students, Kim catalogued the ideals of the school. The school was supposed to allow students to become "full people," and to know the world. The more one showed discipline and allegiance, the more one could hope, "at the proper time," to fulfill one's promise, he said. But something beyond the surface meaning suggested itself in his speech. The speaker admonished students that they should not "imitate the two young men who escaped from the Lycée and found themselves in Bac Ninh."[39]

The ideal student was seemingly contrasted with two truant students who had fled across the river to Bac Ninh province, an organizational center for the Viet Minh. The brief mention, inadvertently perhaps, allowed the absent presence of the two runaways to pervade the end-of-the-year proceedings. Pham went on to admonish, "if your employment is inferior to that of which you feel capable, be patient and tell yourselves that men of value are always superior to that which they are commanded to do." He continued, "do not sacrifice yourself for an idea, because ideas must be beautiful and you must be absolutely sure of them." With the absence of the absconding students invoked in the assembly, we can imagine the students pondering and criticizing the limits of their teacher's message. While listening to Pham, wouldn't the students in the assembly have contemplated those radical "beautiful ideas" about freedom that made their classmates abscond to Bac Ninh? More is said and more is heard in settings of colonial power than how the words read on the page.

Pham's statement to students that "ideas must be beautiful and you must be absolutely sure of them" held a double meaning in the context of the rising spirit of anti-colonial nationalism. Revolutionary action against French protectorate rule was already a great concern by the end of the First World War, as the French education policy was implemented. In 1926, more than 100 students of the Collège de l'Indochine were expelled for participating in the movement to mourn the death of nationalist leader Phan Chu Trinh. A strike ensued at the Collège, alerting the French authorities to the possibility of revolutionary action by the students. By the 1930s, the French authorities in Vietnam were alarmed by the predominant role of students and teachers taking part in anti-colonial movements and activities.[40] So, as students listened to the Prize Day speech, we must wonder about what was being communicated between Pham and the student audience, even as the French administrators looked on.

ANTI-COLONIAL RESPONSES

Anti-colonial struggle was expressed in the physical actions of colonized people, but also in the manifestation of their consciousness – their systems of knowledge, collective memory, and art.[41] Because colonial powers pursued educational projects in overdrive from the 1880s onwards, it only made sense that the domain of cultural life should also serve as a major battleground in the emerging anti-colonial movements of the time. Anti-colonialism reached new heights by the 1920s and 1930s, with interwoven mobilizations for cultural renewal and socio-economic transformation.

Across the overseas French empire, if Vietnam was a major center for educational policy and anti-colonial responses in the decades after the First World War, so too were the French African and Caribbean colonies. A group of Black French students met in Paris in the 1930s as they pursued graduate degrees in France's most prestigious institutions. Chief among them were Léopold Sédar Senghor, from Senegal, Aimé Césaire, from Martinique, and Léon-Gontran Damas, from French Guiana. Together, and surrounded by a larger group of French-speaking Black students, they formed the Negritude cohort. Negritude was an intellectual and political movement for the assertion of Pan-Africanist cultural identity, and for the strident declaration of intercontinental Black anticolonialism. All three of these leaders were educated in assimilationist French colonial schools, where they were subjected to French racism and brainwashing. The legacies of slave-owning and slave-trading still reverberated through French society, just as French Afrophobia deeply informed its colonial policies across Africa.

Yet, from deep within the substrate of French imperial anti-Black racism, the Negritude group boldly criticized French imperial culture for its arbitrary rule and for its hypocritical assertion of republican virtues of equality and liberty. The group came to insist on decolonization as a project in self-expression, self-determination, self-respect, spiritual emancipation, and racial awakening. And Negritude comprised just one network of Pan-African internationalism. Other Black thinkers organized themselves around emerging institutions of the fledgling Soviet state, such as the League against Imperialism. Others still "practiced diaspora," as Brent Hayes Edwards captured it, through literary and political networks anchored in Harlem but tied to centers in Paris, London, Kingston, and Port of Spain.[42]

Collective-action movements among workers and toilers developed across all regions of the Colored world – from South America and the Caribbean, to North America and Latin America, to Black Europe, to Africa, Asia, and the Pacific Islands. And, ironically, imperial regimes of education, such as the one in Hanoi, or in Fort-de-France, Martinique, provided conceptual travel routes for the "beautiful ideas" of young radicals. Resistance involves direct engagement with colonial power, and more. Whether we think of students such as the Mexica actors learning Spanish plays, Black enslaved and free people learning Christian scripture, or Vietnamese youth learning in French *lycées*, education can also serve as a weapon of the diversely oppressed.[43] Colonized peoples study colonizers' plays, literatures, and cultures to first learn their codes, before they begin to disrupt, and even destroy, the colonizers' scripts.[44]

CHAPTER 7

Debt

I N THE SUMMER OF 1944, at the Bretton Woods resort facility in New
Hampshire, USA, the United Nations Monetary and Financial Conference convened. The goal of the conference was monumental: to establish a new international monetary regime after the Second World War,
amidst the rubble of the world order. Some 730 delegates gathered at
Bretton Woods, and the participants included the influential economists
John Maynard Keynes of the United Kingdom and Harry Dexter White
and Henry Morgenthau of the United States of America. The outcome of
the Bretton Woods conference was the creation of two new powerful
institutions: the World Bank (at the time called the International Bank
for Reconstruction and Development) and the International Monetary
Fund (IMF). Bretton Woods inaugurated an international system in which
capital flows of American and European banks came to constrain the
economic sovereignty of the emerging postcolonial nation-states of the
Global South. Since their creation at Bretton Woods in 1945, and especially since the 1970s, the World Bank and the IMF have been instruments
of American and western European monetary imperialism as the chief
stewards of Third World debt, imposing "structural readjustment" programs on the countries of the Global South. After centuries of colonial
extraction, and amidst the ruins of the Second World War, Bretton Woods
re-established a global financial system in which former colonies were
locked in debt to victorious Western imperial powers, centrally the USA,
for whom the very condition for their capital accumulation was the exercise of racial and colonial violence.[1]

W. E. B. Du Bois, the African American philosopher, upon reading the Bretton Wood proposals in 1945, wrote in a penciled note:

There is in the Bretton Woods proposals so far as I can gather no reference to colonies or colonized conditions. Yet colonies are economic rather than solely political problems. 750 millions of people, a third of mankind live in colonies. Cheap colonial labor and materials are basic to post-war industry and governance. Was this matter mentioned in any form at Bretton Woods?[2]

Du Bois trenchantly spoke of the unspoken, asking about the forms of financial colonialism emerging in the 1940s.[3] Even as empires fell in the aftermath of the Second World War, particular forms of credit and debt continued to bind disconnected spaces and times together, like particles around financial nuclei. Bankers of colonial capitalism establish and sustain the force fields of credit and debt relations between colonizers and colonized. The substance of our contemporary world continues to vibrate with financial colonialism and the invisible forms of empire it sustains. For example, between 2010 and 2018, countries of the Global South have seen their public debt payments increase by 85 percent. Today, postcolonial countries suffer under crippling debt-to-income ratios.[4] This trend is part of a much longer colonial legacy. Over the past centuries, colonial wars have increasingly come to be fought in the "invisible" realm of finance and debt. The impact of this atomic colonialism, although hidden on one level, is manifest all around us in everything that we see.

FINANCIALIZED FUTURES

The legacies of financial colonialism are long – much longer than we may think. Since the late fifteenth century, cities in Europe have served as hubs for the financial and insurance services of the new colonialism. Antwerp became the first major European center for financial services associated with overseas colonization, providing the model for the money exchanges in London and Amsterdam.[5] Bankers in Amsterdam and London established the first stock exchanges in permanent session, which served as places for information exchange and for settling credit and debt relations. In the 1500s, Venice, Genoa, Lyons, Lisbon, Seville, and Lübeck all developed important exchanges.[6] Dealers and traders, merchants and financiers met together to drink sweetened cocoa, coffee and tea, and to smoke tobacco, ingesting plantation products and the labor of colonized peoples as they pored over commodity lists and made decisions about which colonial ships to insure and which products to consign.

Europe was not historically exceptional in its use of money or credit for long-distance trade. But it is the violent intensification of how prices, money, and credit came to operate that defines the distinctiveness of the new colonialism of European traders. Under slavery, prices were applied to African people, who were dehumanized and exchanged as things. For wage laborers, prices were applied to labor time. Different forms of colonial coercion and racial differentiation were employed to "cheapen" the price of labor in capitalist economies. By the nineteenth century, capitalist economies had transformed the majority of human beings on earth into slaves, coolies, bonded laborers, or low-paid, coerced, wage workers.[7] This is the financial dimension of the new colonialism we have been tracking throughout this book.

In the 1500s, a particular kind of financial and economic expert, more hidden than the swashbuckling conqueror, was busily at work making the new colonialism possible: the merchant banker. This money professional dealt in current and future stocks, handled shares, organized storage space, planned shipping lines, and made insurance arrangements. The business of colonialism was driven by the commodifying imperative to evaluate, to appraise, to categorize, and to price in the pursuit of profit. Merchant bankers graded commodities with calibrated measures. They carried out fundamental financial operations to make colonial people and goods into tradable commodities, and to calculate marginal profits across transoceanic distances. And profit could also be made by banking on the future. New World exploits amplified speculation activity, and the returns on these futures.[8]

Colonizing groups, through the use of these financial technologies, developed transactional ways of thinking about social relations. These new ways of thinking about social relationships differed from Indigenous conceptions of custom, mutuality, obligation, and interdependence.

Through practices of commodification and tabulation, things became valuable because they could be exchanged for other things, or exchanged for a price.[9] Colonial capitalists saw lucrative returns on investment in theft, exploitation, and extraction from a variety of racialized and Indigenous communities.

The new colonialism relied on banking technologies to financialize the future. Until the establishment of the Wissel Bank (Exchange Bank) in 1609, and the Amsterdam Loan Bank in 1614, commercial credit in Holland was generally furnished by wealthy merchant families. But with the establishment of the first incorporated exchange banks, the speed with which money supply could be raised and invested, and the scale on which credit could be issued, vastly increased. With the coming of the exchange banks in the 1600s, finance was rapidly professionalized, serving to accentuate and accelerate colonial expansion overseas.[10]

The expansion of concentrated financial services in Amsterdam had military preconditions and consequences. Banking activity stimulated the expansion of maritime war in colonial domains. And wars of plunder overseas also generated profits that benefited speculators in northern Europe. From the 1610s to the 1660s, the Dutch became the most important mercantile and military colonial force on earth. They established fortified bases across the coasts of the Indian Ocean, Africa, and the Americas, including at the ports of New Amsterdam (today's New York) and Fort Zeelandia (today's Taiwan).[11] At the same time, English investors expanded commerce in their new plantations across the West Indies and North America, anxiously seeking to overtake the Dutch as the commercial masters of the world.[12]

Amidst the silver boom of the 1600s, new kinds of non-bullion financial instruments came increasingly into circulation, including different kinds of promissory notes, bills of exchange, stocks, and bonds. As a result, credit and debt relations expanded across colonial divides.[13] Financiers played an important role in the deeper and deeper penetration of the mercantile principle into the realm of life.

Investors relied on evolving financial tools, including insurance, to lessen the hazard associated with shipwreck, fire, and premature death on the high seas and in colonial domains.[14] Huge amounts of money had to be secured in the face of high levels of risk in order to pay for long voyages, to hedge against the risk of shipwreck and the loss of crews in far distant seas. Money was secured to prepare for the contingencies of violent wars that European mercenaries would wage in the pursuit of enterprise. For example, "bottomry loans" were issued by the new commercial banks of the Netherlands in the 1500s that served to finance long-distance shipping enterprises through an early mix of maritime insurance and venture capital investment.

Bottomry loans were a means of "hypothecating," or pledging, a ship to secure a commercial transaction. Ship captains seeking to buy cargo could obtain loans from investors by offering the keel, or bottom, of their ships as collateral. The practice allowed ships to be provisioned with a large amount of up-front credit on their outward journey. They would be forced to pay a high level of interest on the profits of their colonial spoils upon return. But if the ship were lost at sea, ship-owners would be free of liability.[15]

Soon, new modes of controlled trading, such as bulk trading, also developed. Bulk trading was a means of quickly mobilizing lucrative commodities, such as sugar, corn, tobacco, and cotton, in order to maximize profit. Commodities were quickly purchased in bulk by merchants, shipped to huge warehouses across Atlantic Europe, and then subdivided and sold on to other retailing merchants. With such controlled trading, big merchants were able to more easily and efficiently meet demand without the long delays common when dealing with a myriad distribution networks ranging over vast seascapes.

Other kinds of financial practices included "buying ahead." Because the prices for natural products could change drastically depending on harvests, shipwrecks, weather, and a huge number of other contingencies, merchants in Amsterdam developed the technique of buying ahead, or on deposit, which came to be colorfully nick-named "buying herrings before they are hatched."[16] Merchants in the trading centers of western Europe bought German and Spanish wools or Italian silks up to twenty-four months ahead of delivery. This foreshadowed the rise of options trading on the large agricultural commodity markets of the nineteenth century. Merchants would speculate on what would bring a good profit under future conditions. Investors could then play with fortune and fate. Forces that once were seen to control the dealings of mortals were now seemingly being tempted by them.[17]

These developments generated the need for new technologies to distribute goods according to long-term contracts. Merchants stream-lined systems of stockpiles, warehouses, and shared-ownership ships for their cargoes. By the early 1600s, large-scale incorporated entities emerged to pool investment capital. These joint-stock companies stimu-lated even greater potential for speculation and greater impetus to forcibly extend commodification, industrious activity, and profiteering on new colonial frontiers.[18]

A "financial revolution" developed among European colonial powers from about 1620 to 1720.[19] The British government's capacity to take out huge loans and fund large-scale and expensive wars increased after the creation of the Bank of England in 1694. The French state attempted to do the same, forming the Banque Générale in 1716.[20] These bank institu-tions, heavily reliant on joint-stock companies, were deeply invested in colonial trade from the very start.[21] The Dutch East India Company, the British East India Company (also known as "John Company"), the British West India Company, the British Royal Africa Company, and the French Mississippi Company were a few of the sixteen most powerful joint-stock companies of the 1700s.[22] These companies had complex governance structures, and the codification of company law led to an emergent, though contested, international legal order cast in the image of European enterprise.[23] Joint-stock companies offered avenues for everyday folk in the metropoles to profiteer from colonial exploitation at a distance.[24] They were military bodies, banks, insurance firms, and government administrations all wrapped into one. The Dutch East India Company became the richest and most impressive military force in Southeast Asia. And by the 1700s, the British East India Company commanded an army more powerful than those of many Asian empires and European states.[25]

THE SECRET LIFE OF MONEY

As money became a new kind of abstract "fetish" in Western societies, people increasingly spoke of it as if it had a life of its own. In 1707, Daniel Defoe parodied this new public attitude, writing:

> O Money, Money! What an influence hast thou on all the affairs of the
> quarrelling, huffing part of this world, as well as upon the most plodding

part of it! Without thee parliaments may meet, and councils sit, and kings contrive, but it will all be to no purpose, their councils and conclusions can never be put in execution![26]

Personified money became something that had to be "managed" by states and "responsibly stewarded" by bankers. It lived and breathed and endeavored to rule.

Money, according to the economic historian Karl Polanyi, arose as a chief new "fictitious commodity" in the late 1700s.[27] Whereas, earlier, currency had been understood as a store of value, as a means of exchange, or even as a materialization of spiritual or cultic power, money was now morphing into something new: an independent abstract entity that was seen to have a life of its own independent of social relations.[28] Through colonial capitalism, money was "disembedded" from social context.

The violent consequences were first felt in the colonial world before they hit the imperial centers. For example, by the 1700s, paper money was widely used in the British North American colonies before it came to be extensively employed in England. Mortgages were widely imposed in the colonial world before they came to Europe. Land banks first emerged in America in the late 1600s, before arriving in England.[29] And joint-stock companies were first developed by rising imperial states in order to fund the expansion of colonial wars and the penetration of their trades. Important developments in the history of finance, such as "sinking funds" and insurance policies, developed so as to facilitate and support new kinds of relations between financial centers in Europe and industrial centers in the colonial world.[30]

The new colonialism, from the start, was a speculative, and thus financial, project. Ships returned to their home docks with exotic goods and with news of heretofore undiscovered countries, or with human trophies in the forms of servants and slaves. And these lucrative, yet risky, exploits stirred up hopes of wild profits. New financial instruments, such as stocks, changed incentives and encouraged merchants and investors to engage in higher-risk enterprises across uncharted waters and into unmapped terrains. Merchant mercenaries, backed by their financiers, became tempters of fate, all in the pursuit of profit.[31]

INTERNATIONAL MONEY SYSTEMS

As trade with India and China was growing by leaps and bounds in the late eighteenth century, European bullion drained towards Asia.[32] Yet, this growing trade imbalance with Asia went along with the rise of the world economic supremacy of western European states. By 1850, Britain had achieved superpower status in the production and trade of manufactures. And by 1900, British exchange banks financed more than half of world trade.[33]

By the end of the 1700s, most of the world used either a silver currency standard or a bimetallic currency standard, in which silver and gold coin were interchangeable and in accepted use. However, during the eighteenth and nineteenth centuries, vast amounts of gold were mined and minted, while silver supplies tapered off. By the mid nineteenth century, the "gold rushes" of Brazil, Canada, California, South Africa, Australia, and New Zealand had created a flood of gold bullion, which began to compete with silver bullion as the preferred store of value on a global scale. As gold began to flood international money markets, the use of silver-backed money became increasingly disadvantageous for countries producing for international imperial markets.[34] The choice of whether to base national currency on silver reserves or on gold became a major topic of monetary policy, but also an expression of changing relations between world powers. France created the Latin Monetary Union in 1867 to coordinate international trade among countries that maintained the bimetallic standard pegged to both silver and gold.

But the economic and military superpower of the eighteenth and nineteenth centuries, Great Britain, had already established an international monetary regime anchored by its own currency, the gold-backed pound sterling. In 1844, the Bank Charter Act guaranteed that Bank of England notes were exchangeable for gold, marking the inauguration of an international "gold standard." By the 1870s, Britain had become the undisputed center of the international capitalist world economy. In order for other countries to beneficially engage in international trade, to consign and sell goods, and to obtain credit, they were effectively forced to adopt the gold standard as the basis for valuation. The pound sterling won the "beauty pageant" of international money markets.[35]

The gold standard made gold the effective *numéraire*, or basic unit of international monetary exchange, and the British pound arose as the most secure monetary equivalent of gold. The gold standard took over the world in the 1880s, and this was coterminous with the immense political clout of urban commercial classes across European and the colonial world. Germany joined the gold standard in 1871, followed by the USA in 1879 and Japan in 1896. Nation-states across Latin America began to use the British pound and the American dollar as their main basis for valuation. Monetary policy was decided in favor of industrialists, bankers, and city-dwelling middle classes.[36]

These shifts in monetary policy went along with the rising imperial penetration of European and North American money markets and economic interests into colonized dependent societies. In other words, the spread of the gold standard meant the diminished economic autonomy of many polities across the emerging Global South. Even nominally sovereign empires, such as the Ottoman empire, became tightly welded to the financial decisions made in European imperial centers.

The British, Dutch, French, and German empires created fixed, permanent exchange rates between the currencies of their colonies and the metropolitan currency; or they simply replaced Native currencies with imperial currency. In 1898, India's silver rupee was pegged to the British pound at the rate of 1 shilling and 4 pence per rupee.[37] Pegged colonial currencies had the overall effect of making it easier for imperial centers to extract financial wealth from their colonies. And the pegged rupee served to enable India to more effectively pay the "Home Charges" debt to Britain. These charges were steep, amounting to a total of about £920.94 million between 1879 and 1925, representing debt interest, the cost of administrative equipment, pensions to retired officials, and military expenses.[38] Imperial monetary policies regulated the ways in which colonized societies were forced to pay their colonizers to service their own conquest.

WEAPONIZED DEBT

Debt relations made it increasingly possible for imperial bankers, merchants, and intermediaries to degrade the sovereignty of the people they ensnared, and to impose domination in the present with the threat of recrimination and punishment in the future.[39] Debt collection was militarized in the nineteenth century. Only because French gunboats were positioned at Haiti's shores in 1825 did President Boyer of Haiti agree to France's demand to pay 150 million francs to compensate the French nation for Haitian independence. As David Graeber aptly put it, "debt . . . can also be a way of punishing winners who weren't supposed to win."[40] To pay this *indemnité*, Haiti took out a loan, financed by French and American banks, and the payments ended only in 1947, after 122 years. British, French, and Spanish gunboats waited on the coast of Mexico in 1861 to collect debt payments from the Mexican state. Militarized debt collection with gunboats was also employed against the Ottoman empire in 1881, when British, French, and German banks set up an oversight institution in Istanbul to manage Ottoman state accounts.

Debt collection continued to serve as a pretext for the incursions of private creditors and imperial states into the affairs of other sovereign polities. In 1887, British and French banking institutions established a company to collect and supervise assigned revenues of the Greek state.[41] A year later, French gunboats assaulted the north coast of Madagascar as they began their takeover of the island and its finances from the native royal house. Meanwhile, in 1902, Britain, Germany, and Italy imposed a naval blockade on Venezuela, sinking Venezuelan ships in order to extract debt payments. Gunboats were employed extensively by the American government after 1898 as it extended its colonial expansion overseas and deeper into the Caribbean, and Central and Southern America, and across Hawaii, Guam, and the Philippines.[42] International financial arrangements benefiting imperial financiers and business leaders were literally imposed at the barrel of the gun.

In the early 1900s, under Presidents Roosevelt and Taft, the US government began "dollar diplomacy" as a formal foreign-policy approach in Asia, Latin America, Central America, and the Caribbean. This was America's moment of international imperial expansion after the Spanish–American War of 1898.[43] During the early twentieth century, the USA occupied the Dominican Republic, Cuba, Panama, Haiti, and Nicaragua on the pretext of resolving supposed internal fiscal "disorder" and "disarray." All of these incursions were accompanied by banking protocols and the imposition of debt relations to the advantage of American lenders. The Guatemalan Loan of 1907, the Haitian Loan of 1910, and the Nicaraguan Loan of 1913 are among the many examples.[44]

In 1914, the USS *Machias* dropped anchor off the harbor of Port-au-Prince, Haiti. US marines invaded the country and went directly to the Banque Nationale d'Haiti to forcibly remove $500,000 worth of gold from its vaults. Marines loaded the cash onto their ships and transported it directly to American banks in New York. The reason, purportedly, was to claim assets required to pay off Haiti's national debt. Debt collection provided the alibi for American imperial intervention, robbing from Haiti's national accounts. American formal occupation of Haiti lasted until the 1930s, while its informal occupation lasts to this day.[45]

PUBLIC DEBT AND COLONIALISM

The late 1800s was a period of great sovereign debt crises. A sovereign debt crisis caused the "silent surrender" of the Ottoman empire to Western banking authorities.[46] The colonizing force of European banks hit the Ottoman empire from the 1850s onwards, as European powers waged the Crimean War across Ottoman lands. The financial consequences of the Crimean War were disastrous for the public finances of the Ottoman empire. European financial institutions, backed by European gunboats and military forces, contributed to the demise of the Ottoman state over the following five decades, leading to the Turkish revolution.[47]

The "Oriental" Ottoman state was considered disorganized, effete, and decayed, according to Orientalist cultural perceptions in Europe. In 1854, the Ottoman government began its practice of selling long-term bonds on European financial markets as a way of raising money. The government's borrowing financed new infrastructure during the modernizing *Tanzimat* reforms, and the payment of military expenses resulting from the Crimean War. In 1854, 1855, and 1858, the Ottoman state took out major foreign loans from British and French banks.

Yet, already by 1865, Ottoman debt payments were almost as high as its income. The Ottoman state obtained no fewer than fifteen large loans between 1854 and 1874, subordinating itself to the requirements of

European lenders.[48] After two decades of digging itself into a deep debt crisis, the government declared a moratorium on the payment of its debts of £252 million sterling, equaling 60 percent of government revenues. The 1875 Ottoman default on loan repayments led to what has been called "colonization through lending."[49] European bankers – such as those at the Rothschild and Barings Banks – and representatives of European states imposed an early form of "structural adjustment" on the Ottoman empire, foreshadowing the role of the World Bank and the IMF across the Global South a century later.

The council of the Ottoman Public Debt Administration (OPDA) was established in 1881 at the urging of gunboats off the coast of Istanbul. A council of the OPDA included banking representatives from six principal crediting countries: France, Germany, Austria, Italy, Britain, and the Netherlands. The huge operation consisted of between 35 and 189 European administrators directing some 8,000 local assistants. The OPDA, as a competing finance ministry within the Ottoman state, directed state funds towards the payment of the public debt. In finance, as in the military, a small number of people command vast armies.[50]

The OPDA aimed to stabilize the monetary policy of the Ottoman empire and to salvage the Ottoman reputation in international borrowing. However, the Ottoman state entered a debt trap, as creditors called for major adjustments that deepened indebtedness; this exacerbated Ottoman dependency on foreign capital in order to maintain its economic reputation on the international money markets. Despite all the interventions supposedly made in the name of fiscal responsibility, Ottoman finances were again on the verge of default by 1910.[51]

The OPDA also fashioned policy, promoting the cultivation of silk, tobacco, and salt production. European bankers took control of major sources of tax collection from the Ottoman state, defining customs rates, trade tax rates, and the level of revenues from patents. The OPDA signed contracts with European banks for large-scale, capital-intensive infrastructure projects that promised strong returns for investors.

Sovereign debt crises were spreading across Latin America around this time. In the 1880s, the Argentinian government borrowed funds from foreign bankers in order to construct railroads and other public works. In order to fund these modernization endeavors, the Argentinian state became the fifth-largest sovereign borrower in the world. Argentina defaulted on nearly £48 million of debt in 1890. The default was followed by the intervention of an international banking group, led by Rothschilds Bank, that restructured the country's debt obligations.[52] Debt crises spread to Paraguay, Uruguay, and Brazil in the 1890s.[53]

The period of the OPDA takeover, and other bank interventions on the peripheries of European empires, coincided with the enormous industrial, commercial, and financial expansion of capitalist warfare, as huge amounts of European capital sought new colonial frontiers for investment. The British economist, Charles Kenneth Hobson, in *The Export of Capital* (1914), took stock of the explosion of British foreign investment. He recognized the central role of capital investment in colonialism:

> History shows that capital may be used for purposes of exploitation in the worst sense of the word. European relations with India in earlier times, and in more recent years with parts of Africa and South America, are particularly flagrant examples. Capital has been employed in numerous instances to drain countries of their resources, to weaken them economically, and to degrade them morally.[54]

Finance involved visible and invisible warlike practices, whereby foreign sovereign peoples were welded to European financial imperatives. Financial tools deceptively transformed sites of extraction and dispossession into sites of debt repayment, as the colonized were made to compensate their colonizers. The societies of the colonized were punctured; the states of the colonized, surveilled; and the colonized themselves, subjected to ruination so that financiers could collect their return on investment and their interest on loans.

COLONIAL BONDS

Consider the image of an Ottoman bond from 1903 (Figure 7.1). By purchasing bonds like these, European banks funded the construction of the Baghdad Railway and other major infrastructure works, putting the Ottoman empire in a relationship of sustained long-term debt to

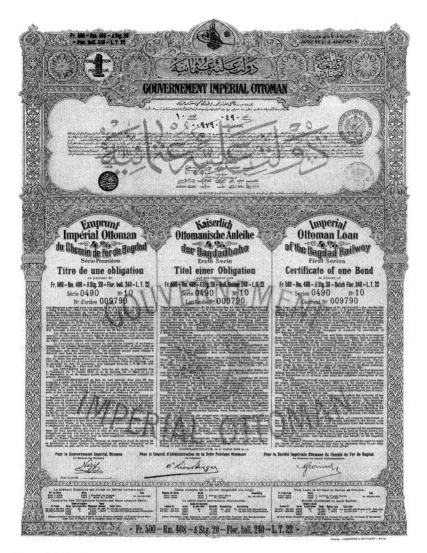

Figure 7.1 Bond of the imperial Ottoman government, 1903. HADB, SG23/18. Used with permission of the Deutsche Bank Historical Institute, Frankfurt am Main, Germany.

European powers, and opening it up to meddlesome intervention. The Baghdad Railway project of 1903, but also the financial debt it generated, was the main mechanism for German imperial influence over Turkey. Meanwhile, the French built debt-funded railways across east and west Africa, Indochina, Madagascar, Guyana, French Somalia, New

Caledonia, and Réunion. The British built railways across British India, British Malaya, Kenya, South Africa, and British West Africa, funded by debt payments of the colonized.

This Baghdad Railway bond, one in a series of 5,400 and worth 10,000 francs, is not only a financial document, but also a colonial and racial leash. The dependence of generations of Turkish taxpayers on Western banks is wrapped up in this piece of paper, as the payment of Ottoman-era debts continued all the way to the 1950s.[55] The bond issue makes reference to the foreign supervisory organization, the OPDA.[56] A full one-third of Ottoman state revenues came under its control. European bankers believed their "more perfect material development" entitled their intervention into the economic domains of "un-civilized and half-civilized peoples."[57] Orientalism informed their modes of investment across the colonial divide. Relations of credit and debt became a major means through which colonial force worked itself out in international relations.

This Ottoman bond is part of a hidden web of colonial relations that connects with other sites of exploitation. Many of the Deutsche Bank officials employed in running the OPDA were also heavily involved in financial colonialism in the German African colonies. Karl Helferrich, a banking executive and colonial administrator in the Ottoman empire (beginning in 1906), also played a major role in German East Africa (present-day Burundi, Rwanda, and Tanzania). In 1903, just as the Ottoman bonds were issued, Helferrich helped establish colonial monetary policy in German East Africa, the economy of which had strong pre-existing monetary ties with India, and in fact used the Indian rupee. But as Germany began the formal colonization of the territory after the Berlin Conference of 1885, colonial administrators moved to replace the British Indian rupee with a new German colonial currency. Helferrich eventually created a fixed exchange rate between the German mark and what came to be known as the "Helferrich rupee." One effect of fixing the exchange rate was that wages to African laborers were reduced, while prices for consumer goods remained unchanged. Helferrich's efforts brought about effective price inflation, and served as a contributing factor to the Maji Maji uprising that broke out in 1905.[58]

Despite the disastrous effects of Helferrich's policies, he continued to serve as a high-level colonial financial administrator and in 1906 became chief financial overseer of the construction of the Baghdad Railway, issuing a new series of bonds to finance the huge project. When he returned to Germany from Turkey in 1908, Helferrich became a deputy director of Deutsche Bank in Berlin, and soon thereafter a full director. He was celebrated as a colonial captain of Deutsche Bank, going on to serve as secretary to the German treasury during the First World War. The invisible threads of finance wove the private sector, the colonial sector, and the state sector together in German acts of imperial warfare, which they called *Weltpolitik*, culminating in the outbreak of belligerencies of 1914.[59]

INVISIBLE WEAPONS

Finance allowed for the expansion of invisible forms of colonialism – colonialism that takes place through the use of inscrutable technologies. Monetary regimes serve to open up colonized societies so they feed imperial metropoles. European and American governments and banks use financial instruments and relationships to undermine, and eventually dismantle, the sovereignty of other governments in the world that they deem to be less "fiscally responsible." This disregard for the sovereignty of other nations takes place along an imposed line of racial and colonial difference.

Just as had been the case in the lead-up to the First World War, and was resurrected at the time of the Bretton Woods conference in the aftermath of the Second World War, sovereign debt crises across Latin America, Africa, and Asia solidified a global financial nexus of Western banks at the expense of the social well-being of the Global South's sovereign peoples. Caught in debt traps to Western lenders, colonized countries have to open themselves up more and more to foreign investors, exacerbating the surrender to the bare-faced economic exploitation of imperial force.[60]

W. E. B. Du Bois puzzled over the proceedings of the Bretton Woods conference of 1944–5. How could an international gathering to decide the economic reconstruction of the whole world after the destruction of the Second World War, and chartered by the United Nations, not foreground the question of equity and reparations for the colonial world? Du

Bois' considerations were elaborated in an essay he published in his column in the *Chicago Defender* newspaper on March 17, 1945. In his article, he observed that the meaning of economic well-being and "development" had been "narrowed" by American officials at the conference:

> Unconsciously narrowing the meaning of currency, trade and economics to matters and movements which do not include the emotions, feelings, wishes and desires of human beings we became suddenly and curiously technical and found ourselves discussing rates of exchange, policies of investment, the stabilization of currencies, the raising of capital private and public for restoring war losses and securing post-war profits.[61]

Du Bois suggested that the very formulation of economic solutions in terms of disembedded finance alone, without reference to history or social context, conspired to disable reflection on questions of social well-being and equity. By contrast, Du Bois insisted that monetary and fiscal policies should be discussed in terms of social economies:

> I insist on the contrary that the human will cannot be plotted by calculus but is subject to incalculable casual change and that the profits of investment are entirely subordinate to the income of workers, their conditions of work, their forms of enjoyment and the voice which they are given in the conduct of industry – that these things are basic to democracy.[62]

Du Bois disrupted the discourse at Bretton Woods:

> I therefore took occasion to interrupt the discussion of financial science, the attitude of the American Bankers association and the gold standard to ask this question: There is in the Bretton Woods proposals so far as I can gather no reference to colonies or colonial conditions. Yet, colonies are economic rather than solely political problems. Seven hundred and fifty millions of people, a third of mankind, live in colonies. Cheap colonial labor and materials are basic to post-war industry and finance. Was this matter mentioned in any form at Bretton Woods?[63]

From the Bretton Woods policy leadership, Du Bois received an emphatic "no" in answer to his question. And this prompted him to ask, "Is the restoration of the world after this war a matter of private profit or public welfare? Is the safe investment of capital more important than wages, health, and education for the masses of the people both in colonies and in civilized states?" Indeed, it is a matter of public economic welfare to redress histories of colonialism and inequality.

Du Bois found that the very conventions of abstraction in American neoclassical liberal economics were intrinsically deceptive. Postcolonial nation-states experimented with alternatives to such financial deceptiveness after the Second World War. Among these postcolonies, new, regional alternatives arose, such as the West Indian Federation, the Latin American and Caribbean Economic System, and the proposal for a Union of African States. The political scientist Adom Getachew has shown how, in the 1970s, still invigorated by the spirit of the Bandung Non-Aligned Meeting of 1955, leaders of developing countries used the United Nations as a platform to define and publicize their vision of a new international system of trade and finance.[64] Third World economic planners called their vision the New International Economic Order (NIEO). This visionary system would surpass the terms of Bretton Woods and serve the development goals of postcolonial societies. The NIEO asserted "the right to development" of nations across Latin America, Africa, and Asia, calling for global regulatory frameworks to limit the reach of Western banks and multinational corporations. The NIEO specifically referred to decolonization as a process that international institutions such as the United Nations were responsible to help complete, which included the global redistribution of financial and technological assets from rich to poor countries, and the international payment of reparations to the Third World for the historical expropriations of colonial powers.[65]

Within this internationalist framework, Third World leaders also understood the importance of local and rooted economic uplift. They prioritized bank nationalization to equitably distribute credit access and state resources among peasants and rural folk. Jamaica provides a good example. Prime Minister Michael Manley inaugurated the Jamaica Development Bank and nationalized the Commercial Bank, allocating special loans for small enterprises, offering tax rebates for training workers, and extending credit to the countryside. However, by the early 1980s, this kind of development-oriented national banking had become untenable.

Institutions such as the World Bank forced indebted postcolonial nation-states to open up to international capital investment and control – what Manley called the foreign "money bind."[66] Structural readjustment policies imposed by the World Bank and IMF required governments to slash spending on social services, to cut education programs and medical services, and to rely increasingly on the services of Western NGOs. Over the course of the 1990s, under the pressure of the prevailing economic order, as well as long-standing proxy wars and interventionism by Western imperial powers, the bloc of internationalist solidarity devoted to the NIEO began to fray.[67]

Fiscal stimulus packages and the structural readjustment policies imposed by the IMF and World Bank crushed nationalized banking and national development schemes in favor of control by foreign banks and NGOs. Today, the number of poor countries facing sovereign debt crises grows. In 2018, of the fifty-nine poorest countries in the world, twenty-four were in debt crisis or tipping towards one. At the time of writing, countries such as Chad, Eritrea, Somalia, South Sudan, and Zimbabwe, as well as Caribbean countries (including Jamaica, Barbados, and Antigua), can pay their financial debts only by cutting deep into their national operating budgets.[68] In Southeast Asia, Laos, Malaysia, Cambodia, and Vietnam face heavy debt burdens. European states, such as Greece, Spain, Portugal, and Ireland, face similar difficulties. At least up until 2019, the fiscal policy of twelve African nations was still subject to decisions made by an imperialist French Central Bank.[69] Meanwhile, countries in the Caribbean, in Africa, and in Southeast Asia serve as extraterritorial zones for parking the lucre of global elites in tax havens and off-shore accounts.[70] The great financialization that began in the 1980s and led to the great recession of 2008 indicates that we live in a period in which banks, and the global capital they command, play a truly imperial role in global governance, interrupting and degrading the possibility for equitable economic and societal development of nation-states across the globe.[71] The extreme expansion of the power and wealth of financial classes today goes hand in hand with the extreme and exacerbating disenfranchisement of the poor.[72]

Yet, late twentieth-century efforts to establish a New International Economic Order also remind us of the persistent, recurring, and concerted efforts in decolonization taking place beyond the dominant international order.[73] From the 1950s to the 1980s, Third World economic leaders pursued a new world order of self-determination and solidarity, and of mutual aid and equity, within frameworks of international law and finance. The creation of progressive, redistributive, and equitable international regimes that nurture local sovereignties and redress colonial dispossession is still our work for the future, just as much as it is a legacy of the decolonizing struggle of our past.

CHAPTER 8

Space

I N 1960, during the era of formal decolonization when nation-states across Latin America, Africa, and Asia declared independence, US American government officials quietly set up meetings with their British counterparts to inquire about the small island of Diego Garcia in the middle of the Indian Ocean. The island had been inhabited since the 1780s by the descendants of enslaved African people, brought there by French-Mauritian planters. The Pentagon wanted to take possession of the island in order to build a military base. In 1964, the United Kingdom agreed to partition Diego Garcia from the rest of the surrounding Chagos Archipelago, and gave this sequestered territory an exceptional status. It also received an exceptional name: BIOT, or British Indian Ocean Territory.

For the peoples of the Chagos Islands this act of partition and renaming had fateful consequences. The UK conspired to remove the Native peoples of Diego Garcia from their lands and waters, and to prepare the newly engineered "BIOT" for USA military occupation. In 1973, some 2,000 Chagossians (or Ilois people) were expelled from their islands, and removed 1,300 miles away to Mauritius and the Seychelles. During the expulsions, British military officers herded the dogs of the Chagossian families and exterminated them en masse.[1] That same year, the USA completed the core of its military base on Diego Garcia, which would eventually become one of its most important overseas operation sites. The US military established Camp Justice and nicknamed the base its "footprint of freedom." The base immediately served as a central post for

US military operations in the last phases of the Vietnam War. More recently, it helped launch wars in Iraq and Afghanistan, and has become a CIA "black site" for covert operations and extrajudicial detainments of suspected enemies of the US state.[2]

The Chagossians were viewed as refugees and unwanted aliens in the societies that received them. Many fell into debt and poverty. Some Chagossians migrated to the UK, where their families were trapped in extensive immigration proceedings, which tangle up the grandchildren of those original Chagossian expellees even today. Chagossians have been forced to work in menial and slave-like labor conditions, and been criminalized by both the Mauritian and UK states. The "Give Us Back Diego!" movement emerged in Mauritius beginning in the 1980s, creating a tense constellation of protest between Chagossian activists and Mauritian politicians. The groups have different objectives, the former seeking repatriation back home and self-government, and the latter demanding the extension of Mauritian state control over Diego Garcia. And yet the very persistence of the *Rann nu Diego!* movement, as it is called in Chagossian Kreol, points to the living pulse of decolonization that is the counterpoint to ongoing colonial dispossession. Prominent women leaders organized the Chagossian movement from the start, including Aurélie Talate (1941–2012), Rita Bancoult (1921–2016), and Charlesia Alexis (1934–2012). They led hunger strikes and petition movements, and created the Chagos Refugees Group. Charlesia Alexis was also a well-known singer of Chagossian *séga* music, performing at the intersections of art and activism. For example, in 2014, Alexis performed this *séga* song:

> When I lived in Diego, I was like a beautiful bird in the sky
> Since I've been in Mauritius
> We are living a worthless life
> Help me my friend, help me to sing
> To send our message to the world
> (*Stealing a Nation*, 17:30)

The lyrics express longing and loss. Alexis describes the shock and vulnerability of expulsion as feeling like being snatched from out of the sky. At the same time, Alexis evokes a politics of friendship with her lyrics, "help me my friend/ help me to sing/ to send our message to the world." The song is a vigil for what has been lost, while simultaneously evoking friendship and affiliation as a means of recognizing the possibilities of the future. Charlesia Alexis was a major leader of hunger strikes, street protests, and grassroots organizing through the Chagos Refugees Group. She brought together different "repertoires of contention," in a way that resonates with other colonial experiences of partition and expulsion.[3] Amahl Bishara has shown how Palestinians in Gaza and the West Bank, facing the 2014 Gaza war, used a variety of distinct repertoires of contention, including vigils, marches, commemorations, songs, stone-throwing, and direct confrontations to demand justice and envision freedom. As Bishara observes, the forms by which communities assert themselves under colonial oppression involve a varied repertoire that contradicts the varied forms of colonial violence functioning on local, regional, and diasporic levels.[4]

GEOPOLITICAL RE-ENGINEERING

Geopolitical interventions aim to re-organize and re-engineer social spaces of land and sea, and the Indigenous sovereignties arrayed across them. Colonial interventions often involve the construction of canals, bridges, and railways to impose new conduits of connection. Yet, colonial geopolitics can also draw partitions, build walls, and impose blockades and bans to halt and disrupt mobility. Colonial force in the age of geopolitics seeks to penetrate the lands and the bodies of sovereign peoples, and to control their mobilities. It also pursues the re-engineering of local, regional, international, and planetary relations through power plays of walls and bridges.

Nigerian historian A. I. Asiwaju writes of the African experience of "political surgery," as communities have been separated against their will. People of "common ancestry . . . strong kinship ties, shared socio-political institutions and economic resources, common customs and practices" were divided from each other by the ruling lines of colonial administrators. Across Africa, since the Great Partitions of the late 1800s that divided up the continent among European imperial competitors, families have been divided, and people forcibly removed from their lands.

Geopolitics severs social, cultural, and ecological tissues. In sub-Saharan Africa, this reiterates the social pain and depletion of severed kin relations caused by the centuries-long slave trade.[5]

Chagossian Islanders trace their histories on Diego Garcia to the slave trade, as French colonizers brought enslaved Africans to the island in the 1790s. The Chagossian protests remember multiple experiences of social dismemberment. These include the severing and displacement caused by US militarism in the Indian Ocean, the racial politics of the Mauritian state, British imperial expansion in the Indian Ocean, and the legacies of French slavery. Toni Morrison calls the work of remembering in the midst of ongoing colonial violence and denial, the work of "re-memory." It is itself an essential form of grassroots activism and survival.[6]

MAPS OF POWER

When geographic domains are re-engineered, they are also reimagined. The colonial reimagination of territory has a long history. A general transformation in the practice of drawing maps began in the 1500s, as new colonization in the Americas and in Asia called forth the need for practices of legitimation.[7] Technologies of geographic mapping became more precise and standardized. Cartographers began representing new kinds of information, especially topographical and nautical information. Eventually, maps also included information on hydrology, population, and political geography. The map became a tool to gain both an overview of, and a detailed miniaturized perspective onto, terrains in which colonial force planned to make incision and to construct new colonial sectors of state dominion.[8]

Colonial force, under the conditions of racial capitalist globalization, does not just seek to conquer labor, land, and sea. It re-engineers territories, ecologies and social life in ways that disadvantage and threaten certain communities, exacerbating their vulnerability to death in order to advantage and enrich dominant groups. From the late 1400s onwards, we have observed how colonialism generated new frontiers for its operation, and produced new kinds of spaces for ventures in racialization, conquest, and rule. Colonialism operates both by fusing huge scales of land and sea together into "sectors" of domination, and by paring power down to the smallest archipelagoes and the finest frontier lines by "surgical" warfare.[9]

Since the eighteenth century, the idea of engineering space on a large scale preoccupied colonial state powers. Since then, colonial forces have aspired to coordinate control over ports, oceanic arenas, expanses of land, airspace, and even outer space to achieve "full spectrum" dominance.[10] This desire for spatial command has had much to do with changing technological possibilities of warfare, but also with the colonial compulsion for commodification and accumulation. As new technologies develop to engineer and securitize space, so too have the means to destroy enemy "space" become more decisive. The visualizing of warfare has changed over time with the ability to reimagine "enemy territory." War looks different when fought with long guns, versus machine guns, versus ballistic missiles, versus airplane bombers, versus chemical weapons, versus drones. (See Figures 8.1 and 8.2.)[11]

The geographer Derek Gregory defines a space of exception as "one in which a particular group of people is knowingly and deliberately exposed to death through the political-juridical removal of legal protections and affordances that would otherwise be available to them."[12] He reminds us that these spaces "assume no single form." They have taken the shape of concentration camps, but also of plantation enclosures and prison complexes. But they also take the form of partition lines and borderlands, where the sovereign right to life of some human beings is suspended, in ways that produce economic, symbolic, or even psychic value for dominating communities. These same walled and policed spaces and tracts of colonialism, however, also call forth new forms of endurance, meaning-making, and transformation among the oppressed.[13] The securitization of enfranchised citizens, that is, the urge to defend citizens against real or imagined threats, drives the ongoing sequestering of racialized and colonized subjects in zones of containment and vulnerability.

The use of massive violence came to be discussed by colonizing states as a kind of prophylactic or disinfectant practice by the end of the nineteenth century. Geopolitical might became increasingly technologized and incisive. In 1865, the massacre of Black, Indian, and Indigenous Jamaicans during the Morant Bay rebellion was justified by General Eyre

Figure 8.1 Aurel Stein, aerial photograph of Balad Sinjar, Iraq (1938). ASA/3/7. 12.14 F/6IN 4000. Used with permission of the British Academy.

as a means of smiting the "outrages" spreading across the Eastern provinces.[14] Fear of the contagion of fanaticism and rebellious "outrages" also justified British terrorization campaigns in Uganda in 1952–60 during the war against the Mau Mau.[15] New kinds of space were produced through the massive violence used to eradicate colonial "terrorists." The United States of America engaged in its own massive machine-gun wars across Central America in the early 1900s as it forced polities along its southern border into its imperial penumbra. And an ongoing global campaign of high-tech US counterinsurgency against "terror" inaugurated the twenty-first century, in the wake of September 11, 2001.[16]

Capitalist interests play an important role in promoting preemptive warfare. John Hobson in his book *Imperialism* (1905) wrote of what he

dronestagram

Figure 8.2 James Bridle, "Dronestagram," 2012–15. Used with permission of James Bridle, and Instagram. Map data: Google.

called the "parasites of empire," the military-industrial complex that feeds off of war as a means of profit. "Although the new Imperialism has been bad business for the nation," he wrote, "it has been good business for certain classes and certain trades within the nation."[17] Powerful states carried out the construction of huge infrastructure projects, but specific classes and interest groups within these states did the handiwork. War is the health of the colonial state.[18]

During the Cold War, imperialist governments developed "proxy warfare" as one of their most successful practices of geopolitical incision. For example, even as the Congo became independent in 1960, Belgian special forces, supported by the USA, backed the rise of Moise Tshombe and the assassination of the democratically elected Patrice Lumumba. A decade later, covert American forces manipulated political developments in Egypt, Afghanistan, Somalia, and elsewhere. Across the Global South, the CIA, in the context of the Cold War, created paramilitary commando squads, funded arms trading, and sabotaged public infrastructures in ways that were intended to keep the helms of postcolonial states within the hands of strongmen that the USA could trust and control. Many countries in the postcolonial world, from the 1970s to our own day, experienced or continue to experience dictatorial rule. The oppression of Third World peoples by oligarchs and army juntas has been politically expedient for the USA and European powers in their effort to maintain geopolitical supremacy.[19]

Today, in the age of drone warfare and digital media, American geopolitical objectives are conceived as what historian David Immerwahr terms a "war of points."[20] These points include bases, ships, and platforms. Most characteristic of drone warfare are the "personality strikes," aimed at taking out specific individuals based on their GPS coordinates. "Targeted killing" and "surgical warfare" make war seem clean and precise, when it is always a matter of fire and blood for the weak and the targeted.

Since September 11, 2001, tribal areas of Pakistan have become the most targeted zone in the world for "covert" CIA drone warfare. Between 2005 and 2015 there were approximately 414 recorded drone strikes, officially killing 4,000 people in Pakistan's Federally Administered Tribal Areas (FATA). These fatal engagements resonate with historical precedent.[21] This same region of South Asia was the site of British aerial policing in the 1920s and 1930s, and was viewed back then, too, as the terrain of insurgent tribes.

FATA was designated as an exceptional zone by the British colonial government, outside the regular rule of colonial law. In the 1920s, the Royal Air Force bombarded this region to eliminate insurgencies. Summary killing carried out from the sky was considered to be appropriate for "savage tribes," claimed the RAF chief of the air staff. In the 1980s, this same area became a center for CIA sponsorship of Central Asian militants against the Soviet Union. Since 2004, the region has been reframed as a collection of points for "surgical" drone strikes. However, the hygienic language is mere cellophane covering over devastation: the number of noncombatants who have been killed due to strikes is estimated in the thousands, and the effects of air terrorization continue to ripple through the psyche of people across the region.[22] The geographic patterns of destruction under colonization reverberate – no, detonate – across time.

CANAL CONSTRUCTION

Large-scale colonial operations in the late nineteenth century were justified as projects in bringing civilization and progress to the "savage" and "semi-civilized" races. By the time the Suez Canal was dredged in the 1860s, vast ecological arenas were permanently transformed through the colonial impulse to forcibly project capitalist principles into the realm of production and life.[23] The Middle East was also a major colonial target for large-scale projects in carving up land and engineering seas. It became one of the most important arenas of geopolitics in the nineteenth and twentieth centuries.[24] Migrant laborers excavated and built the canal between 1859 and 1869. Ferdinand de Lessep, who designed the Canal, believed that the project to connect the Mediterranean to the Indian Ocean was a *pensée morale*, or an ethical vision, to suture the backwards Orient closer to the forward-moving West.

The canal served capitalist and military objectives. The Suez Canal opened in 1869, and became the major shipping route between the Atlantic and the Indian Ocean thereafter – a superhighway between world regions.[25] British, French, German, Austrian, Italian, and Russian naval colonialism erupted across this domain leading to the First World War. Geopolitics led to warfare between states, even as it purported to carve out spheres of influence to preserve international peace. In the imperial war games that developed by the late nineteenth century, military and financial executives saw whole populations, seas, mountain passes, desert expanses, and (eventually) aerial zones as pieces on their chessboards.[26]

The US government pursued the construction of the Panama Canal in the early twentieth century, inspired by the Suez. By 1898 and the conclusion of the Spanish–American War, the USA practiced aggressive overseas expansion. The USA sought to make the Caribbean Sea into its imperial lake, and to transform the countries of the Caribbean and Central America into de facto colonies. The Panama Canal project represented an imperial transportation utopia for American officials and the general public. American experts developed maps, surveys, and other kinds of scientific reports about Panama in advance of cutting the canal. Novels, paintings, and exhibitions laid out a utopian vision of colonial expansion that fantasized about the vital economic and cultural power afforded by a direct route between the Atlantic and the Pacific Oceans.[27]

The idea of a canal across Panama, joining the Pacific with the Atlantic Ocean, was an old one, initially advanced in 1826 by Latin American nationalist leader Simón Bolivár, at the Conference of Panama. Bolivár thought of Panama as the center of the Americas, as a bullseye of trade and communication for emerging independent Latin American countries. This concept resurfaced in a very different way in the context of the Monroe Doctrine and of increasing westward Anglo-American settler expansion. The USA forcibly annexed Texas from Mexico in 1845. In 1848, the Guadeloupe–Hidalgo Treaty concluded the Mexican–American War, resulting in the Anglo-American swallowing of Alta California and Nuevo México, and the "closing of the western frontier."

Mexico lost almost half its land to the United States during *la Invasión Norteamericana*. Yet, the Mexican nation-state, declaring its independence in 1821, was itself a settler colonial formation. Centuries of Spanish colonization had created a multi-layered social hierarchy, in which proximity to European ethnic traits and Hispanocentric cultural norms were prized. And yet, many of those who fought for Mexican independence against the Spanish crown were from Indigenous communities. Mexican independence had signified for many of the freedom fighters a wish to break away from this colonial caste system. As historian María Josefina Saldaña-Portillo explains, over the course of the new nation's first decades, genocidal Mexican settler colonial impulses set in. The Mexican state defined itself against the so-called "indios bárbaros," the racialized term used by incorporated Mexican citizens to name all Native peoples – whether Apache, Comanche, Kiowa, or Seri.[28]

Not only did North American Westward Expansion result in the violent incursion of one settler state into the affairs of another, but the conflagration took place in ways that exposed Native communities in the border regions to the brunt of the violence. The Tohono O'odham and Hopi peoples, and other Pueblo peoples, saw their lands confiscated as they were assigned to reservations on mere fractions of their ancestral terrains. Native homelands were partitioned in the process of North American accession. Fierce resistance by the Apache followed, which was met with genocidal war maneuvers by the US state in the areas of today's New Mexico and Arizona. US Army Dragoons attacked Apache villages, destroyed crops and livestock, and slaughtered women, children, and noncombatants. Settler militaries called this the "first way of war," which entailed unlimited wars of extravagant violence, bullying, rape, and indiscriminate killing. Settlers said the first way of war was proper for engagements with enemies in Indian Country.[29]

It was in this context of colonial expansion, in the 1850s, that Senator James Buchanan proposed a policy of mass migration of Anglo-Americans to Central America. Militarized Anglo-centric Pan-Americanism led the USA to take over the Panama Canal construction. Work on the Panama Canal began in 1903, and had important ties to the Suez Canal engineers. Ferdinand de Lesseps initiated the Panama Canal project. The Canal was to be a lock-type canal, connecting the deep salt water between two oceans. The American phase of construction of the Panama Canal began in 1904, after the French had already excavated 78 million cubic yards. It took sixteen years before the canal was fully opened to the first ships, at a cost of $379 million.[30] And the United States also pursued other similar projects in Central America, including the Nicaragua Canal from San Juan del Norte to Brito beginning in 1916.[31] The USA solely controlled the Panama Canal between 1914 and 1979.

Colonel George Washington Goethals, a US army general and engineer, oversaw the Panama Canal construction. President Roosevelt gave him sweeping command and authority in 1908. The Panama Canal Act of 1912 cemented Goethals' control over all parts of the canal enterprise. Goethals wanted the zone to be "like a large corporate enterprise . . . and not the government of a local republic."[32] His words indicate how closely military interests, corporate interests, and governmental strategy interwove with each other.

In order to build the canal, the Americans flooded the Chagres River basin and displaced more than 20,000 dwellers, forming a new artificial body of water, Lake Gatún.[33] Residents of the region fled to the new waterline, and most were subsequently evicted by the American Canal Zone administration. Panamanian people entered diaspora, losing their customary economies and their communities. At least twenty-one villages between Gatún and Matachín were inundated with the flooding of the canal route.[34] Canal dredging involved infrastructural engineering on a massive scale. In order to ship out vast amounts of dirt generated by the dig, the Panama Railroad was extended. Fortifications grew along the length of the canal, with nine operational fortifications established at each end of the canal by 1912. US military bases immediately followed.

A segregated corps of migrant workers built the canal. The Jim Crow-era labor system, based on a post-Civil War racial division of labor, divided the workforce up by racial group. The hardest tasks fell to Black workers and indentured workers from India and China. Always thinking about labor through racial categories, American officials interpreted the reluctance of local Panamanians to take canal construction jobs as a sign of their "indolence" and "laziness." "The native Isthmian [Panamanian] will not work," declared one American colonial official.[35] The Panama Canal commission, early on, brought Asian indentured laborers to the canal, even though anti-Chinese exclusionary laws were in place. While American society wanted to benefit from the cheap labor of Chinese and Indian bodies, it also did not wish to admit them into the nation as rights-bearing persons. American authorities developed strategies to simultaneously mobilize Asian laborers and to maintain their exclusion. Asian migrants to Panama, some arriving as canal workers, but others as merchants and small-scale enterpreneurs, were seen as permanent outsiders and transient aliens. Nevertheless, Chinese Panamanians set down roots and created a new diasporic culture in the canal zone in opposition to these colonial designs.[36]

While White workers were placed on what was called the "Gold Roll," Colored workers were sequestered on the "Silver Roll." In February 1908, the Americans closed the Gold Roll to non-Americans and Blacks. This meant that Americans were paid in gold dollars, while other workers received Colombian silver pesos. The general manager of the Panama Railroad, Hiram Slifer, explained in a letter that, "[he had been] endeavoring to transfer all Negroes from the Gold to the Silver roll."[37] It was the commission's policy "to keep employees who are undoubtedly Black or belong to mixed races on the Silver rolls." At the end of 1909, after protesting the White supremacist policy of the commission, Panamanian nationals were allowed back onto the Gold Roll.[38] Caribbean migrant workers and Asian indentured workers, however, were never allowed onto this Roll. And they were paid even less than all other ethnic groups on the Silver Roll.[39]

Black laborers worked in gangs, with White foremen overseeing them, as on plantations.[40] Notice the positions of the figures in this photograph from the Panama Canal construction zone (Figure 8.3). The camera looks down on the workers as they labor in the pit. The three men in the foreground are occupied with heavy work. They seem to be plying, digging, and shoveling. A fourth worker bends down in front of them, and we only see a small wedge of his face in profile. Meanwhile, in the distance, a group of men gaze back at the photographer. They maneuver a hose, and as they do so, they pause to look back at the documenting camera. At the vanishing point of the photograph sits another Caribbean worker, perhaps stealing a moment of repose. He is almost hidden from the camera's view, despite occupying the optic focal point. And his moment of repose may also be hidden from the view of the only person in the photograph whose gaze is returned at the same level as the camera: the White foreman standing on the rock mass above the pit. The foreman is the surveilling overseer and the disciplinarian on the worksite. Labor discipline was viciously enforced in the canal zone. This

26 J¹⁰³ Balboa Terminals. Dry Dock Nº1. Grouting rock under pressure and grouting anchorage rails under caisson sill. North end of sill. Mch. 29/915.

Figure 8.3 "Balboa terminals." Courtesy National Archives of the United States of America, Washington, DC, photo no. 185.G.255.

image suggests, however, the everyday hiding places of racialized laborers carved out in plain sight, as workers took extended breaks, or dragged their feet, or intentionally broke equipment.

WALLS

Colonial force divides space as one of its fundamental practices. If the massive building of canals and great passageways featured in the transportation utopias of colonial power, then the drawing of partition lines across sovereign peoples' territories was the paradoxical counterthrust of geopolitical engineering. The colonizer's acts of partition produce "aliens," "migrant poor," "illegals," "refugees," "asylum seekers," and "violators" on the borderlands.[41] Along these borders, new technologies of state-organized enforcement arise, including holding cells, camps, prisons, and monitoring centers. The partitioning of territory establishes borders that cut straight through historically interwoven communities.

By the late nineteenth century, colonial bureaucrats wielded immense power to partition territory, and this power continues into our time. For example, the French cartographer, Regnault de Lannoy de Bissy, passed the nib of his pen over the map of vast communities of Africans in the late nineteenth century. He designed the maps showing the new partition lines of Africa negotiated at the Berlin Conference.[42] During this dawning partition fever, imperial lords in Europe carved up the whole continent of Africa according to their own arrangements with each other. The General Act of the Conference of Berlin, signed on February 26, 1885, divided interwoven societies of the African continent among the British, French, Belgians, Portuguese, Italians, and Germans, in ways that have lasting effects today. Over the coming two decades, African sovereign lands were carved up 27 different ways, and claimed by European powers.

How can colonized societies undergo political surgery by colonial lords and not be disfigured? Viceroy Curzon partitioned Bengal in 1905 and created two new provinces with a stroke of his pen.[43] In 1921, the British partitioned Northern Ireland from the Republic of Ireland. In 1947, the British drew the Radcliffe Line across the Indus Valley and the Gangetic Plain, partitioning the new, noncontiguous state of Pakistan from India to both its east and west. The Durand Line

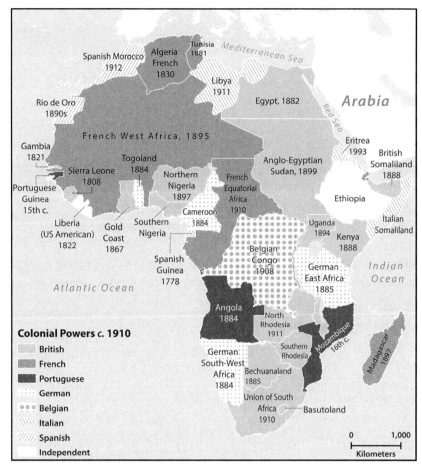

Figure 8.4 Colonial divisions of Africa, c. 1910. Created by the Tufts Data Lab: Carolyn Talmadge, Deirdre Schiff, Patrick Florance.

partitioned Pakistan from Afghanistan to its west. And the Macmahon Line was drawn to separate India from China. In these different cases, drawing lines created zones of exception, massive population displacements, and lasting violence along borderlands.[44]

The United Nations voted to partition Mandatory Palestine in 1947, but failed to implement a responsible partition plan. With no procedure put in place for how the partition should happen, the Israeli army filled the vacuum and implemented its own militarized partition scheme in 1948, called Plan D. This led to mass Palestinian expulsions and deaths.[45]

Today, we see how this conjuncture of imperial geopolitics and Israeli settler colonialism has led to the sequestering of Muslim Palestinians in the Gaza Strip and the West Bank, and the erection of the highly militarized Green Wall around the West Bank. The wall is an instrument in separating Palestinian communities from each other, keeping the Palestinian population in a state of exception.

The United States of America's militarized southern border and Israeli barrier construction in the West Bank and Gaza are juxtaposed by physical walls erected across post-Apartheid South Africa; Saudi Arabia's concrete barrier across its border with Yemen; and the barbed-wire border fence along the India–Pakistan border. The political theorist Wendy Brown notes that the rise of wall construction reflects panicked colonial ventures for control in the face of ungovernable circulations and social transformation. The new walling that is taking place today, suggests Brown, is part of a "global landscape of flows and barriers ... that divide richer from poorer parts of the globe" in ways that operate within nation-states and across national boundaries.[46]

FREEDOM IS A PLACE

Apartheid, the regime to inequitably divide and police space between White settlers and Black communities in South Africa, became official policy in 1948. But its roots date back to Dutch and British colonization in the mid 1800s, as Indigenous Africans were displaced and sequestered through settler colonial war. Dutch settlers, known as Afrikaaners, found in Apartheid a common cause to invent and strengthen their national identity. Formal legal apparatuses to restrict the movements of Africans were established alongside infrastructures to make sure Blacks would continue to labor for White South Africans in their homes and office spaces. The division of Apartheid was also gendered. Black women's mobility in public space was relatively more restricted and imperiled. The South African writer, Miriam Tlali, explores the cramped spaces, and the many experiences of sexual harassment and violation, in which Black South African women were ensnared because of Apartheid. The restricted trains, buses, and ferries were places in which women were vulnerable to assault. Tlali's stories about the embodied violence that characterized the Apartheid regime, alongside the high-frequency detentions and curfews, show freedom is a matter of place, and also of gender. The space-based experience of freedom is intersectional, forged in ongoing ways, out of racial, colonial, and gendered oppression.[47]

Military, financial, political, and patriarchal power create different kinds of geopolitical incisions into land and sea, but also into people's families and communities.[48] From the nineteenth century to our own time, the processes of geopolitical re-engineering have been justified by the paradoxical logics of simultaneously creating new infrastructures for mobility, and new blockages to disrupt and impede mobility. As Wendy Brown notes, the new colonialism simultaneously creates exceptional spaces for unleashing the "vital power" of transport and of "physical barricades" to stop mobility. Both of these geopolitical drives rely on the exposure of racialized and gendered communities to heightened vulnerability to death, and on the severing of their communities' fibers. Ongoing warfare produces a strength-effect – a feeling of being strong – for anxious ruling groups so set on preserving the inequitable and unsustainable colonizer's "peace."

At the time of writing, the United Kingdom still claimed sovereignty over the Chagos Islands, and the United States still used Diego Garcia as its military "footprint." The Chagossians are still banished from their land. Speaking from Mauritius in 2018, Olivier Bancoult, the leader of the Chagos Refugee Group (CRG), recalled the day in 1968 when members of his family, having come to Mauritius for medical assistance, were informed by authorities that they could never return home. His father still had the padlock to their home in his pocket. The British state's removals of Chagossian peoples have caused generations of hardship for the displaced. Yet, Bancoult remembered especially the political strength of Chagossian women during the removals, as they led the protests and organized the CRG. And while that first generation of activists has passed away, younger generations are tirelessly at work. Bancoult's mother was Rita Bancoult, one of the original Chagossian leaders in exile. Her son ended his 2018 TED talk in Mauritius in a way that reverberated with a speech of the Civil Rights leader, Martin Luther King, but also with the futuristic words of his mother, Rita Bancoult, and the women leaders of the movement: "I have a dream. One day Chagossians will be on Chagos. And I will never give up."[49]

CHAPTER 9

Body

I N 1972, the Black Panther Party extended its People's Free Medical Clinic program across Oakland, California, USA. Community organizers and activists worked in mobile clinics to screen thousands of people for sickle cell anemia and to provide basic preventive care.[1] The Black Panther Party viewed health as an inalienable right, much as Martin Luther King had articulated it during the Civil Rights Movement eight years earlier. A community of healers cared for the sick in their community, as volunteers manned clinics and did outreach and health education in homes, churches, and parks. Black Panthers in the 1970s emphasized the continuities between racial oppression, socio-economic exploitation, and disease. Black Panther healthcare arose in response to systematic medical discrimination in the United States against Black folk. Sociologist Alondra Nelson shows how African American activists built alternative institutions to the so-called "separate but equal" segregated hospital system of the United States that actively withheld equitable medical care from Blacks. Ideas about "therapeutics" and "health" emerged over the course of hundreds of years of colonialism and racialization. In fact, the racialized bodies of oppressed groups were often depleted, or even destroyed, in order to develop the therapies and cures that afforded the enfranchised citizenry its health. The work of the Black Panther Party Medical Clinics, then, did not just distribute healthcare, but also disrupted the underlying definition of Western therapeutics. The Clinics enacted a new social meaning of "health" and "care." Their decolonizing practice involved the establishment of parallel facilities, alternative initiatives, and autonomous organizations to counteract the inequitable distribution of social goods.

We can gather an overall impression of the effects of colonial forces by looking at what they do to living human bodies: displacing them, alienating them, dispossessing them from their native lands, commodifying them, regulating them, extracting their labor, killing them, and using them as a means for colonizers' ends. Colonial power, over the course of centuries, came to penetrate the body at deep levels. Michel Foucault, in his many works, explored how, ever since the late 1700s, medical and moral apparatuses in Western societies "[endeavored] to administer, optimize, and multiply" life, and to submit it to increasing controls and regulations.[2] The late 1700s marked a historical transition, away from societies organized by feudal privileges and the exercise of arbitrary dread force, to ones activated by the doctrine of citizens' rights and liberal forms of self-discipline. Hospitals, schools, legal systems, prisons, and policy-making institutions conceived of the human body as an entity to be maximally improved and controlled. Intervention into the functioning of bodies worked out in the colonies in particular ways.

If geopolitical power was busy cutting canals, building bridges, and damming rivers on a mega scale, biopolitical power was preoccupied with making incisions into bodies, engineering reproduction rates, and tunneling into the biochemical realm of human life on the most intimate scale. Colonial biopower, to elaborate one of Foucault's terms, is the governmental power to re-engineer colonized bodies in ways that serve modern racial capitalist interests.[3] The optimization of vitality for selected, dominant groups depends on the intensified extraction from and violation of colonized groups. Colonial biopower pursues what we might call, following the author Octavia Butler, "xenogenesis," or the reproduction of the colonizer's life through the bodies of its colonized Others.[4] Colonial projects presented themselves in the past, as they do today, as pursuits of order, hygiene, cure, and vitality. Health and disease, after all, are medical concepts, but also social constructs. Cures – whether for illness, idleness, or ignorance – deceptively defined how colonized peoples were supposed to benefit from the experience of colonization. No wonder that colonialism in the nineteenth century came to be associated with the use of Western soap.[5]

Colonial empires in the nineteenth century administered healthcare to colonial subjects. Medical officers of the British Indian army, for example, devoted significant efforts to addressing the threat of epidemics of such diseases as malaria, cholera, plague, and influenza among British and Indian troops. Given racialized ideas about the supposed European vulnerability to the weather of the tropics, White soldiers were afforded better treatment and therapies to promote their health, such as retreat to the sanatoriums and rest houses in the "hill station" towns of the Himalayan foothills. The British government believed that Indians, supposedly inured to environments "saturated in specific filth," did not require the same treatment as their more "civilized" and "fragile" European counterparts.[6] The era of widespread public healthcare for South Asians really only commenced at the turn of the twentieth century, in the context of the huge plague epidemic spreading across port cities in 1896.[7]

But long before this, during the colonization of the Americas, Whites traveling to the colonies believed they were headed to places of "miasma," noxious air, and putrefaction. Europeans wrote incessantly about the fragility of their physical constitutions in the torrid tropics.[8] Colonial administrators said the enslaved, by contrast, only needed to be pressed out of the fetid slave ships and briefly "seasoned" on the plantations before hard labor commenced. For centuries, enslaved Africans were intentionally exposed to disease and left to die with impunity.[9]

In the 1800s, as professional medical experimentation emerged in the United States, the enslaved were widely used as non-consensual test subjects. Sometimes therapies were administered, but other times, therapies were withheld, or disease and pain intentionally inflicted, in order to study their effects. For the colonized, interventions never involved consent. The colonized body was thus used as a commodified vessel for the aims of researchers – as human instrumentation.[10]

QUARANTINE

Colonial strategies of detention and containment informed the emerging practices of public health. Quarantine, as a means to reduce the spread of disease, developed as a new medical technique of nineteenth-century empires during the time of accelerating seaborne travel and commerce.[11] The practice of detaining and inspecting sea vessels was common across the Atlantic by the early 1700s. But, beginning in the 1800s, colonial governments began to inspect migrant populations on "quarantine islands," offshore containment areas, before passengers were allowed to disembark at harbor. The rise of indentured labor and of large-scale free travel by sea – such as with Islamic hajj pilgrimage to Mecca – became the focus of European colonial public health panics about bodily surveillance and regulation.[12]

Europeans spoke of "Asiatic cholera," and believed that it threatened to invade their homelands: "The Asiatic cholera, profiting, like man, from the modern discoveries, makes its incursions much easier than fifty years ago, and it spreads afar with all the rapidity of steamships and railway."[13] European medical researchers identified the origin of specific diseases, including yellow fever and plague, with the Orient. In 1865, Muslim pilgrims, or hajjis, from around the world were subjected to a massive quarantine program in the midst of fear about cholera outbreaks.

At international sanitary conferences, such as that held at Constantinople in 1866, European delegates decided to use the practice of quarantine to control the spread of cholera contagion. A ten-day quarantine was imposed on all people traveling to Mecca. Pilgrims on ships had to disembark on one of the quarantine islands in the Persian Gulf, such as Kamaran Island, and wait ten days to see whether cholera symptoms developed. Those who came overland by the caravan route were detained in Mecca itself. Other pilgrims, departing from so-called "sanitary ports," such as from the British colony of Singapore, were exempted from the arduous quarantine, as their ships traveled with "clean bills of health."[14] Only if hajjis went through quarantine, or traveled from one of the European "sanitary ports" in Asia, could they continue on to Mecca.

The conditions of the quarantine were awful. People were held in cramped spaces and without sufficient food. A report from the 1866 conference insisted that the Orient's "populations, most of the time itinerant and nomad, cross the borders unceasingly. ... These populations only subject themselves to material force and do not have the least respect for the law, be it sanitary or civil."[15] Such fixed racial stereotypes spuriously made "Orientals" into the carriers of the globe's diseases. But, what's more, they employed the Asian body as a container into which they poured fretful European anxieties about the superconnected world order, pulsating with the derangements of colonial power and war capitalism.

Acts of division, separating the space of the "clean" from the "dirty," or of the "vulnerable" from the "dangerous," played out across different colonial domains. Colonial medicine focused on sequestering the racialized sick, removing them, and incarcerating them under strict control in spaces where their bodies could be manipulated and transgressed. In late nineteenth-century Australia, people of all races suspected of infection were interned in quarantine camps and "leper colonies." Whites were quarantined together, while Chinese and Indigenous communities were grouped in separate quarantine locations. Chinese persons under quarantine were de-individualized in the official records. They simply became "Chinamen" in medical reports, while the names for the quarantined White Australians were registered. Chinese people were housed in specially constructed tents, not in the buildings for White patients. They were compulsorily vaccinated; meanwhile, consent was sought from Whites. Australian hospitals had wards for so-called "ordinary people" and "ward pavilions for dark races."[16]

By the end of the nineteenth century, the government of the United States of America was also collecting, containing, and secluding Chinese, Indian, and Hispanic migrants in quarantine zones along its southern borders. Geopolitical and biopolitical practices of colonial rule interwove. Nayan Shah's work explores the details of colonial race and public health in turn-of-the-century California. Angel Island, off the coast of San Francisco, served as a major site for the inspection of Chinese immigrants to the USA between 1900 and 1940. Medical professionals carried out a battery of tests on steerage passengers, not only to determine whether they harbored contagions, but now also to scrutinize their fitness, vitality, and eligibility for admission to the American settler state.

During the inspections, men were separated from women. Officers inspected the men's teeth, ears, and noses, conducted a stethoscope examination of the chest, and then "completely stripped" the men in order to "reveal any abnormalities below the waist." After 1910, new procedures were introduced. All detainees were forced to line up at the toilets and were "required to furnish a specific of feces for hookworm examination." The migrants were then given denim uniforms to wear as their clothes were fumigated. The 1924 Johnson–Reed Act implemented a new deportation policy focused especially on the southwest border with Mexico. Latino migrants confronted biomedical technologies of surveillance and command. In the wake of the 1924 anti-Asian Immigration Act, Mexican migrants emerged as the largest low-wage workforce in the American West. Protocols on the southwest border now included the imposition of compulsory sanitization baths.[17] And in 1929 new laws were passed to criminalize Mexican migration to the USA on grounds of "unlawful entry." By the end of the 1930s, tens of thousands of Mexican people were imprisoned for immigration crimes.[18] The specter of the "illegal alien" emerged in American political debate, and a corps of border control agents within US Immigration Services was established to defend the settler citizens against this newly fabulated threat to their security.[19]

VACCINATION

Over the course of the nineteenth century, colonial governments increasingly presented themselves as the protectors of their colonial subjects, especially through their management of health interventions. In addition to quarantine protocols, colonial governments also carried out inoculation and vaccination campaigns. The talk of curing the infected Native helped to justify an expansion in surveillance techniques, and the penetration of colonial command into increasingly intimate domains of social and personal life. From the level of populations, to the family level, to the epidermal level, colonialism produced new dimensions of bodily space within which to exercise colonial command, and to police, divide, contain, and cleanse.

Contagious diseases such as cholera, smallpox, and plague were major threats to the circulatory principles of free trade and liberal commerce. Smallpox, colloquially called the "speckled monster," was caused by the variola virus. In the 1840s, as with so many other diseases, European medical science considered smallpox an Oriental illness. The irony here of course was that European settlers brought smallpox to the Americas in the 1500s and 1600s, decimating Native populations.[20] Smallpox played a crucial role in the Spanish settlement of Peru and in the settlement of North America. Portuguese traders carried smallpox to west Africa in the late fifteenth century. The virus traveled to Australia on British settler colonist ships when they arrived in 1788, killing 20 to 50 percent of the Indigenous people who contracted it. But despite its long history, European science projected the problem onto the colonized, and into the colonized – into the embodiments of Chinese indentured migrants, Muslim religious pilgrims, and the "menace" and dirtiness of the racialized Other.

Research by Robert Koch and Louis Pasteur in the 1860s led to breakthroughs in medical science, helping to develop the germ theory of disease. This bacteriological revolution uncovered how diseases spread through microscopic pathogens, and prescribed new medical techniques, especially vaccination, as the cure.[21] Some practitioners from the Pasteur Institute in Paris soon oriented themselves to the colonial world. Adrien Loir, for example, was an epidemiologist in Paris, and Pasteur's nephew. In 1888, he traveled to Australia and oversaw vaccination programs against smallpox. New South Wales, on the eastern coast of the Australian continent, received its allocation of smallpox vaccine from Bombay, where the British Indian government had its main medical laboratory. But while Loir was inoculating humans with the smallpox vaccine, he simultaneously led the campaign to infect the rabbit population with "chicken cholera" in a major attempt at "vermin eradication." A public health scientist and a biopolitical engineer, Loir aspired to master and manage the biological vectors of bacteria not only in humans, but also in cows, rabbits, and fowl. He soon traveled to other colonial domains, to Tunisia and to Canada, to implement colonial public health policies there.

As Adrien Loir worked to deliver the smallpox vaccine to Native communities in Australia, he and his Native assistants traveled with the vaccine in a cubed wicker basket like the one in Figure 9.1. Colonial medics used this kind of basket in places as distant as India, Southeast Asia, and the Pacific Islands. Woven by local artisans, the basket suggests ways that the delivery of cures to Indigenous populations stimulated

Figure 9.1 "Basket to carry vaccine in Asia." A617815. Wellcome Collection. Science Museum, London, UK. Used with permission of Science Museum / Science and Society Picture Library.

indigenizing practices and negotiations. The vaccination basket speaks of the biopolitical expressions of colonial rule, and the participation of the colonized in their own cures.

What might it have been like to be a colonial subject and to encounter a basket like this and the vial of smallpox vaccine inside of it? The arrival of the basket may have gone along with other procedures of intimate conquest: the invasion of the home, and the non-consensual application of the vaccine. Yet, there would also have been cases in which the hand-woven basket containing the vaccine would have stirred up a feeling of relief, and a hope for remedy, among the colonized. In some cases, it would be brought to villages or rural areas by local nurses or community members. And the coming of the vaccine might be accompanied by other forms of Asian or Indigenous healing practice, woven with the community's own ideas of healing.

For example, smallpox badly affected the tribal communities of Orissa in the east of India in the late nineteenth century. Initially, Native Adivasi people tried to resolve the disease through cultural practices, including rituals to appease the gods. However, when this did not work, they sought out the colonial administrators from local towns and asked for a *sircari* (or state-administered) smallpox vaccine. Indigenous peoples in India sought out British colonial medicine.[22] Yet, among the Adivasi community, this went along with the intensified practice of supplication to their goddess, Dharma Pinnu, the goddess of smallpox.

These two endeavors went hand in hand for the tribal peoples of Orissa: vaccination and ritual. Even though the *sircar*, or government, was synonymous with colonial oppression, the Indigenous still made a calculated choice to accept its smallpox cure. The Indigenous negotiated their own narratives of what healing involved, and they also availed themselves of what the colonial state had to offer. The colonial government was simultaneously revered and contested by the colonized for the public health initiatives it brought. And yet, these cures did not supplant or replace Native traditions, including tribal medicine, Islamic Yunani, and Hindu Ayurveda. Rather, the *sircari* medicine, often transported in wicker baskets, wove into pre-existing ways of telling about healing.

The anthropologist Anna Tsing suggests that acts of healing are also acts of storytelling. "Health" is a biomedical process, but also a narrative practice, by which communities tell themselves about, and also holistically enact, healing and repair. The stories that heal can be multiple, and contradictory, and are passed on by caregivers to convalescents, and across generations of community. This patchwork of stories about health and healing unfolds like a knotted fabric across the history of colonialism.[23]

PRISONS

Colonialism compulsively seeks captives, placing racialized groups in institutions of containment. Prisons are places of neglect and enforced vulnerability to premature death; but they had been represented since the late eighteenth century as enclosures of social hygiene, to safeguard the enfranchised body of citizens from the "disorderly" flesh of the colonized. In addition, prisons served as centers of non-consensual experimentation, in which the bodies of the criminalized were used to develop therapeutics for the well-being of the imperial citizenry. In India, medical doctors studied the etiology, or the causation pathways, of such diseases as dysentery, enteric fever, tuberculosis, and hookworm infection by experimenting on prison populations.[24] Prophylactic drug trials were administered to prisoners first, such as the tests for inoculation against plague, cholera, and typhoid. Prisoners' bodies were used to produce medical data about disease, but also about diet, and eventually about psychology and personality, serving to affirm the self-perception of British dominant groups as modernizing and progressive.[25]

Ideas about sickness surpassed physical or bodily conditions. Colonizers also sought to correct the "moral sickness" of the colonized in penal facilities and carceral zones. Correction itself was supposed to be a certain kind of cure, healing the moral character of those groups deemed to be diseased in spirit. In the 1600s, the Dutch East India Company established the first penal colonies, such as at Robben Island off the coast of today's Cape Town, and at St. Helena Bay and Saldanha Bay.[26] The British penal system across the Indian Ocean and the Pacific Ocean emerged just as that empire shifted its attention from its western colonies (many of which it lost after the American Revolutionary War) to its emerging colonies across Asia. Already by the 1780s, islands off Australia, Prince of Wales Island (Penang), and Mauritius were used as penal colonies for prisoners from Bengal. The French empire created *bagnes* (overseas penal colonies) in New Caledonia in the Pacific, and in French Guiana around the same time.[27]

Overall, more than 90,000 convict laborers were shipped from India overseas between 1787 and 1900.[28] In 1807, Indian convicts were sent to Mauritius in order to provide labor for public works projects. Colonial prisons spread across the Indian Ocean in the nineteenth century. After the great rebellion in India of 1857, the penal settlement in the Andaman Islands emerged as a prison for rebels and dissidents.[29] Here, alongside Singapore and Rangoon, the "terrorists," "fanatics," and eventually the so-called "criminal tribes" who rebelled against British rule were locked up. Putting people in prison was about suppressing dissent and insurgency. On the Andaman Islands, prisoners became forced laborers in the cultivation of coconuts, tea, coffee, cocoa, hemp, and teak. The ideology of work was central to the Andaman prison. Work was supposed to rehabilitate the convict. Prisoners complied, but they also sabotaged and shirked the forced labor regime, and combined together to voice petitions against ill-treatment. Meanwhile, across the American South after 1865, after the Civil War and the 13th amendment to the US Constitution ending slavery, authorities criminalized and incarcerated Black men and women at an unprecedented rate. Under the convict leasing system, begun in the wake of emancipation, state governments contracted out prisoners, mostly Black freed people, to companies and private individuals, for manual, industrial, and domestic forced labor. The prison-industrial complex and mass incarceration continued slavery by another name.[30]

REPRODUCTIVE HEALTH

The "microsite of family and intimate space" became a prize target of colonial state intervention.[31] In the second half of the 1800s, around the same time as colonial governments became concerned with containing infectious disease, they also focused intently on attempts to control reproductive life and women's bodies. Colonialism learned how to speak not just of the dictates of death, but also the language of life.[32] Increasingly, imperial states sought to engineer the stability and industry of large numbers of migrant laborers shipped to plantation islands around the world by regulating gender ratios in the colonies. While the indentured labor trade focused almost exclusively on male laborers in the 1830s, this had shifted by the 1860s to new policies aimed at an optimal gender balance (conceived by colonial administrators to be two-thirds men and one-third women) to reduce crime rates, improve industriousness, and promote the "natural replenishment" of labor reserves through childbirth. By the turn of the twentieth century, colonial statecraft had penetrated deep into the sexualities of its colonial subjects through population science and reproductive health technologies.[33]

Colonial governments designed policies to encourage reproduction in some cases and to deter it in others.[34] For example, the rubber plantation industry grew rapidly in Malaya from the 1860s onwards. The British colonial state quickly recognized that it had to develop the means to secure the place of women workers within the migrant population. Imperial administrators believed that the presence of Malayan, Indian, and Chinese women in plantation colonies would bring salutary social effects to worker communities. As a kind of subsidy on the cost of labor, colonial capitalists wanted to benefit from the extra and unpaid carework extracted from women in the social replenishment of the community.[35] By the 1930s, the colonial state had started recruiting local Malay women as midwives to care for *kampong* patients, or patients from the countryside. Plantation women were commanded to work harder, and longer, and to use capacities that were not demanded of plantation men, even as they were always paid less.

SEX WORK

Colonial power wishes to wear the disguise of Hippocrates, the gift-giving harbinger of medical care. But the face under the mask is not that of the benefactor, but the thief. French colonial policy-makers in the protectorate colony of Algeria in the 1840s presented the colony as a place for public health programs. Yet, colonial racist tropes about Arab contagion colored French social utopianism. Medical professionals struggled to contain and cure what they described as the problem of the "syphilitic Arab."[36] Meanwhile, the British Contagious Diseases Acts of 1864 (amended and expanded in scope in 1866 and 1869) focused on regulating the health of European women sex workers across the African and Asian colonies, in order to reduce the spread of syphilis.[37] In both cases, the sexual license of European men in the colonies was left unquestioned.

Following the passage of the 1866 Contagious Diseases Act in Britain, an Indian Contagious Diseases Act was passed in 1868, focusing on the control of European sex workers who transacted with the British Indian army. Queensland, Australia, passed a Contagious Diseases Act in 1868, as did the Straits Settlements (today's Singapore and Malaysia) in 1870.[38] Similar acts were passed covering Gibraltar, Malta, Sudan, Egypt, and Hong Kong. In suppressing the spread of syphilis, women sex workers, and not their clients in the British army, were registered, inspected, policed, and detained for signs of syphilis, and confined to "lock hospitals" if they were found to be affected.[39]

Sciences of sex deployed technologies of intimate surveillance. British soldiers availed themselves of relations with sex workers, even as the British colonial state sought to restrict "impure" sex between its White men and local Indian women. In Bombay, European women sex workers had to be registered in order to trade. Registered prostitutes were required to present themselves every seven days for medical examination using a set of standardized procedures. If symptoms were detected, sex workers were admitted to hospices. There they were instructed to follow a set schedule of waking, eating, and sleeping. And all sex workers were required to present their registration tickets to the authorities upon request.

Yet, the administration of the Contagious Diseases Acts created labyrinthine avenues for its own evasion. Women in the trade denied being prostitutes and claimed marital status when confronted by police or summoned before magistrates. "Dancing girls," wealthier than the average prostitute, often argued that they were more like ballet dancers, and thus not subject to the Acts. Others used bribes and forgery to avoid medical examination. They worked surreptitiously, trying to evade the police in the first place, and playing hide and seek with officers sent to apprehend them. These rebellious acts offer testament to the continuous failings of colonial command over bodies. Attempts at colonial rule inadvertently activated the recalcitrant circuits of unruly life.

MEDICAL APARTHEID

The historian Karen Kruse Thomas shows how White American policy-makers have historically neglected the health of minorities, and yet have used high rates of death and disease in colonial spaces to justify legalized segregation, immigration restrictions, and other forms of discrimination.[40] The Tuskegee trials of the 1930s to 1970s, carried out in Alabama, USA, give us a concrete example of the racial and colonial cunning of medical research. The bodies of African American men in Macon, Alabama, were subjected to long-term experimentation, from 1932 to 1972, to observe and measure the etiology of syphilis.[41] Under the guise of offering free healthcare, government researchers took bodily and biochemical measurements of Black men infected with syphilis without ever telling them they had the disease, and without ever offering medical treatment. Not only did the lives of Black patients not matter to White researchers, but the sickness and death of Black patients was engineered as a means of capturing value – in this case, scientific knowledge about syphilis – to advantage White society in the United States.[42]

As colonial power develops, the logic of mastery recurs, from early ventures in conquest and plunder in the 1400s, to colonial campaigns to engineer human bodies from the 1800s up to our present time. Colonial apparatuses continuously produce new dimensions within which to attempt to take command. From sea to womb, the sites and the interventions of colonial power operate across a vast range of scales. In this sense, the history of colonialism over the past 500 years cannot be described in terms of a spread over geographic space alone, or a linear movement across chronological time. The processes at work are more akin to the unfolding of new spatial dimensions, like an extending concertina, across which colonial power and resistance recur. Because colonialism works in and through bodies and bodily spaces, it has no clear endpoint, no natural limit, no threshold marking its conclusion with a treaty, conference, or declaration.

But, at the same time, the colonized use biomedical technologies to their own ends, to practice forms of recuperation and body ownership. For example, while the medical benefits of genetics research are inequitably distributed to White communities, Black people today use genetics research to new therapeutic ends. Given the history of colonial medicine, Black folk exhibit understandable distrust of the medical system, while also pursuing the newest available cures.[43] And, through ancestry DNA testing, colonized people trace family genealogies and ancestral lines that are otherwise obscured by the obliterations of slavery's history. Communities use these technologies of genetic research to build material and imaginative bridges across the door of no return. While genetic testing produces concepts of racial essentialism based on biochemicals, adenine, cytosine, guanine, and thymine, it also allows Black people to redesign the social meaning of race, and to transform these findings of biomedical science into new cultural significance. A number of reparations cases have emerged since 2002 based on DNA testing, including the case heard in the federal court in Brooklyn to pay reparations to descendants for unpaid slave labor.[44] In 2015, the Community of Caribbean States made reparations claims at the United Nations, and availed itself of genomic arguments to assert that Black Caribbean people living today are descendants of people who were enslaved 150 years ago. Even as genetics research creates new colonial frontiers of appropriation and racialization, it simultaneously also creates new frontlines for resistance and bodily recuperation. For communities traumatized by histories of colonialism, healing is a parallactic project, in which the narratives of repair exist in tension and contradiction. Technology is not just a site of medical intervention. From an Afrofuturistic perspective, technology is a tool for the reclamation of past experiences, and for speculation on future social worlds still for us to imagine.

Epilogue

O N DECEMBER 1, 1962, James Baldwin, the American author and philosopher, wrote a letter to his nephew. It was the 100th anniversary of Emancipation Day. Contending with the accursed destiny of a US prison cell, his namesake, James, suffered a typical and ongoing form of attack by the racial and carceral American state on young Black men. In this letter, Baldwin recognizes the reverberations of colonial violence across successive generations. "I have begun this letter five times and torn it up five times," Baldwin writes. "I keep seeing your face, which is also the face of your father and my brother. . . . Other people cannot see what I see whenever I look into your father's face, for behind your father's face as it is today are all those other faces which were his."[1] In his nephew's struggle against White supremacist American society, James Baldwin perceived an improvisation of other struggles across time.

Baldwin's letter testifies to the ways our colonial and racialized pasts accompany us in the echoing present. And amidst the repeating, percussive rhythm of oppression and resistance, Baldwin asks his nephew to "remember."

> You were a big baby. . . . Here you were to be loved. To be loved, baby, hard at once and forever to strengthen you against the loveless world. Remember that . . .
>
> Please try to remember that what they believe, as well as what they do and cause you to endure, does not testify to your inferiority, but to their inhumanity and fear.

215

Baldwin wishes to save his young namesake from despondency. To "remember" becomes an emancipatory act for Baldwin because it broadens the spirit, allays the fear of abandonment, and dispels the myth of inferiority. "Re-memory," as Toni Morrison coined it, creates space for cognitive freedom. It counteracts not only individual acts of historical forgetting, but also the deeper and more pervasive disavowal and evasion by whole societies of their ongoing colonial histories. Present-day cultures of denial draw life from undead colonial pasts.[2]

Baldwin encourages his nephew to remember, and thus to witness and recognize, that the permanent and ongoing legacies of anti-racist struggle and survival are rooted in the "deep stock" of those who "picked cotton, dammed rivers, built railroads in the teeth of the most terrifying odds." For Baldwin, to "re-member" is to establish firm bodily ground from which to struggle for freedom into the future. If colonialism terrorizes and divides in order to rule, Baldwin performs re-memory – an act of mind, body, and spirit – in order to grasp how the many pieces still hold together.

Baldwin's America was locked in a self-made prison of historical denial and disavowal, incarcerated by the chains of deadly, feigned innocence. The same can be said for all societies rooted in colonialism. We, today, exist in a concert of colonial processes and decolonial struggles. Like the histories of James Baldwin and his nephew, our histories are lived through the echoing remains of oppression and the future-oriented redemption songs, known to the families of the colonized across space and time.

ABOLITION STRUGGLES

In our times, the police killing of Black men, including Trayvon Martin, Michael Brown, and Eric Garner, gave birth to the Black Lives Matter movement. BLM provides a space to mourn the deadly attack on Black folk in the United States by militarized police and the prison-industrial complex, and to organize for the abolition of these oppressions. In 2016, in the United States of America, the police killed 1,092 people, with a median age of 35. Black men are nine times more likely than other Americans to be murdered by police, and each death involves the obliteration of family bonds. In 2019, African Americans were overrepresented in US prisons by 80 percent. Native Americans and Latino Americans are also grossly overrepresented in prison. The US prison is thus a carceral enclosure to exacerbate the vulnerability of specific groups. Among the consequences of criminalization are psychic terrorization, the loss of the vote, and the pile-up of life-long debt. In the United States, incarceration and policing, and the intergenerational pit of debt, continue to serve as colonial technologies of social control to disempower communities of color. Mass incarceration operates through a network of laws, customs, technologies, and ideological stances, to exploit and diminish differentially vulnerable communities in plain sight.[3]

Since 2013 there have been more than 3,000 BLM mobilizations and protests, large and small. Gatherings, art installations, prayer circles, vigils, and new courses at schools, universities, and community centers emphasize grassroots activism. In addition, the international movement for reparations for slavery re-emerges today, reinvigorated by the 200th anniversary in 2007 of the abolition of the British slave trade. Drawing on the long-standing work of Black organizations such as NCOBRA in the USA and PARCOE in Britain, these grassroots organizations demand expanded and equitable access to healthcare, education, housing, and economic justice. Groups such as Project South, based in Atlanta and operating across all thirteen states of the American South, emphasize the community-based mobilization of Black people to put pressure on state representatives, and to promote their own interests, including through mutual aid societies for people's democracy. The colonized and racialized know that the struggle is an old one and also a present-day one, and that "nobody is free until everybody is free."

SOVEREIGN ASSERTIONS

Sovereignty movements by Native peoples arose with the first onslaughts of settler colonial war, and they continue in our time. Native land and water protectors serve an important and life-giving role in today's movements for justice. The Standing Rock mobilization began in January 2016 under the banner *Water Is Life*. Native leaders organized the #NODAPL movement of non-violent resistance to block the construction of the Keystone XL Pipeline and promote reconciliation with the earth. The TransCanada Corporation's Keystone XL Pipeline construction, cutting through North Dakota, South Dakota, and Illinois over 1,172 miles, had already destroyed at least 280 Indigenous architectural and cultural sites, including burial grounds. The mobilization reiterated the ongoing resistance by the Oceti Sakowin people as they have battled the predatory settler United States over the centuries.[4]

The Idle No More (INM) movement, led by Indigenous women in Canada and founded in 2012, began by protesting crude-oil fracking in the Canadian province of Alberta, where the Keystone XL Pipeline originates. The #INM movement has spread across North America in the form of protests, rallies, teach-ins, art exhibitions, and networks of political friendship. Meanwhile, in Central America, such movements as the Quechua Buen Vivir in Ecuador and Bolivia pursue alternative social economies based on Indigenous social philosophies. In India, Indigenous movements against mining and deforestation are fought by communities outside the Hindu caste system. The Naxalite movement in eastern India, across the states of Chhatisgarh, Bihar, Odisha, and Bengal, provides a vivid example. The Naxal decades-long insurgency against bauxite mining by the likes of the Vedanta Resources Corporation led to a moratorium on mining from 2013 to 2018.[5]

PEOPLE'S DEMOCRACY

The brewing politics of many African states today is marked by protest, especially by the mobilization of groups outside the enfranchised and propertied elites. These groups converge together, sometimes in incoherent or temporary ways, to put pressure on established neo-colonial state regimes. Grassroots organizations protest state clientelism and subservience to foreign powers, banks, and NGOs. For example, the Nigerian Occupy movement took shape in 2012. Early that year, the government removed oil subsidies and raised the fuel price. A countrywide strike emerged as labor organizations, student groups, professional organizations, and well-known artists and musicians brought millions of people out on the streets, protesting for ten days. The fuel subsidy was eventually reinstituted, although not to the level demanded by the demonstrators. Here, it was not civil society, nor the arena of formal institutions, that mobilized. Rather, political society, the realm of unofficial, grassroots, and informal organizations, came to the fore on a national scale. Fugitive spaces of hope and as yet unknown possibilities erupt in political society today.[6] The Nigerian demonstrations showed that political society is irreverent and strong, and growing stronger.

In December 2018, an international gathering of grassroots groups came together in Dakar, Senegal. The Université Populaire de L'Engagement Citoyen (UPEC), the Popular University for Civic Engagement, gathered grassroots activists from twenty-five African countries. Balai Citoyen of Burkina Faso, the Y'en a Marre organization of Senegal, and En Aucun Cas of Togo, among others, demanded the end to oligarchies and corruption. The organizations, converging around a popular group of Senegalese musicians, asked for the end of governance by ruling families and of the one-way humanitarianism of Western NGOs, imposing their own visions of social order, as opposed to supporting the visions of the people themselves. UPEC's assertions were visionary, but also historical. Drawing on the demands made by anti-Apartheid activists of the 1960s, those gathered for UPEC 2018 called for:

- All national groups should have equal rights.
- All people should share in the people's wealth.
- Land should be shared by the people who work it.
- All should be equal before the law.
- There should be work and security for all.
- Access to learning and education should be open to all.
- There should be housing for all.
- There should be peace and friendship.

Movements within political society such as this arise from a convergent and assembled array of different groups, positioned in different nation-states, speaking different languages, suffering under differential experiences of urban and rural oppression. In political society, we witness a heterogeneous, and at times incoherent and unstable, coming together of church groups, labor movements, student organizations, local assemblies, and peasant cooperatives.

W. E. B. Du Bois in *Black Reconstruction* (1935) observed that when demands for progressive social change and wealth redistribution are articulated, elites mobilize ideas about racial difference, cultural purity, and national belonging in order to break apart progressive blocs. Ideas about cultural purity, national security, and the fear of the "mobile poor" and "foreigners" are part of a tried and trusted bag of tricks. These tricks seek to disable the possibilities of political friendship among differentially oppressed groups across lines of class, ethnicity, gender and sexuality, and cultural belonging. During Reconstruction (1865–77), amidst the progressive political developments that ushered in elected Black representatives to all levels of electoral bodies across the post-Emancipation US South, the planter class went busily to work reconstructing the plantation order. The counter-revolutionary collusion of the plantocracy helped to arrest the people's democratic development. Jim Crow laws were put in place, including the codified and enforced division of social space between Whites and Blacks, and the systematic deprivation of social goods to Blacks, including good healthcare, housing, and education. Gerrymandering tampered with boundaries of voting districts to hardwire the plantocracy's interests into the electoral system.[7] This pernicious use of ideas about cultural, ethnic, and racial difference, and the conspiracy of law and policy to shore up the interests of elites, operates today across nation-states in many parts of the world. If the twentieth century saw the spread of the nation-state to the four corners of the earth, our twenty-first century lays bare the colonial intent of national elites who seek to prevent equitable social redistribution at all costs, including the perils of self-destruction.

FREEING THE CONSCIOUSNESS

On the other hand, progressive, intersectional, and internationalist mobilization goes back hundreds of years and shows no sign of letting up. In a time of authoritarian populism, we actively witness struggles to occupy the enclosures, to abolish carceral policing, to redistribute wealth, to staunch the infinite push of extractive racial capitalism, and to thwart the tricks of xenophobia, patriarchy, and majoritarian nationalism. Colonialism, in its multiple and asymmetrical forms, does not just entail an attack on different peoples' social economies and lands. It is a war on peoples' families, cultures, spirits, and psyches. In response, disparate colonized groups develop diverse and non-equivalent ways of conceiving struggle against colonialism that surpass the limits of the colonizer's imagination.

The new colonialism, rooted, as we have seen, in the rise of racial capitalism, continually redraws the line between those overrepresented as the fully human, and those supposedly lacking full human status.[8] The colonized – Blacks, Natives, Orientals, Islanders, Queers, Abnormal Whites, and Primitives of the earth – are consigned to the racialized domain of the less-than-human, just as they are socio-economically conscripted into globe-spanning capitalist production regimes. Yet, in unvanquished response to colonial degradation, oppressed peoples transform their conditions of oppression and reclaim their ground through their irreverent politics, art, words, dance, reinventions of tradition, and re-memory, and through the intimate and public performances of their bodies.[9] The work of freeing consciousness from the ongoing effects of colonialism is still unfinished work. Communities of repair and reclamation are all around us, and they are as strong and vibrant as ever.

So, what, in the end, is colonialism? It is a force field of social power and social differentiation that structures societies on a global scale today. This field of forces has emerged over hundreds of years through ongoing capitalist wars, projects in racialized rule, and practices of deception and denial, as well as through continuously countervailing big and small acts of transformative resistance, rebellion, and re-memory. Colonialism is not an amorphous cloud, but a taut social fabric composed of highly differentiated and dissimilar threads, vibrating together in tension. We endeavored to practice parallax to study this tensile fabric of relations: to practice a way of seeing that holds together uneven and discordant perspectives on shared historical legacies. We explored a multiplicity of colonial histories and practices, in different times and places of racial capitalism, juxtaposing forms of resistance that continue to thwart master designs. Colonialism and the irreverent responses of the colonized are recursive, yet also dynamic. In this book, we developed a description of different interlocking colonial histories, each of which had particular and distinctive implications for subjected and oppressed groups, who also contested and transformed these histories. We considered settler colonial conquests and Native acts of resistance in the Spanish Americas, the Anglo-Americas, and the Pacific. We explored histories of racial slavery and anti-Black racism, and African diasporic liberation struggle in the New World. We examined the expansion of racial capitalist empire across Asia, and the contestations of Asian indentured migrants and Asian states from the eighteenth century onwards. We noted forms of the new colonialism that continue to target oppressed groups today, and the decolonizing responses on the part of these groups. As much as colonial forces act upon the colonized, these forces arise as fearful and anxious reactions to the ongoing resistant agencies of the colonized.

We explored the sociological aspects of colonial power under racial capitalism, and the counteractions to that power. Cutting across hundreds of years of the new colonialism, colonial power recurred in dynamically changing forms to occupy, commodify, and alienate; enumerate and catalog; tutor and indoctrinate; indebt and entrap; divide, displace, and contain; and re-engineer, possess, and surveil. The colonized dismantle and resist these colonial techniques of rule through actions and non-participations: protesting, marching, conspiring, rebelling, striking, running away, finding respite, reveling, re-creating, worshiping, resting, foot-dragging, satirizing, reclaiming, memory-working, narrating, re-interpreting, witnessing, and choosing to take part in communities of chosen kinship. If colonial force is structural to the modern world, so too is colonial resistance.[10]

Given the ongoing trajectories of colonial violence under racial capitalism, what does decolonizing liberation look like in our present time and in the future? To answer the question, we look to our pasts. Progressive politics recognizes the asymmetries of situations based on class, gender and sexuality, differential racializations, different generational experience, and different urban and rural locations. Mobilizations around anti-racism, social economies, environment, food, energy, sustainability, bodily freedom, and social justice are in concert today. Food sovereignty movements, agro-ecological movements, environmental justice movements, #MeToo movements, #BLM and #IDL movements, and other social justice movements bring together large, dynamic constellations of political society.

To be in this world in ethical and life-sustaining, as opposed to life-destroying, ways means that we shift and adjust our imagination and our modes of social action.[11] The study of colonialism is both a critical inquiry and a call to action. In 2005, poet laureate Naomi Shihab Nye, daughter of a Palestinian refugee to the United States, published a poem about Black internationalist musician and activist Paul Robeson (1898–1976). The US government blacklisted Robeson in 1950 and denied him permission to travel outside the continental United States due to his "extreme advocacy on behalf of the independence of the colonial peoples of Africa." In 1952, in the context of state surveillance and containment, Robeson traveled to the border with Canada to perform at an event organized by the Union of Mine, Mill and Smelter Workers. He could not cross the border, but he could sing at the line. Colonial processes seek to cut relations and to break connections. Nye's poem, *Cross that Line* (2005), beautifully reminds us of the unsilenced truth:

He sang into Canada.
His voice left the USA
when his body was
not allowed to cross
that line.

Remind us again,
brave friend.
What countries may we
sing into?
What lines should we all
be crossing?
What songs travel toward us
from far away
to deepen our days?[12]

Robeson, himself, after returning from the event at the border, poignantly observed, in a way that resonates across space and time: "Songs of liberation – who can lock them up? The spirit of freedom – who can jail it?"[13] Liberation songs travel to us from the past, and also from the future, to deepen us. The colonized continually find ways to evade and survive the incisions of conquest, the command and containment of governments and militias, and the deceptions of the colonizer's mind, until all are free.

Notes

INTRODUCTION

1 Suzanne Preston Blier, *African Vodun: Art, Psychology, and Power* (University of Chicago Press, 1995).

2 Michel Bouffioux has been doing a great deal to make this story a matter of Belgian debate: www.michelbouffioux.be/lusinga

3 Email correspondence from archivist of Tervuren Museum to the author, May 27, 2019.

4 Sven Augustijnen, *Spectres* (Belgium: ASA Publishers, 2011).

5 See, for example, the Universities Studying Slavery network, https://slavery.virginia .edu/universities-studying-slavery/

6 Immanuel Maurice Wallerstein, *The Modern World-System* (Berkeley: University of California Press, 2011), p. 67.

7 Jorge Luis Borges, "On Rigor in Science," in *Collected Fictions* (New York: Penguin, 1998 [1948]), p. 325.

8 Katherine McKittrick, *Demonic Grounds: Black Women and the Cartographies of Struggle* (Minneapolis: University of Minnesota Press, 2006), pp. 33–34; Mishuana Goeman, *Mark My Words: Native Women Mapping Our Nations* (Minneapolis: University of Minnesota Press, 2013), 158–71.

9 Erna Brodber, *Nothing's Mat* (Mona, JA: University of West Indies Press, 2014).

10 Sylvain Lazarus, *Anthropologie du nom* (Paris: Éditions du Seuil, 1996).

11 Jodi A. Byrd, *The Transit of Empire: Indigenous Critiques of Colonialism* (Minneapolis: University of Minnesota Press, 2011), p. xxxvi; Lisa Lowe, *The Intimacies of Four Continents* (Durham, NC: Duke University Press, 2015), p. 15.

12 Byrd, *Transit of Empire*, p. xxiv; Lowe, *Intimacies of Four Continents*; Grace Kyungwon Hong and Roderick A. Ferguson, *Strange Affinities: The Gender and Sexual Politics of Comparative Racialization* (Durham, NC: Duke University Press, 2011), pp. 4–5; Shona N. Jackson, *Creole Indigeneity: Between Myth and Nation in the Caribbean* (Minneapolis: University of Minnesota Press, 2012); Françoise Lionnet and Shumei Shih, *Minor Transnationalism* (Durham, NC: Duke University Press, 2005), p. 19; Manu Vimalassery and Alyosha Goldstein, "Colonial Unknowing and Relations of Study," *Theory & Event* 20, no. 4 (2017): 1042; Robin D. G. Kelley, "The Rest of Us: Rethinking Settler and Native,"

American Quarterly 69, no. 2 (2017): 267; Natalia Molina, Daniel Martinez HoSang, and Ramón Gutiérrez, eds., *Relational Formations of Race: Theory, Method, and Practice* (Berkeley: University of California Press, 2019).

13 I am interested especially in Byrd's elaboration of the perils of interpreting "parallactic effects" in ways that reduce them to discourses of multiperspectivalism and multiculturalism. Byrd, *Transit of Empire*, p. 54. Also see Lisa Lowe and Kris Manjapra, "Comparative Global Humanities after Man: Alternatives to the Coloniality of Knowledge," *Theory, Culture, and Society* 35, no. 5 (2019): 23–48.

14 Vimalassery and Goldstein, "Colonial Unknowing and Relations of Study," 1042; Lionnet and Shih, *Minor Transnationalism*.

15 Scholars have argued with vigor for decades about the phases and processes of capitalist development. Robert Brenner, commenting on the "transition from feudalism to capitalism" debates of the 1960s and 1970s, argued that modern capitalism emerged in the 1600s through western European agrarian class struggle as "landlord capitalists" overpowered the resistance of "tenant-wage laborers." See Robert Brenner, "Agrarian Class Structure and Economic Development in Pre-Industrial Europe," *Past & Present* 70 (1976): 63. Another group of scholars, following Fernand Braudel, situated the origins of capitalism elsewhere, outside western European homelands in expanding Atlantic commodity frontiers and overseas colonial markets. According to this view, capitalism arose through European maritime commercial mobilities. See Fernand Braudel, *Afterthoughts on Material Civilization and Capitalism*, tr. Patricia Ranum (Baltimore: Johns Hopkins Press, 1979), pp. 39–75. Immanuel Wallerstein in his "world-systems analysis" adopted Braudelian assumptions, but emphasized the role of coercion in histories of expanding European capitalism. Wallerstein depicted successive phases of capitalist development, from "capitalist agriculture," to "mercantilism," to "industrial capitalism," within a larger story of western European state domination over other peoples and polities of the world. See Wallerstein, *The Modern World-System*. Finally, for the purpose of this brief discussion, Giovanni Arrighi argued that the emergence of capitalism is better understood as a series of "systemic cycles" of financial expansion and capital accumulation within empires. See Giovanni Arrighi, *The Long Twentieth Century* (New York: Verso, 1994), pp. 111–48.

However, I look to another group of scholars who decisively critique the western-Europe centrism of many of these accounts, and instead situate the rise of capitalism in the friction of colonial encounters and contestations across the Atlantic and Asia, and in the clashes and interactions between different forms of modern economic activity and political sovereignty beyond the Atlantic fringe of Europe. See Andre Gunder Frank, *Capitalism and Underdevelopment in Latin America: Historical Studies of Chile and Brazil* (New York: Monthly Review Press, 1969), pp. 21–28; Andre Gunder Frank, *Reorient: Global Economy in the Asian Age* (Berkeley: University of California Press, 1998), pp. 278, 279; Cedric J. Robinson, *Black Marxism: The Making of the Black Radical Tradition* (Chapel Hill: University of North Carolina Press, 2000), pp. 19–28. Also see Kenneth Pomeranz, *The Great Transformation: China, Europe and the Making of the Modern World Economy* (Princeton University Press, 2000), pp. 186–210; David Graeber on "great capitalist empires," in David Graeber, *Debt: The First 5,000 Years* (New York: Melville House Publishing, 2012), p. 308.

16 Celso Furtado, *Accumulation and Development: The Logic of Industrial Civilization* (Oxford: M. Robertson, 1983), p. 33.

17 Michael Hardt, *Empire*, ed. Antonio Negri (Cambridge, MA: Harvard University Press, 2000) on "the multitude," p. 393; Jason W. Moore, "The Capitalocene, Part I: On the Nature and Origins of Our Ecological Crisis," *The Journal of Peasant Studies* 44, no. 3 (2017): 594; Françoise Vergès, "Racial Capitalocene," in *Futures of Black Radicalism*, ed. Gaye Theresa Johnson and Alex Lubin (London: Verso, 2017).

18 See foundational texts on racial capitalism in Robinson, *Black Marxism*; C. L. R. James, *The Black Jacobins: Toussaint L'Ouverture and the San Domingo Revolution*, 2nd ed., rev. ed. (New York: Vintage Books, 1963); Eric Williams, *Capitalism and Slavery* (Chapel Hill: University of North Carolina Press, 2014); W. E. B. Du Bois, *Black Reconstruction in America: An Essay toward a History of the Part Which Black Folk Played in the Attempt to Reconstruct Democracy in America, 1860–1880* (New York: Oxford University Press, 2007); Sylvia Wynter, *Black Metamorphosis: New Natives in a New World* (New York: Schomburg Center for Research in Black Culture, n.d.).

19 Ruth Wilson Gilmore, *Golden Gulag: Prisons, Surplus, Crisis, and Opposition in Globalizing California* (Berkeley: University of California Press, 2007), pp. 97–113; Nikhil Singh, "On Race, Violence, and So-Called Primitive Accumulation," *Social Text* 34, nos. 3–128 (2016): 27; L. Morgan Jennifer, "Archives and Histories of Racial Capitalism: An Afterword," *Social Text* 33, no. 4 (2015): 153; Zenia Kish and Justin Leroy, "Bonded Life: Technologies of Racial Finance from Slave Insurance to Philanthrocapital," *Cultural Studies* 29, nos. 5–6 (2015): 630; Peter James Hudson, *Bankers and Empire: How Wall Street Colonized the Caribbean* (University of Chicago Press, 2017); Paula Chakravartty and Denise Ferreira Da Silva, "Accumulation, Dispossession, and Debt: The Racial Logic of Global Capitalism – An Introduction," *American Quarterly* 64, no. 3 (2012): 361.

20 Robinson, *Black Marxism*, p. 121.

21 Sylvia Wynter, "Unsettling the Coloniality of Being/Power/Truth/Freedom: Towards the Human, after Man, Its Overrepresentation – An Argument," *CR: The New Centennial Review* 3, no. 3 (2003).

22 Gilmore, *Golden Gulag*, p. 12.

23 Graeber, *Debt*, p. 332.

24 Singh, "On Race"; Jennifer, "Archives and Histories of Racial Capitalism"; Kish and Leroy, "Bonded Life"; Hudson, *Bankers and Empire*; Chakravartty and Silva, "Accumulation, Dispossession, and Debt."

25 Derek Walcott, *The Star-Apple Kingdom* (New York: Farrar, Straus, Giroux, 1979), p. 47.

26 "Programme for International Student Assessment 2015," The Organisation for Economic Co-operation and Development: www.oecd.org/education/pisa-2015-results-volume-i-9789264266490-en.htm. Information on unemployment rates from the Observatoire national de la politique de la ville 2015 report: www.onpv.fr/zoom/rapport2015

27 Katherine McKittrick, "Plantation Futures," *Small Axe* 17, no. 3 (2013): 1.

28 David R. Roediger, *The Wages of Whiteness: Race and the Making of the American Working Class* (London; New York: Verso, 1991), pp. 16, 17.

29 Alyosha Goldstein, *Formations of United States Imperialism* (Durham, NC: Duke University Press, 2014), pp. 2–5.

30 Patricke Wolfe, "Settler Colonialism and the Elimination of the Native," *Journal of Genocide Research* 8, no. 4 (2006): 389.

31 Jane Burbank and Frederick Cooper, eds., *Empires in World History: Power and the Politics of Difference*, ed. Frederick Cooper (Princeton University Press, 2010), pp. 153–62.

32 Celso Furtado, *Development and Underdevelopment* (Berkeley: University of California Press, 1964), 32.

33 Joseph Conrad, *Heart of Darkness* (Cambridge University Press, 2018 [1902]), p. 5.

34 Stephanie E. Smallwood, "The Politics of the Archive and History's Accountability to the Enslaved," *History of the Present* 6, no. 2 (2016).

35 Saidiya Hartman, "Venus in Two Acts," *Small Axe* 12, no. 2 (2008): 3; Lisa Lowe, "History Hesitant," *Social Text* 33, no. 4 (2015): 87; Lowe, *Intimacies of Four Continents*.

36 Judith Butler, *Frames of War: When Is Life Grievable?* (London: Verso, 2010), pp. 165–84.

CHAPTER 1

1 Bernal Díaz del Castillo, *The Conquest of New Spain* (Nendeln: Kraus Reprint, 1967), p. 39.

2 Stuart B. Schwartz, "Cities of Empire: Mexico and Bahia in the Sixteenth Century," *Journal of Inter-American Studies* 11, no. 4 (1969): 616.

3 Ricardo Padrón, *The Spacious Word: Cartography, Literature, and Empire in Early Modern Spain* (University of Chicago Press, 2004), p. 45; Tzvetan Todorov, *The Conquest of America: The Question of the Other* (Norman: University of Oklahoma Press, 1999).

4 Clements R. Markham, *Reports on the Discovery of Peru* (New York: B. Franklin, 1963), pp. 44–52; Johannes Fabian, *Time and the Other: How Anthropology Makes Its Objects* (New York: Columbia University Press, 1983), pp. 21–25.

5 J. B. Harley, *The New Nature of Maps: Essays in the History of Cartography* (Baltimore: Johns Hopkins University Press, 2001), pp. 178–95; Denis Wood, *Rethinking the Power of Maps* (New York: Guilford Press, 2010).

6 J. E. Staller, "Dimensions of Place: The Significance of Centers of the Development of Andean Civilization: An Exploration of the Ushnu Concept," in *Pre-Columbian Landscapes of Creation and Origin*, ed. J. E. Staller (New York: Springer, 2008), p. 275; Marisol de la Cadena, *Earth Beings: Ecologies of Practice across Andean Worlds* (Durham, NC: Duke University Press, 2015).

7 Laurence Roudart and Marcel Mazoyer, *Large-Scale Land Acquisitions* (Leiden: Brill, 2016), pp. 11–13.

8 J. Blaut, "Colonialism and the Rise of Capitalism," *Science and Society* 53, no. 3 (1989): 260.

9 *Ibid.*, 267.

10 Dale Tomich, "Rethinking the Plantation Concepts and Histories," *Review* 34, nos. 1–2 (2011): 15.

11 Kenneth Pomeranz, *The Great Divergence: China, Europe, and the Making of the Modern World Economy* (Princeton University Press, 2000), p. 264.

12 Kari Polanyi Levitt, *The Great Transformation* (Boston: Beacon Press, 1957).

13 Celso Furtado, *Development and Underdevelopment* (Berkeley: University of California Press, 1964); Patricia Seed, *American Pentimento: The Invention of Indians and the Pursuit of Riches* (Minneapolis: University of Minnesota Press, 2001), p. 100.

14 George Fadlo Hourani, *Arab Seafaring in the Indian Ocean in Ancient and Early Medieval Times*, ed. John Carswell (Princeton University Press, 1995), p. 51; K. N. Chaudhuri, *Asia before Europe: Economy and Civilisation of the Indian Ocean from the Rise of Islam to 1750* (Cambridge University Press, 1990); Engseng Ho, *The Graves of Tarim: Genealogy and Mobility across the Indian Ocean* (Berkeley: University of California Press, 2006), p. 98.

15 Chaudhuri, *Asia before Europe*; Sanjay Subrahmanyam, *The Portuguese Empire in Asia, 1500–1700: A Political and Economic History*, 2nd ed. (Chichester: Wiley-Blackwell, 2012); André Wink, *Al-Hind: The Making of the Indo-Islamic World* (Boston: Brill Academic Publishers, 2002), pp. 36–64.

16 Denis Cosgrove, "Mapping New Worlds: Culture and Cartography in Sixteenth-Century Venice," *Imago Mundi* 44, no. 1 (1992): 65.

17 Marco Polo, *The Travels of Marco Polo*, ed. R. E. Latham (Harmondsworth: Penguin Books, 1958).

18 Geoffrey Parker, *The Military Revolution: Military Innovation and the Rise of The West, 1500–1800* (New York: Cambridge University Press, 1996), p. 45.

19 Subrahmanyam, *The Portuguese Empire in Asia*, p. 43; Ronald Findlay and Kevin O'Rourke, *Power and Plenty* (Princeton University Press, 2007), p. 145.

20 The *cartaz* system soon gave way by the 1550s to the concessionary system, whereby Portuguese merchants turned their attention to asserting permanent control over ports, such as at Macau.

21 Bailey W. Diffie, *Prelude to Empire: Portugal Overseas before Henry the Navigator* (Lincoln, NE: University of Nebraska Press, 1960), p. 9; C. R. Boxer, *Portuguese Conquest and Commerce in Southern Asia 1500–1750* (London: Variorum Reprints, 1985).

22 Biblioteca Nacional de Portugal Sintra, 20 de Setembro de 1570, COD. 801, f. 142–44.

23 Sugata Bose and Ayesha Jalal, *Modern South Asia: History, Culture, Political Economy*, ed. Ayesha Jalal, 3rd ed. (London: Routledge, 2011); Patricia Risso, *Merchants and Faith: Muslim Commerce and Culture in the Indian Ocean* (Boulder: Westview Press, 1995), p. 85.

24 Daviken Studnicki-Gizbert, *A Nation upon the Ocean Sea: Portugal's Atlantic Diaspora and the Crisis of the Spanish Empire, 1492–1640* (Oxford University Press, 2007), p. 18; Daniel Pratt Mannix, *Black Cargoes: A History of the Atlantic Slave Trade, 1518–1865* (New York: Viking Press, 1962), pp. 4–5.

25 Hugo Grotius, *Freedom of the Seas or, the Right Which Belongs to the Dutch to Take Part in the East Indian Trade* (New York: Oxford University Press, 1916 [1609]), p. 11; John Selden, *Mare Clausum: The Right and Dominion of the Sea in Two Books*, ed. James Howell and Marchamont Nedham (London: Andrew Kembe and Edward Thomas, 1663).

26 Adrian Finucane, *The Temptations of Trade: Britain, Spain and the Struggle for Empire* (Philadelphia: University of Pennsylvania Press, 2016), p. 16; Arturo Giráldez, *The Age of Trade: The Manila Galleons and the Dawn of the Global Economy* (Lanham: Rowman & Littlefield, 2015); Dennis Owen Flynn, Arturo Giráldez, and James Sobredo, *European Entry into the Pacific: Spain and the Acapulco–Manila Galleons* (Aldershot: Ashgate, 2001); Benito J. Legarda, *After the Galleons: Foreign Trade, Economic Change & Entrepreneurship in the Nineteenth-Century Philippines* (Quezon City: Ateneo de Manila University Press, 1999); Sanjay Subrahmanyam, "Holding the World in Balance: The Connected Histories of the Iberian Overseas Empires, 1500–1640," *The American Historical Review* 112, no. 5 (2007): 1373.

27 Jan Glete, *War and the State in Early Modern Europe: Spain, the Dutch Republic and Sweden as Fiscal–Military States, 1500–1660* (London: Routledge, 2002), p. 84; Kenneth R. Andrews, *Trade, Plunder, and Settlement: Maritime Enterprise and the Genesis of the British Empire, 1480–1630* (Cambridge University Press, 1984).

28 Andrew Lipman, *The Saltwater Frontier: Indians and the Contest for the American Coast* (New Haven: Yale University Press, 2015), p. 99; Renisa Mawani, *Across Oceans of Law: The Komagata Maru and Jurisdiction in the Time of Empire* (Durham, NC: Duke University Press, 2018), p. 119; Frederick Cooper and Ann Laura Stoler, *Tensions of Empire: Colonial Cultures in a Bourgeois World* (Berkeley: University of California Press, 1997), p. 5.

29 Roger C. Smith, *Vanguard of Empire: Ships of Exploration in the Age of Columbus* (New York: Oxford University Press, 1993); James F. Shepherd and Gary Walton, *Shipping, Maritime Trade, and the Economic Development of Colonial North America* (Cambridge University Press, 1972), p. 72.

30 Irene Silverblatt, *Modern Inquisitions: Peru and the Colonial Origins of the Civilized World* (Durham, NC: Duke University Press, 2004), p. 105.

31 T. C. F. Hopkins, *Confrontation at Lepanto: Christendom vs. Islam* (New York: Forge, 2006).

32 Luis Gorrochategui Santos, *The English Armada: The Greatest Naval Disaster in English History* (London: Bloomsbury Academic, 2018), pp. 7–12; Felipe Fernández-Armesto, *The Spanish Armada: The Experience of the War in 1588* (Oxford University Press, 1988).

33 David Parrott, *The Business of War: Military Enterprise and Military Revolution in Early Modern Europe* (Cambridge University Press, 2012), pp. 27–31; Michael Duffy, *The Military Revolution and the State, 1500–1800* (University of Exeter, 1980), pp. 2–3.

34 Nelson Maldonado Torres, *Against War: Views from the Underside of Modernity* (Durham, NC: Duke University Press, 2008), pp. 164–86.

35 Gloria Elizabeth Chacón, *Indigenous Cosmolectics: Kab'awil and the Making of Maya and Zapotec Literatures* (Chapel Hill: University of North Carolina Press, 2018), p. 26.

36 Boone, "Introduction: Writing and Recording Knowledge," in Elizabeth Hill Boone and Walter Mignolo, *Writing without Words: Alternative Literacies in Mesoamerica and the Andes* (Durham, NC: Duke University Press, 1994), p. 21.

37 José de Acosta, *Natural and Moral History of the Indies* (Durham, NC: Duke University Press, 2002).

38 Walter Mignolo, *The Darker Side of the Renaissance: Literacy, Territoriality, and Colonization*, 2nd ed. (Ann Arbor: University of Michigan Press, 2003), pp. 127–69.

39 Derek Walcott, *Omeros* (New York: Farrar, Straus, Giroux, 1990), p. 75.

40 Gene Tucker, "Place-Names, Conquest, and Empire: Spanish and Amerindian Conceptions of Place in the New World" (University of Texas at Arlington: PhD Dissertation, 2011), p. 70; Charles Whitney, "The Naming of America as the Meaning of America: Vespucci, Publicity, Festivity, Modernity," *Clio* 22, no. 3 (1993): 195.

41 Heather Streets-Salter and Trevor R. Getz, *Empires and Colonies in the Modern World: A Global Perspective* (New York: Oxford University Press, 2016).

42 Macarena Gómez-Barris, *The Extractive Zone: Social Ecologies and Decolonial Perspectives* (Durham, NC: Duke University Press, 2017), p. xvii.

43 Ernesto Laclau, "Feudalism and Capitalism in Latin America," *New Left Review* 1, no. 67 (1971): 19.

44 Tamar Herzog, *Frontiers of Possession: Spain and Portugal in Europe and the Americas* (Cambridge, MA: Harvard University Press, 2015), pp. 253–55; Philip Stern and Carl Wennerlind, *Mercantilism Reimagined: Political Economy in Early Modern Britain and Its Empire* (Oxford University Press, 2014).

45 Ronald Batchelder and Nicolas Sanchez, "The Encomienda and the Optimizing Imperialist: An Interpretation of Spanish Imperialism in the Americas," *Public Choice* 156, no. 1 (2013): 45.

46 Héctor Díaz Polanco, *Indigenous Peoples in Latin America: The Quest for Self-Determination* (Boulder: Westview Press, 1997), p. 45; Seed, *American Pentimento*, p. 132; María Josefina Saldaña-Portillo, *Indian Given: Racial Geographies across Mexico and the United States* (Durham, NC: Duke University Press, 2016), p. 37.

47 Susan E. Ramírez, *The World Upside Down: Cross-Cultural Contact and Conflict in Sixteenth-Century Peru* (Stanford University Press, 1996), p. 72.

48 Mónica Brito Vieira, "Mare Liberum vs. Mare Clausum: Grotius, Freitas, and Selden's Debate on Dominion over the Seas," *Journal of the History of Ideas* 64, no. 3 (2003): 367.

49 Martin Lynch, *Mining in World History* (London: Reaktion Books, 2002).

50 Eduardo Galeano, *Open Veins of Latin America: Five Centuries of the Pillage of a Continent*, 25th anniversary ed. Foreword by Isabel Allende (New York: Monthly Review Press, 1997), p. 23; P. J. Bakewell, *Mines of Silver and Gold in the Americas* (Aldershot: Variorum, 1997).

51 A. Kobata, "The Production and Uses of Gold and Silver in Sixteenth- and Seventeenth-Century Japan," *Economic History Review* 18, no. 2 (1965): 253.

52 Paula Zagalsky, "The Potosí Mita: An Unchanged Colonial Imposition within a Context of Multiple Transformations," *Chungara* 46, no. 3 (2014): 375.

53 Christine D. Beaule, *Frontiers of Colonialism* (Miami: University Press of Florida, 2017); Ward Stavig, "Continuing the Bleeding of These Pueblos Will Shortly Make Them Cadavers: The Potosí Mita, Cultural Identity, and Communal Survival in Colonial Peru," *The Americas: A Quarterly Review of Inter-American Cultural History* 56, no. 4 (2000): 529.

54 Silvia Rivera Cusicanqui, "Ch'ixinakax Utxiwa: A Reflection on the Practices and Discourses of Decolonization," *South Atlantic Quarterly* 111, no. 1 (2012): 96.

55 Richard Jurin, "The Unending Frontier: An Environmental History of the Early Modern World," *The Journal of Environmental Education* 35, no. 1 (2003): 54.

56 Legarda, *After the Galleons*.

57 Immanuel Maurice Wallerstein, *The Modern World-System* (Berkeley: University of California Press, 2011), p. 189.

58 Birgit Tremml, *Spain, China and Japan in Manila, 1571–1644: Local Comparisons and Global Connections* (Amsterdam University Press, 2015), p. 99.

59 Linda A. Newson, *Conquest and Pestilence in the Early Spanish Philippines* (Honolulu: University of Hawaii, 2009), p. 37.

60 Tatiana Seijas, *Asian Slaves in Colonial Mexico: From Chinos to Indians* (New York: Cambridge University Press, 2014), pp. 73–108.

61 Galeano, *Open Veins of Latin America.*

62 Tremml, *Spain, China and Japan in Manila*, p. 106; Birgit Tremml, "The Global and the Local: Problematic Dynamics of the Triangular Trade in Early Modern Manila," *Journal of World History* 23, no. 3 (2012): 555.

63 Robert C. Smith, "Colonial Towns of Spanish and Portuguese America," *Journal of the Society of Architectural Historians* 14, no. 4 (1955): 3; John Lynch, "The Institutional Framework of Colonial Spanish America," *Journal of Latin American Studies* 24, no. 1 (1992): 69.

64 Serge Gruzinski, *Les quatre parties du monde: Histoire d'une mondialisation* (Paris: La Martinière, 2004).

65 Dennis Carr, *Made in the Americas: The New World Discovers Asia* (Boston: Museum of Fine Arts, 2015).

66 Vicente L. Rafael, *Contracting Colonialism: Translation and Christian Conversion in Tagalog Society under Early Spanish Rule* (Durham, NC: Duke University Press, 1993).

67 Eric R. Wolf, *Europe and the People without History* (Berkeley: University of California Press, 1982), p. 153.

68 Rainer F. Buschmann, *Navigating the Spanish Lake: The Pacific in the Iberian World, 1521–1898* (Honolulu: University of Hawaii Press, 2014), p. 63.

69 Gómez-Barris, *The Extractive Zone*, p. 45; María Elena Martínez, *Genealogical Fictions: Limpieza De Sangre, Religion, and Gender in Colonial Mexico* (Stanford University Press, 2008).

70 Saldaña-Portillo, *Indian Given*; Mary Louise Pratt, *Imperial Eyes: Travel Writing and Transculturation* (London: Routledge, 1992), pp. 172–200.

71 Martínez, *Genealogical Fictions*, p. 25; Ben Vinson, *Before Mestizaje: The Frontiers of Race and Caste in Colonial Mexico* (New York: Cambridge University Press, 2018), p. 70.

72 Charles F. Walker, *The Tupac Amaru Rebellion* (New York: Oxford University Press, 2016), p. 46.

73 Saldaña-Portillo, *Indian Given*; Jose Rabasa, "Of Zapatismo: Reflections on the Folkloric and the Impossible in a Subaltern Insurrection," in *Without History: Subaltern Studies, the Zapatista Insurgency, and the Specter of History* (University of Pittsburgh Press, 2010), p. 41.

CHAPTER 2

1 Natick Indian petition, 1748, Massachusetts State Archive. Information on Ebenezer Felch was recorded later in the *Natick Bulletin*, May 21, 1909.

2 On refusal, see Audra Simpson, *Mohawk Interruptus: Political Life across the Borders of Settler States* (Durham, NC: Duke University Press, 2014), p. 25.

3 Jean O'Brien, "Natick," in *Early Native Literacies in New England: A Documentary and Critical Anthology*, ed. Kristina Bross and Hilary Wyss (Boston: University of Massachusetts Press, 2008), p. 125.

4 On "low-frequency" resistance, see Saidiya V. Hartman, *Scenes of Subjection: Terror, Slavery, and Self-Making in Nineteenth-Century America* (New York: Oxford University Press, 1997); James C. Scott, *Weapons of the Weak: Everyday Forms of Peasant Resistance* (New Haven: Yale University Press, 1985).

5 On legacies of warfare, see Jean Comaroff and John L. Comaroff, *Law and Disorder in the Postcolony* (University of Chicago Press, 2006), p. 20.

6 Jean M. O'Brien, *Dispossession by Degrees: Indian Land and Identity in Natick, Massachusetts, 1650–1790* (Cambridge, MA: Harvard University Press, 1997).

7 Philip Joseph Deloria, *Playing Indian* (New Haven: Yale University Press, 1998); Kevin Bruyneel, *The Third Space of Sovereignty: The Postcolonial Politics of U.S.–Indigenous Relations* (Minneapolis: University of Minnesota Press, 2007), p. 13.

8 Patrick Wolfe, "Settler Colonialism and the Elimination of the Native," *Journal of Genocide Research* 8, no. 4 (2006): 387.

9 Roxanne Dunbar-Ortiz, *An Indigenous Peoples' History of the United States* (Boston: Beacon Press, 2014), p. 220.

10 Jodi A. Byrd, *The Transit of Empire: Indigenous Critiques of Colonialism* (Minneapolis: University of Minnesota Press, 2011), p. xxxv.

11 Patrick Wolfe, *Settler Colonialism and the Transformation of Anthropology: The Politics and Poetics of an Ethnographic Event* (London: Cassell, 1999), p. 390; Lorenzo Veracini, *Settler Colonialism: A Theoretical Overview* (Houndmills, Basingstoke: Palgrave Macmillan, 2010), p. 16.

12 Jean M. O'Brien, *Firsting and Lasting: Writing Indians out of Existence in New England* (Minneapolis: University of Minnesota Press, 2010), p. xv.

13 Bruyneel, *The Third Space of Sovereignty*, p. xvi.

14 Mishuana Goeman, *Mark My Words: Native Women Mapping Our Nations* (Minneapolis: University of Minnesota Press, 2013), p. 3; Gerald Robert Vizenor, *Manifest Manners: Narratives on Postindian Survivance* (Hanover: University Press of New England, 1994).

15 Thomas Hobbes, *Hobbes's Leviathan* (Oxford: Clarendon Press, 1958), p. 96.

16 Sarah Barber and David Smith, "Regicide and Republicanism: Politics and Ethics in the English Revolution, 1646–1659," *Historical Journal* 46, no. 2 (2003): 31.

17 Kenneth Pomeranz, *The Great Divergence: China, Europe, and the Making of the Modern World Economy* (Princeton University Press, 2000), p. 264.

18 Lisa Blee and Jean M. O'Brien, *Monumental Mobility: The Memory Work of Massasoit* (Chapel Hill: University of North Carolina Press, 2019), p. 202.

19 Paul Corcoran, "John Locke on Native Right, Colonial Possession, and the Concept of *Vacuum Domicilium*," *The European Legacy* 23, no. 3 (2018): 238.

20 Jill H. Casid, *Sowing Empire: Landscape and Colonization* (Minneapolis: University of Minnesota Press, 2005), p. 95; Margaret Strobel, *European Women and the Second British Empire* (Bloomington: Indiana University Press, 1991).

21 Cotton Mather, *The Life and Death of John Eliot* (Boston: John Dunton, 1691), p. 82; Cotton Mather, *The Wonders of the Invisible World: Being an Account of the Tryals of Several Witches Lately Executed in New-England and of Several Remarkable Curiosities Therein Occurring,* 2nd ed. (Boston: John Damon, 1693), p. 1.

22 John Locke, *Second Treatise of Government,* ed. C. B. Macpherson (Indianapolis: Hackett, 1980).

23 O'Brien, *Dispossession by Degrees,* p. 21.

24 Peter Benes and Jane Montague Benes, eds., *New England and the Caribbean* (Deerfield: Dublin Seminar for New England Folklife, 2012).

25 Lisa Tanya Brooks, *Our Beloved Kin: A New History of King Philip's War* (New Haven: Yale University Press, 2018), p. 17; Paul Chaat Smith, *Everything You Know about Indians Is Wrong* (Minneapolis: University of Minnesota Press, 2009), p. 75.

26 Comaroff and Comaroff, *Law and Disorder in the Postcolony.*

27 O'Brien, *Dispossession by Degrees,* p. 29.

28 K-Sue Park, "Money, Mortgages, and the Conquest of America," *Law & Social Inquiry: Journal of the American Bar Foundation* 41, no. 4 (2016): 1006.

29 Brenna Bhandar, *Colonial Lives of Property: Law, Land, and Racial Regimes of Ownership* (Durham, NC: Duke University Press, 2018).

30 Park, "Money, Mortgages, and the Conquest of America."

31 Eric Evans, *The Contentious Tithe: The Tithe Problem and English Agriculture, 1750–1850* (Boston: Routledge & K. Paul, 1976), p. 161.

32 Jennifer J. Baker, *Securing the Commonwealth: Debt, Speculation, and Writing in the Making of Early America* (Baltimore: Johns Hopkins University Press, 2005).

33 Stephanie Fitzgerald, "'I Wunnatuckquannum, This Is My Hand': Native Performance in Massachusett Language Indian Deeds," in *Native Acts: Indian Performance, 1603–1832,* ed. Joshua David Bellin and Laura L. Mielke (Lincoln, NE: University of Nebraska, 2012), p. 145.

34 Max Weber, *The Protestant Ethic and the Spirit of Capitalism: With Other Writings on the Rise of the West,* ed. Stephen Kalberg, 4th ed. (New York: Oxford University Press, 2009).

35 O'Brien, *Dispossession by Degrees,* p. 92.

36 Blake A. Watson, "The Impact of the American Doctrine of Discovery on Native Land Rights in Australia, Canada, and New Zealand," *Seattle University Law Review* 34 (2011): 507; Colin G. Calloway, *Pen and Ink Witchcraft: Treaties and Treaty Making in American Indian History* (Oxford University Press, 2013).

37 O'Brien, *Dispossession by Degrees,* pp. 29, 32.

38 Daniel R. Mandell, *King Philip's War: Colonial Expansion, Native Resistance, and the End of Indian Sovereignty* (Baltimore: Johns Hopkins University Press, 2010), p. 13.

39 William Cronon, *Changes in the Land: Indians, Colonists, and the Ecology of New England,* ed. John Demos (New York: Hill and Wang, 2003), p. 42.

40 Brooks, *Our Beloved Kin,* p. 35.

41 Wolfe, "Settler Colonialism and the Elimination of the Native," 388.

42 Alyssa Mt. Pleasant, "After the Whirlwind: Maintaining a Haudenosaunee Place at Buffalo Creek, 1780–1825" (University of Cornell: PhD Dissertation, 2007), p. 10.

43 Keith H. Basso, *Wisdom Sits in Places: Landscape and Language among the Western Apache* (Albuquerque: University of New Mexico Press, 1996), p. xv.

44 Dee Brown, *Bury My Heart at Wounded Knee: An Indian History of the American West*, 30th anniversary ed. (New York: H. Holt, 2001), p. 5.

45 Tiya Miles, *Ties That Bind: The Story of an Afro-Cherokee Family in Slavery and Freedom*, 2nd ed. (Oakland: University of California Press, 2015); Kendra Taira Field, *Growing up with the Country: Family, Race, and Nation after the Civil War* (New Haven: Yale University Press, 2018).

46 Arthur Derosier, *The Removal of the Choctaw Indians* (Nashville: University of Tennessee Press, 1981), p. 23; Clyde Adrian Woods, *Development Arrested: The Blues and Plantation Power in the Mississippi Delta* (London: Verso, 1998), p. 43; Walter Johnson, *River of Dark Dreams: Slavery and Empire in the Cotton Kingdom* (Cambridge, MA: Harvard University Press, 2013); Matthew Pratt Guterl, *American Mediterranean: Southern Slaveholders in the Age of Emancipation* (Cambridge, MA: Harvard University Press, 2008).

47 Alexis de Tocqueville, *Democracy in America*, ed. Arthur Goldhammer (New York: Penguin Putnam, 2004), ch. 18.

48 *Cherokee vs. Georgia*, paragraph 60.

49 Ned Blackhawk, *Violence over the Land: Indians and Empires in the Early American West* (Cambridge: Harvard University Press, 2006).

50 Patrick Wolfe, *Traces of History: Elementary Structures of Race* (London: Verso, 2016), p. 35.

51 Alfred W. Crosby, *Ecological Imperialism: The Biological Expansion of Europe, 900–1900*, 2nd ed. (Cambridge, MA: Cambridge University Press, 2004); Richard Grove, *Ecology, Climate and Empire: Colonialism and Global Environmental History, 1400–1940* (Cambridge University Press, 1997).

52 Brooks, *Our Beloved Kin*, p. 27.

53 C. A. Bayly, *Imperial Meridian: The British Empire and the World, 1780–1830* (London: Longman, 1989).

54 Peter Veth, Peter Sutton, and Margo Neale, *Strangers on the Shore: Early Coastal Contact in Australia* (Canberra: National Museum of Australia, 2008).

55 Boyd Hunter, "The Aboriginal Legacy," in *The Cambridge History of Australia*, ed. Alison Bashford and Stuart Macintyre (Port Melbourne: Cambridge University Press, 2013), p. 73.

56 Epeli Hau'ofa, *We Are the Ocean: Selected Works* (Honolulu: University of Hawaii Press, 2008), p. 11; Lynette Russell, *Roving Mariners: Australian Aboriginal Whalers and Sealers in the Southern Oceans* (Albany: University of New York Press, 2012); Tracey Banivanua-Mar, *Decolonisation and the Pacific: Indigenous Globalisation and the Ends of Empire* (Cambridge University Press, 2016).

57 Judy Campbell, *Invisible Invaders: Smallpox and Other Diseases in Aboriginal Australia, 1780–1880* (Carlton South: Melbourne University Press, 2002).

58 Elizabeth A. Povinelli, *Labor's Lot: The Power, History, and Culture of Aboriginal Action* (University of Chicago Press, 1993), p. 24; Noel Dyck, ed., *Indigenous Peoples and the Nation-State: "Fourth World" Politics in Canada, Australia, and Norway* (St. John's, Canada: Institute of Social and Economic Research, 1985); George Manuel, *The Fourth World: An Indian Reality* (Minneapolis: University of Minnesota Press, 2019), p. 13.

59 Leigh Dale, "Empire's Proxy: Sheep and the Colonial Environment," in *Five Emus to the King of Siam: Environment and Empire*, ed. Helen Tiffin (Amsterdam: Rodopi, 2008), p. 9.

60 Jim Endersby, "A Garden Enclosed: Botanical Barter in Sydney, 1818–39," *British Journal for the History of Science* 33, no. 3 (2000): 313.

61 Sylvia Morrissey, "The Pastoral Economy, 1821–1850," in *Essays in Economic History of Australia, 1788–1939*, ed. James Griffin (Brisbane: Jacaranda, 1967), p. 58.

62 Stanley L. Engerman, *Terms of Labor: Slavery, Serfdom, and Free Labor* (Stanford University Press, 1999).

63 Wolfe, *Traces of History*, p. 208.

64 Morrissey, "The Pastoral Economy," p. 58.

65 Sarah Carter, *Imperial Plots: Women, Land, and Spadework of British Colonialism on the Canadian Prairies* (Winnipeg: University of Manitoba Press, 2016).

66 Renisa Mawani, *Across Oceans of Law: The Komagata Maru and Jurisdiction in the Time of Empire* (Durham, NC: Duke University Press, 2018).

67 Matthew H. Edney, *Mapping an Empire: The Geographical Construction of British India, 1765–1843* (University of Chicago Press, 1997).

68 Caroline Elkins and Susan Pedersen, *Settler Colonialism in the Twentieth Century: Projects, Practices, Legacies* (New York: Routledge, 2005); Achille Mbembe, *On the Postcolony* (Berkeley: University of California Press, 2001).

69 Ahmad H. Sa'di and Lila Abu-Lughod, eds., *Nakba: Palestine, 1948, and the Claims of Memory* (New York: Columbia University Press, 2007).

CHAPTER 3

1 Jason Daniels, "Recovering the Fugitive History of Marronage in Saint Domingue, 1770–1791," *The Journal of Caribbean History* 46, no. 2 (2012): 121; Robin Blackburn, *The Overthrow of Colonial Slavery, 1776–1848* (London: Verso, 1988); Jean Fouchard, *The Haitian Maroons: Liberty or Death* (New York: E. W. Blyden Press, 1981); Carolyn E. Fick, *The Making of Haiti: The Saint Domingue Revolution from Below* (Knoxville: University of Tennessee Press, 1990), p. 25.

2 John K. Thornton, "'I Am the Subject of the King of Congo': African Political Ideology and the Haitian Revolution," *Journal of World History* 4, no. 2 (1993): 183.

3 M. Neocosmos, *Thinking Freedom in Africa: Toward a Theory of Emancipatory Politics* (Johannesburg: Wits University Press, 2016), pp. 70–72.

4 Sylvia Wynter, *Black Metamorphosis: New Natives in a New World* (New York: Schomburg Center for Research in Black Culture, n.d.), p. 127.

5 David Patrick Geggus, *The Impact of the Haitian Revolution in the Atlantic World* (Columbia: University of South Carolina, 2001); Ada Ferrer, *Freedom's Mirror: Cuba and Haiti in the Age of Revolution* (New York: Cambridge University Press, 2014); David Barry Gaspar and David Patrick Geggus, *A Turbulent Time: The French Revolution and the Greater Caribbean* (Bloomington: Indiana University Press, 1997), p. 5; Julius Sherrard Scott, *The Common Wind: Afro-American Currents in the Age of the Haitian Revolution*, ed. Marcus Rediker (London: Verso, 2018), p. 118.

6 Cedric J. Robinson, *Black Marxism: The Making of the Black Radical Tradition* (Chapel Hill: University of North Carolina Press, 2000), p. 148.

7 Saidiya V. Hartman, *Scenes of Subjection: Terror, Slavery, and Self-Making in Nineteenth-Century America* (New York: Oxford University Press, 1997).

8 J. E. Inikori and Stanley L. Engerman, *The Atlantic Slave Trade: Effects on Economies, Societies, and Peoples in Africa, the Americas, and Europe* (Durham, NC: Duke University Press, 1992), p. 481.

9 William St. Clair, *The Door of No Return: The History of Cape Coast Castle and the Atlantic Slave Trade* (New York: BlueBridge, 2007), p. 232.

10 Afonso I to João III, October 18, 1528. António Brásio, *Monumenta Missionaria Africana: Africa Ocidental* (Lisbon: Agência Geral do Ultramar, 1952–88).

11 Sylviane A. Diouf, *Fighting the Slave Trade: West African Strategies* (Athens, GA: Ohio University Press, 2003), p. 137.

12 On insurrections at sea, see Maggie Montesinos Sale, *The Slumbering Volcano: American Slave Ship Revolts and the Production of Rebellious Masculinity* (Durham, NC: Duke University Press, 1997), pp. 1–29; Greg Grandin, *The Empire of Necessity: Slavery, Freedom, and Deception in the New World* (New York: Metropolitan Books/Henry Holt and Company, 2014).

13 Omise'eke Natasha Tinsley, "Black Atlantic, Queer Atlantic: Queer Imaginings of the Middle Passage," *GLQ: A Journal of Lesbian and Gay Studies* 14, nos. 2–3 (2008): 191.

14 Dedication in Toni Morrison, *Beloved* (New York: Alfred A. Knopf, 1987); Stephanie E. Smallwood, "The Politics of the Archive and History's Accountability to the Enslaved," *History of the Present* 6, no. 2 (2016): 19.

15 Stephanie E. Smallwood, *Saltwater Slavery: A Middle Passage from Africa to American Diaspora* (Cambridge, MA: Harvard University Press, 2007), p. 16.

16 Orlando Patterson, *The Sociology of Slavery: An Analysis of the Origins, Development, and Structure of Negro Slave Society in Jamaica*, 1st American ed. (Rutherford: Fairleigh Dickinson University Press, 1969), pp. 152–58.

17 Smallwood, *Saltwater Slavery*.

18 *Ibid.*

19 Wynter, *Black Metamorphosis*, p. 27.

20 Jennifer L. Morgan, *Laboring Women: Reproduction and Gender in New World Slavery* (Philadelphia: University of Pennsylvania Press, 2004), p. 50.

21 Olaudah Equiano, *The Interesting Narrative and Other Writings*, ed. Vincent Carretta, rev. ed. (New York: Penguin Books, 2003).

22 Walter Johnson, *Soul by Soul: Life inside the Antebellum Slave Market* (Cambridge, MA: Harvard University Press, 1999), p. 138.

23 Laird Bergad, *The Comparative Histories of Slavery in Brazil, Cuba, and the United States* (Cambridge University Press, 2001), p. 159.

24 Eric Williams, *Capitalism and Slavery* (Chapel Hill: University of North Carolina Press, 2014), pp. 7–9.

25 St. Clair, *The Door of No Return*, p. 4.

26 Carina E. Ray, *Crossing the Color Line: Race, Sex, and the Contested Politics of Colonialism in Ghana* (Athens, GA: Ohio University Press, 2015).

27 Roquinaldo Amaral Ferreira, *Cross-Cultural Exchange in the Atlantic World: Angola and Brazil during the Era of the Slave Trade* (New York: Cambridge University Press, 2012), p. 52.

28 Richard B. Allen, "European Slave Trading, Abolitionism, and 'New Systems of Slavery' in the Indian Ocean," *PORTAL: Journal of Multidisciplinary International Studies* 9, no. 1 (2012): 190.

29 See the stool belonging to the Denkyira ruler at the Leiden Museum Volkenkunde, Object acquisition number: RV–230–1685.

30 Inikori and Engerman, *The Atlantic Slave Trade;* Nathan Nunn and Leonard Wantchekon, "The Slave Trade and the Origins of Mistrust in Africa," *American Economic Review* 101, no. 7 (2011): 3225.

31 J. E. Inikori, *Forced Migration: The Impact of the Export Slave Trade on African Societies* (New York: Africana Publication, 1982), p. 53.

32 Fred D'Aguiar, *Feeding the Ghosts* (London: Chatto & Windus, 1997), p. 113.

33 Ray, *Crossing the Color Line*, pp. 34–46.

34 Kofi Asante, *"Purchased Allies" or "Thorns in the Side of the Government"?: African Merchants and Colonial State Formation in the Nineteenth-Century Gold Coast* (Evanston, IL: Northwestern University, 2016), p. 70; J. T. Lever, "Mulatto Influence on the Gold Coast in the Early Nineteenth Century: Jan Nieser of Elmina," *African Historical Studies* 3, no. 2 (1970): 253.

35 Nieser, Letter to Liverpool, Accra, June 2, 1803, Nationaal Archief, Nederlandse Bezittingen op de Kust van Guinea, 1133.

36 Dionne Brand, *A Map to the Door of No Return: Notes to Belonging* (Toronto: Vintage Canada, 2002), p. 4.

37 Sidney W. Mintz, *Sweetness and Power: The Place of Sugar in Modern History* (New York: Viking, 1985); Walter Johnson, *River of Dark Dreams: Slavery and Empire in the Cotton Kingdom* (Cambridge, MA: Harvard University Press, 2013), pp. 209–44; Doreen B. Massey, *Space, Place, and Gender* (Minneapolis: University of Minnesota Press, 1994).

38 On plantation science, see Kris Manjapra, "Plantation Dispossessions: The Global Travel of Agricultural Racial Capitalism," in *American Capitalism: New Histories*, ed. Sven Beckert and Christine Desan (New York: Columbia University Press, 2016), p. 361; Prakash Kumar, *Indigo Plantations and Science in Colonial India* (Cambridge University Press, 2012).

39 C. L. R. James, *The Black Jacobins: Toussaint L'Ouverture and the San Domingo Revolution*, 2nd ed., rev. ed. (New York: Vintage Books, 1963), p. 86; Sidney W. Mintz, "Was the Plantation Slave a Proletarian?," *Fernand Braudel Center Review* 2, no. 1 (1978): 81.

40 Clyde Adrian Woods, *Development Arrested: The Blues and Plantation Power in the Mississippi Delta* (London: Verso, 1998), p. 67.

41 Mintz, *Sweetness and Power*, p. 74.

42 Derek Walcott, *Omeros* (New York: Farrar, Straus, Giroux, 1990), p. 259.

43 Giorgio Riello and Prasannan Parthasarathi, *The Spinning World: A Global History of Cotton Textiles, 1200–1850* (Oxford University Press, 2009).

44 John D. Garrigus, *Before Haiti: Race and Citizenship in French Saint-Domingue* (New York: Palgrave Macmillan, 2006), p. 7.

45 Morgan, *Laboring Women*, p. 71.

46 Tera W. Hunter, *Bound in Wedlock: Slave and Free Black Marriage in the Nineteenth Century* (Cambridge, MA: The Belknap Press of Harvard University Press, 2017), pp. 72–74.

47 Jennifer L. Morgan, "Partus Sequitur Ventrem," *Small Axe: A Caribbean Journal of Criticism* 22, no. 1 (2018): 1.

48 Martha S. Santos, "'Slave Mothers,' Partus Sequitur Ventrem, and the Naturalization of Slave Reproduction in Nineteenth-Century Brazil," *Tempo* 22, no. 41 (2016): 467.

49 Alan Watson, "The Origins of the Code Noir Revisited (Slavery Laws in the French Colonies)," *Tulane Law Review* 71, no. 4 (1997): 1041.

50 Alexandra A. Chan, *Slavery in the Age of Reason: Archaeology at a New England Farm* (Knoxville: University of Tennessee Press, 2007), pp. 47–57.

51 James, *The Black Jacobins*.

52 Elizabeth M. Deloughrey, "Yam, Roots, and Rot: Allegories of the Provision Grounds," *Small Axe: A Caribbean Journal of Criticism* 15, no. 1 (2011): 61.

53 Mintz, "Was the Plantation Slave a Proletarian?," 81.

54 Vincent Brown, *The Reaper's Garden: Death and Power in the World of Atlantic Slavery* (Cambridge, MA: Harvard University Press, 2008), p. 129.

55 Hartman, *Scenes of Subjection*, p. 67.

56 *Ibid.*, p. 73.

57 Woods, *Development Arrested*, p. 129.

58 *Ibid.*

59 *Ibid.*

60 Paul Gilroy, "'Living Memory': An Interview with Toni Morrison," *City Limits* 31 (March–April 1988).

61 Toni Morrison, *Song of Solomon* (New York: Knopf, 1977), p. 49.

62 Gilroy, "'Living Memory'"; Paul Gilroy, *The Black Atlantic: Modernity and Double Consciousness* (Cambridge, MA: Harvard University Press, 1993), p. 79.

63 Christopher Schmidt-Nowara, *Empire and Antislavery: Spain, Cuba, and Puerto Rico, 1833–1874* (University of Pittsburgh Press, 1999).

64 Manisha Sinha, *The Slave's Cause: A History of Abolition* (New Haven: Yale University Press, 2016), p. 2.

65 Michael Craton, *Testing the Chains: Resistance to Slavery in the British West Indies* (Ithaca, NY: Cornell University Press, 1982), p. 335.

66 Richard S. Dunn, *A Tale of Two Plantations: Slave Life and Labor in Jamaica and Virginia* (Cambridge, MA: Harvard University Press, 2014), p. 4; James, *The Black Jacobins*, p. 12.

67 Thomas C. Holt, *The Problem of Freedom: Race, Labor, and Politics in Jamaica and Britain, 1832–1938* (Baltimore: Johns Hopkins University Press, 1992), pp. 56–65, 126; W. E. B. Du Bois, *Black Reconstruction in America: An Essay toward a History of the Part Which Black Folk Played in the Attempt to Reconstruct Democracy in America, 1860–1880* (New York: Oxford University Press, 2007), p. 381; Patterson, *The Sociology of Slavery*, p. 273.

68 Radiclani Clytus, "Envisioning Slavery: American Abolitionism and the Primacy of the Visual" (Yale University: PhD Dissertation, 2007).

69 Sojourner Truth, *Narrative of Sojourner Truth*, ed. Olive Gilbert and Frances W. Titus (New York: Arno Press, 1968), p. 82.

70 Harriet A. Jacobs, *Incidents in the Life of a Slave Girl* (New York: Penguin Books, 2000), p. 55.

71 Christina Elizabeth Sharpe, *In the Wake: On Blackness and Being* (Durham, NC: Duke University Press, 2016).

72 Hartman, *Scenes of Subjection*, p. 79.

73 I am grateful to Kofi Yao Agorkor for developing this formulation. Lecture at XR London, May 25, 2019.

CHAPTER 4

1 Hugh Tinker, *A New System of Slavery: The Export of Indian Labour Overseas, 1830–1920* (London: Oxford University Press, 1974).

2 Lisa Yun, *The Coolie Speaks: Chinese Indentured Laborers and African Slaves in Cuba* (Philadelphia: Temple University Press, 2008), p. 118.

3 Lauren A. Benton, *Law and Colonial Cultures: Legal Regimes in World History, 1400–1900* (Cambridge University Press, 2004), p. 31.

4 Frank Broeze, ed., *Bridge of the Sea: Port Cities of Asia from the 16th–20th Centuries* (Honolulu: University of Hawaii Press, 1989), p. 11.

5 K. N. Chaudhuri, *Trade and Civilisation in the Indian Ocean: An Economic History from the Rise of Islam to 1750* (Cambridge University Press, 1985).

6 Hyunhee Park, *Mapping the Chinese and Islamic Worlds: Cross-Cultural Exchange in Pre-Modern Asia* (Cambridge University Press, 2012), p. 7.

7 Kerry Ward, *Networks of Empire: Forced Migration in the Dutch East India Company* (Cambridge University Press, 2009), p. 127.

8 Johan Mathew, *Margins of the Market: Trafficking and Capitalism across the Arabian Sea* (Oakland: University of California Press, 2016), pp. 12–18.

9 Holden Furber, *Bombay Presidency in the Mid-Eighteenth Century* (New York: Asia Publishing House, 1966), pp. 66–69.

10 Philip J. Stern, *The Company-State: Corporate Sovereignty and the Early Modern Foundation of the British Empire in India* (New York: Oxford University Press, 2011), p. 124.

11 *Ibid.*

12 Madhavi Kale, *Fragments of Empire: Capital, Slavery, and Indian Indentured Labor Migration in the British Caribbean* (Philadelphia: University of Pennsylvania Press, 1998), p. 21.

13 John Brewer, *The Sinews of Power: War, Money, and the English State, 1688–1783*, 1st American ed. (New York: Knopf, 1989), 1994.

14 Daniel Baugh, "Great Britain's 'Blue-Water' Policy, 1689–1815," *The International History Review* 10, no. 1 (1988): 33.

15 Sugata Bose, *A Hundred Horizons: The Indian Ocean in the Age of Global Empire* (Cambridge, MA: Harvard University Press, 2006), p. 36.

16 Sanjay Subrahmanyam and C. A. Bayly, "Portfolio Capitalists and the Political Economy of Early Modern India," in *Merchants, Markets and the State in Early Modern India*, ed. Sanjay Subrahmanyam (Delhi: Oxford University Press, 1990), pp. 59–64.

17 Javier Laviña and Michael Zeuske, *The Second Slavery: Mass Slaveries and Modernity in the Americas and in the Atlantic Basin* (Berlin: Lit, 2014), pp. 113–42.

18 C. A. Bayly, *Empire and Information: Intelligence Gathering and Social Communication in India, 1780–1870* (Cambridge University Press, 1999), p. 3.

19 Patricia Risso, *Merchants and Faith: Muslim Commerce and Culture in the Indian Ocean* (Boulder: Westview Press, 1995).

20 Kenneth Pomeranz, *The Great Divergence: China, Europe, and the Making of the Modern World Economy* (Princeton University Press, 2000), p. 281.

21 Adam Smith, *Wealth of Nations* (Buffalo: Prometheus Books, 1991), p. 493.

22 *Ibid.*, p. 350.

23 Lisa Lowe, *The Intimacies of Four Continents* (Durham, NC: Duke University Press, 2015), pp. 1–21, 101–33. For a discussion of theories of liberalism, see Uday Singh Mehta, *Liberalism and Empire: A Study in Nineteenth-Century British Liberal Thought* (University of Chicago Press, 1999), pp. 120–22.

24 Michael Tomz, *Reputation and International Cooperation: Sovereign Debt across Three Centuries* (Princeton University Press, 2011), pp. 114–57; P. J. Cain, *British Imperialism: Crisis and Deconstruction, 1914–1990*, ed. A. G. Hopkins (London: Longman, 1993); Mike Hill and Warren Montag, *The Other Adam Smith* (Stanford University Press, 2015).

25 Serkan Demirbas, "The Treaty of Balta Limani's Role in Anglo-Ottoman Relations during the Mehmet Ali Problem," *Journal of History School* 8, no. 24 (2015): 233.

26 Rana Behal, *One Hundred Years of Servitude: Political Economy of Tea Plantations in Colonial Assam* (New Delhi: Tulika Books, 2014).

27 Ajay Parasram, *Becoming the State: Territorializing Ceylon, 1815–1848* (Ottawa: Carleton University, 2017), p. 191.

28 G. R. Knight, "John Palmer and Plantation Development in Western Java during the Earlier Nineteenth Century," *Journal of the Humanities and Social Sciences of Southeast Asia* 131, no. 2 (1975): fn. 65, 327.

29 Eric Tagliacozzo, *Secret Trades, Porous Borders: Smuggling and States along a Southeast Asian Frontier, 1865–1915* (New Haven: Yale University Press, 2005), p. 186.

30 Timothy Brook and Bob Tadashi Wakabayashi, *Opium Regimes: China, Britain, and Japan, 1839–1952* (Berkeley: University of California Press, 2000), p. 32; Carl A. Trocki, *Opium, Empire, and the Global Political Economy: A Study of the Asian Opium Trade, 1750–1950* (London: Routledge, 1999).

31 Song-Chuan Chen, *Merchants of War and Peace: British Knowledge of China in the Making of the Opium War* (Hong Kong University Press, 2017), pp. 1–10.

32 Lowe, *Intimacies of Four Continents*, p. 103; Alain Le Pichon, *China Trade and Empire: Jardine, Matheson & Co. and the Origins of British Rule in Hong Kong, 1827–1843* (London: British Academy, 2006).

33 Julia Lovell, *The Opium War: Drugs, Dreams and the Making of China* (London: Picador, 2011).

34 David Northrup, *Indentured Labor in the Age of Imperialism, 1834–1922* (Cambridge University Press, 1995), p. 55.

35 Sophia Kopela, "Port–State Jurisdiction, Extraterritoriality, and the Protection of Global Commons," *Ocean Development & International Law* 47, no. 2 (2016): 89.

36 Antony Anghie, "Finding the Peripheries: Sovereignty and Colonialism in Nineteenth-Century International Law," *Harvard International Law Journal* 40, no. 1 (1999).

37 Tinker, *A New System of Slavery*, p. 61.

38 Northrup, *Indentured Labor in the Age of Imperialism*, p. 63.

39 Walton Look Lai, "The Chinese Indenture System in the British West Indies and Its Aftermath," in *The Chinese in the Caribbean*, ed. Andrew R. Wilson (Princeton: M. Wiener Publishers, 2004), p. 12.

40 Walter Rodney, "Plantation Society in Guyana," *Review* 4, no. 4 (1981): 646. Marcel Van Der Linden, "Re-Constructing the Origins of Modern Labor Management," *Labor History* 51, no. 4 (2010): 511–13.

41 Walton Look Lai, *Indentured Labor, Caribbean Sugar: Chinese and Indian Migrants to the British West Indies, 1838–1918* (Baltimore: Johns Hopkins University Press, 1993), p. 87.

42 David Northrup, "Migration from Africa, Asia, and the South Pacific," in *The Oxford History of the British Empire*, ed. William Roger Louis (Oxford University Press, 1998), p. 92.

43 Yun, *The Coolie Speaks*, p. 28.

44 Edward W. Said, *Orientalism*, 25th anniversary ed. with a new preface by the author (New York: Vintage Books, 1994), pp. 49–110; Mahmood Mamdani, *Good Muslim, Bad Muslim: America, the Cold War, and the Roots of Terror* (New York: Three Leaves Press, 2005).

45 Andrea Smith, "Heteropatriarchy and the Three Pillars of White Supremacy: Rethinking Women of Color Organizing," in *Incite! Anthology*, ed. INCITE! Women of Color Against Violence (Durham, NC: Duke University Press, 2016).

46 Leonard Wray, *The Practical Sugar Planter: A Complete Account of the Cultivation and Manufacture of the Sugar-Cane* (London: Smith, Elder and Co, 1848), p. 82.

47 Manu Karuka, *Empire's Tracks: Indigenous Nations, Chinese Workers, and the Transcontinental Railroad* (Oakland: University of California Press, 2019), pp. 40–59.

48 Persia Campbell, *Chinese Coolie Emigration* (London: Anti-slavery and Aborigines' Protection Society, 1924); Andrew Gyory, *Closing the Gate: Race, Politics, and the Chinese Exclusion Act* (Chapel Hill: University of North Carolina Press, 1998).

49 Ryan Dearinger, *The Filth of Progress: Immigrants, Americans, and the Building of Canals and Railroads in the West* (Oakland, CA: University of California Press, 2016), p. 165.

50 Karuka, *Empire's Tracks*, p. 74.

51 Moon-Ho Jung, *Coolies and Cane: Race, Labor, and Sugar in the Age of Emancipation*, ed. Muse Project (Baltimore: Johns Hopkins University Press, 2006).

52 Arnold Meagher, "The Introduction of Chinese Laborers to Latin America: The 'Coolie Trade,' 1847–1874," (University of California, Davis: PhD Dissertation, 1975), p. 1.

53 Ronald T. Takaki, *Strangers from a Different Shore: A History of Asian Americans*, updated and rev. ed. (Boston: Little, Brown, 1998), p. 99.

54 Nayan Shah, *Contagious Divides: Epidemics and Race in San Francisco's Chinatown* (Berkeley: University of California Press, 2001), p. 57.

55 Mae M. Ngai, *Impossible Subjects: Illegal Aliens and the Making of Modern America* (Princeton University Press, 2004), p. 68.

56 Earl Lovelace, *Salt: A Novel* (New York: Persea Books, 1997).

57 Tejaswini Niranjana, Surabhi Sharma, and Remo, *Jahaji Music: India in the Caribbean* (Mumbai: SurFilms, 2007); Richard Fung, *Dal Puri Diaspora* (Toronto: V. Tape, 2012); Prabhu Mohapatra, "The Hossay Massacre of 1884: Class and Community among Indian Immigrant Labourers in Trinidad," in *Work and Social Change in Asia: Essays in Honour of Jan Breman*, ed. Arvind N. Das and Marcel van der Linden (Delhi: Manohar, 2003).

58 I am inspired by how Christina Elizabeth Sharpe writes about "the weather" in her *In the Wake: On Blackness and Being* (Durham, NC: Duke University Press, 2016).

CHAPTER 5

1 Carl Linnaeus, "Reflections on the Study of Nature," *The Columbian Magazine (1786–1790)* 3, no. 3 (1789): 3; see Arthur O. Lovejoy, *The Great Chain of Being: A Study of the History of an Idea* (Cambridge, MA: Harvard University Press, 2001), p. 183.

2 Allan Megill, "Theological Presuppositions of the Evolutionary Epic: From Robert Chambers to E. O. Wilson," *Studies in History and Philosophy of Biological & Biomedical Science* 58 (2016): 27.

3 Carl Linnaeus, *Reflections on the Study of Nature*, tr. J. E. Smith (Dublin: L. White, 1786), p. 13.

4 The mystical Hermetic tradition in Europe dated back many centuries to Platonic thought, and believed that God's intelligence could be revealed in all creation. See R. van den Broek and Wouter J. Hanegraaff, *Gnosis and Hermeticism from Antiquity to Modern Times* (Albany: State University of New York Press, 1998).

5 Lovejoy, *The Great Chain of Being*, p. 234.

6 Pehr Kalm, *Travels into North America*, tr. John Reinhold Forster (London: T. Lowndes, 1772). See also the discussion about Linnaean natural history travel writing as mediating colonial encounter in Mary Louise Pratt, *Imperial Eyes: Travel Writing and Transculturation* (London: Routledge, 1992), pp. 24–37.

7 Pehr Kalm, *Travels into North America, Containing Its Natural History*, ed. Johann Reinhold Forster, 2nd ed. (London: T. Lowndes, 1772).

8 Linnaeus, "Reflections on the Study of Nature."

9 H. V. Bowen, *The Business of Empire: The East India Company and Imperial Britain, 1756–1833* (Cambridge University Press, 2006), p. 159.

10 David Blackbourn, *The Conquest of Nature: Water, Landscape, and the Making of Modern Germany* (New York: Norton, 2006), pp. 77–120.

11 Richard Harry Drayton, *Nature's Government: Science, Imperial Britain, and the "Improvement" of the World* (New Haven: Yale University Press, 2000), pp. 85–128.

12 Edward W. Said, *Orientalism*, 25th anniversary ed. with a new preface by the author (New York: Vintage Books, 1994), p. 84.

13 *Ibid.*, pp. 300–1.

14 C. A. Bayly, *Empire and Information: Intelligence Gathering and Social Communication in India, 1780–1870* (Cambridge University Press, 1999).

15 Hermann von Schlagintweit, *Results of a Scientific Mission to India and High Asia* (Leipzig: F. A. Brockhaus, 1862–82), p. 41.

16 Arthur MacGregor, *Sir Hans Sloane: Collector, Scientist, Antiquary, Founding Father of the British Museum* (London: Published for the Trustees of the British Museum by the British Museum Press in association with Alistair McAlpine, 1994), pp. 232–38.

17 Maya Jasanoff, *Edge of Empire: Lives, Culture, and Conquest in the East, 1750–1850* (New York: Knopf, 2005), pp. 177–210.

18 *Acquisitions by the British Museum*, vol. III, no. 5 (London: British Museum, 1880), p. 95; *Acquisitions of British Museum*, vol. IV, no. 9 (London: British Museum, 1890), p. 432; Dennis Duerden, "The 'Discovery' of the African Mask," *Research in African Literatures* 31, no. 4 (2000).

19 Andrew Zimmerman, *Anthropology and Antihumanism in Imperial Germany* (University of Chicago Press, 2010), p. 87.

20 William Whewell, "The General Bearing of the Great Exhibition on the Progress of Art and Science," in W. Whewell et al., *Lectures on the Results of the Great Exhibition of 1851* (London: D. Bogue, 1852), p. 14.

21 John M. MacKenzie, *Museums and Empire: Natural History, Human Cultures and Colonial Identities* (New York: Palgrave Macmillan, 2009), p. 2.

22 David Cannadine, *Ornamentalism: How the British Saw Their Empire* (New York: Oxford University Press, 2001).

23 Rainer Christoph Schwinges, ed., *Humboldt International: Der Export des deutschen Universitätsmodells im 19. und 20. Jahrhundert* (Basle: Schwabe & Co., 2001), pp. 6, 82–96; Tamson Pietsch, *Empire of Scholars: Universities, Networks and the British Academic World, 1850–1939* (Manchester University Press, 2013), p. 18.

24 See Suzanne L. Marchand, *German Orientalism in the Age of Empire: Religion, Race, and Scholarship* (Cambridge University Press, 2009).

25 Susanne Zantop, *Colonial Fantasies: Conquest, Family, and Nation in Precolonial Germany, 1770–1870* (Durham, NC: Duke University Press, 1997); Kris Manjapra, *Age of Entanglement: German and Indian Intellectuals across Empire* (Cambridge, MA: Harvard University Press, 2014).

26 Ayesha Jalal, *Self and Sovereignty: Individual and Community in South Asian Islam since 1850* (London: Routledge, 2000).

27 William Wilson Hunter, *The Indian Musalmans* (New Delhi: Rupa & Co., 2002 [1871]).

28 "While the most fanatical of the Musalmans have thus engaged in overt sedition, the whole Muhammadan community has been openly deliberating on their obligation to rebel." Quoted from W. W. Hunter, *The Indian Musalmans* (Delhi: Rupa & Co., 2002 [1871]), p. 1.

29 Amir Khan, *The Great Wahabi Case* (Calcutta: R. Cambray, 1899); Benjamin Hopkins, "A History of the 'Hindustani Fanatics' on the Frontier," in *Beyond Swat: History, Society and*

Economy along the Afghanistan–Pakistan Frontier, ed. Benjamin Hopkins and Magnus Marsden (New York: Columbia, 2013), pp. 39–43.

30 Helen James, "The Assassination of Lord Mayo: The 'First' Jihad?," *International Journal of Asia Pacific Studies* 5, no. 2 (2009): 2.

31 Boyd Hunter, "The Aboriginal Legacy," in *The Cambridge History of Australia*, ed. Alison Bashford and Stuart Macintyre (Port Melbourne: Cambridge University Press, 2013), p. 1.

32 Ayesha Jalal, *Partisans of Allah: Jihad in South Asia* (Cambridge, MA: Harvard University Press, 2008), pp. 83, 114.

33 Manjapra, *Age of Entanglement*.

34 Laleh Khalili, *Time in the Shadows: Confinement in Counterinsurgencies* (Stanford University Press, 2013); Hamid Dabashi, *Brown Skin, White Masks* (London: Pluto, 2011), pp. 112–24.

35 Manjapra, *Age of Entanglement*, pp. 17–40.

36 Jürgen Zimmerer, *Von Windhuk nach Auschwitz? Beiträge zum Verhältnis von Kolonialismus und Holocaust* (Berlin: Lit, 2011), pp. 22–25; David Ciarlo, "Picturing Genocide in German Consumer Culture, 1904–10," in *German Colonialism and National Identity*, Michael Perraudin and Jürgen Zimmerer (New York: Routledge, 2011), pp. 69–87.

37 David Arnold, *Colonizing the Body: State Medicine and Epidemic Disease in Nineteenth-Century India* (Berkeley: University of California Press, 1993), pp. 61–115.

38 Achille Mbembe, "Necropolitics," *Public Culture* 15, no. 1 (2003): 11.

39 Isabel V. Hull, *Absolute Destruction: Military Culture and the Practices of War in Imperial Germany* (Ithaca, NY: Cornell University Press, 2005), pp. 85–92; Jeremy Sarkin-Hughes, *Germany's Genocide of the Herero: Kaiser Wilhelm II, His General, His Settlers, His Soldiers* (Cape Town: UCT Press, 2011).

40 K. Schwabe, *Der Krieg in Deutsch-Südwestafrika, 1904–1906* (Berlin: Verlag von C. A. Weller, 1907).

41 Holger Stoecker and Andreas Winkelmann, "Skulls and Skeletons from Namibia in Berlin," *Human Remains and Violence: An Interdisciplinary Journal* 4, no. 2 (2018).

42 Paul Bohannan, quoted in Jerry Gershenhorn, *Melville J. Herskovits and the Racial Politics of Knowledge* (Lincoln: University of Nebraska Press, 2004), p. 50.

43 For example, William Benjamin Smith and Robert Bennet Bean at Tulane University.

44 John David Smith, "Felix von Luschan," in *Germany and the Americas: Culture, Politics, and History*, ed. Thomas Adam and Will Kaufman (Santa Barbara: ABC-CLIO, 2005), p. 152.

45 Felix von Luschan, *Völker, Rassen, Sprachen* (Berlin: Welt-verlag, 1922).

46 John David Smith, "I Would Like to Study Some Problems of Heredity: Felix von Luschan's Trip to America, 1914–1915," in *Felix von Luschan (1854–1924): Leben und Wirken eines Universalgelehrten*, ed. Peter Ruggendorfer and Hubert Szemethy (Vienna: Böhlau, 2009), p. 706.

47 W. E. B. Du Bois to Felix von Luschan, December 21, 1914, Du Bois Papers, University of Massachusetts, Amherst.

48 Anonymous, "The First Universal Race Congress in London, England," *The American Missionary* 45, no. 9 (September 1911): 323–24.

49 W. E. B. Du Bois, *The World and Africa: An Inquiry into the Part Which Africa Has Played in World History; Enlarged Edition, with New Writings on Africa, 1955–61* (New York: International Publishers, 1965), p. 5.

50 *Ibid.*, p. 4.

51 Immanuel Kant, "What Is Enlightenment?," in *Kant's Political Writings*, ed. and trans. Hans Reiss (Cambridge University Press, 1970 [1784]), p. 2; Michel Foucault, "What Is Enlightenment?," in *The Foucault Reader*, ed. Paul Rabinow (New York: Pantheon Books, 1984).

CHAPTER 6

1 Joshua David Bellin and Laura Mielke, eds., *Native Acts: Indian Performance, 1603–1832* (Lincoln, NE: University of Nebraska Press, 2011).

2 Diana Taylor, *The Archive and the Repertoire: Performing Cultural Memory in the Americas* (Durham, NC: Duke University Press, 2003), p. 70.

3 *Ibid.*, p. 30; Stuart Hall, "Identity: Community, Culture, Difference," in *Cultural Identity and Diaspora*, ed. Jonathan Rutherford (London: Lawrence & Wishart, 1990), p. 226.

4 María Josefina Saldaña-Portillo, *Indian Given: Racial Geographies across Mexico and the United States* (Durham, NC: Duke University Press, 2016).

5 Lynette Russell, *Colonial Frontiers: Indigenous–European Encounters in Settler Societies* (Manchester: Palgrave, 2001).

6 Ennis Barrington Edmonds, *Caribbean Religious History: An Introduction*, ed. Michelle A. Gonzalez (New York University Press, 2010), pp. 45, 65; Heather D. Curtis, *Holy Humanitarians: American Evangelicals and Global Aid* (Cambridge, MA: Harvard University Press, 2018), p. 81.

7 Mary Prince, *The History of Mary Prince: A West Indian Slave*, ed. Moira Ferguson, rev. ed. (Ann Arbor: University of Michigan Press, 1997), pp. 31, 37.

8 Sojourner Truth, *Narrative of Sojourner Truth*, ed. Olive Gilbert and Frances W. Titus (New York: Arno Press, 1968), p. 114.

9 Imanuel Geiss, *The Pan-African Movement: A History of Pan-Africanism in America, Europe, and Africa* (New York: Africana Publishing Company, 1974), pp. 67–8.

10 Ranajit Guha, *A Rule of Property for Bengal: An Essay on the Idea of Permanent Settlement* (Paris: Le Monde d'Outre-mer, 1963).

11 Karuna Mantena, *Alibis of Empire: Henry Maine and the Ends of Liberal Imperialism* (Princeton University Press, 2010), p. 7; Uday Singh Mehta, *Liberalism and Empire: A Study in Nineteenth-Century British Liberal Thought* (University of Chicago Press, 1999), pp. 120–22.

12 Homi K. Bhabha, *The Location of Culture* (London; New York: Routledge, 2004), pp. 159–64; Partha Chatterjee, *Nationalist Thought and the Colonial World: A Derivative Discourse* (Minneapolis; London: University of Minnesota Press, 1993); David Kopf, *The Brahmo Samaj and the Shaping of the Modern Indian Mind* (Princeton University Press, 1979).

13 Catherine Hall, *Macaulay and Son: Architects of Imperial Britain* (New Haven: Yale University Press, 2012).

14 Ranajit Guha, "The Prose of Counter-Insurgency," in *Selected Subaltern Studies*, ed. Ranajit Guha and Gayatri Spivak Chakravorty (New York: Oxford University Press, 1998), p. 70.

15 Alexis de Tocqueville, *Writings on Empire and Slavery* (Baltimore: Johns Hopkins University Press, 2001), p. 70.

16 Thomas Rid, "Razzia: A Turning Point in Modern Strategy," *Terrorism and Political Violence* 21, no. 4 (2009): 617.

17 Jennifer Pitts, *A Turn to Empire: The Rise of Imperial Liberalism in Britain and France* (Princeton University Press, 2005), pp. 220–25.

18 Jane Griffith, "Of Linguicide and Resistance: Children and English Instruction in Nineteenth-Century Indian Boarding Schools in Canada," *Paedagogica Historica* 53, no. 6 (2017); Charles Leslie Glenn, *American Indian/First Nations Schooling: From the Colonial Period to the Present* (New York: Palgrave Macmillan, 2011), pp. 19–29.

19 Eric Taylor Woods, *A Cultural Sociology of Anglican Mission and the Indian Residential Schools in Canada: The Long Road to Apology* (New York: Palgrave Macmillan US, 2016), p. 10.

20 Captain Richard H. Pratt, "Kill the Indian, and Save the Man" speech, delivered at the 1892 Convention of the National Conference of Charities and Correction.

21 Jacqueline Fear-Segal and Susan D. Rose, eds., *Carlisle Indian Industrial School: Indigenous Histories, Memories, and Reclamations* (Lincoln, NE: University of Nebraska Press, 2016); B. D. Mayberry, *A Century of Agriculture in the 1890 Land-Grant Institutions and Tuskegee University, 1890–1990* (New York: Vantage Press, 1991).

22 Mayberry, *A Century of Agriculture*, p. 108.

23 Louellyn White, "White Power and the Performance of Assimilation: Lincoln Institute and Carlisle Indian School," in *Carlisle Indian Industrial School*, ed. Segal and Rose, p. 106.

24 Pitts, *A Turn to Empire*, pp. 3–6.

25 Hue-Tam Ho Tai, *Radicalism and the Origins of the Vietnamese Revolution* (Cambridge, MA: Harvard University Press, 1992), pp. 171–95; Ranajit Guha, *Dominance without Hegemony: History and Power in Colonial India* (Cambridge, MA: Harvard University Press, 1997), pp. 100–52.

26 Karsten Linne, *Von Witzenhausen in Die Welt: Ausbildung und Arbeit von Tropenlandwirten 1898 bis 1971* (Göttingen: Wallstein Verlag, 2017).

27 Susan Bayly, *Asian Voices in a Postcolonial Age: Vietnam, India and Beyond* (Cambridge University Press, 2007), pp. 35–37.

28 Gail Kelly, "Conflict in the Classroom: A Case Study from Vietnam, 1918–38," *British Journal of Sociology of Education* 8, no. 2 (1987): 191; Micheline Lessard, "Tradition for Rebellion: Vietnamese Students and Teachers and Anticolonial Resistance, 1888-1931" (Cornell University: PhD Dissertation, 1995).

29 Mantena, *Alibis of Empire*, p. 21.

30 Trần Thị Phương Hoa, "From Liberally-Organized to Centralized Schools: Education in Tonkin, 1885–1927," *Journal of Vietnamese Studies* 8, no. 3 (2013): 27.

31 Gail Kelly, "The Transfer of an Education Operation System," in *Educational Technology: Its Creation, Development, and Cross-Cultural Transfer*, ed. R. Murray Thomas and Victor N. Kobayashi (New York: Pergamon Press, 1987).

32 Albert Sarraut, *La mise en valeur des colonies françaises* (Paris: Payot & Cie, 1923), p. 88.

33 Tai, *Radicalism and the Origins of the Vietnamese Revolution*, p. 34.

34 Sophie Quinn-Judge, *Ho Chi Minh: The Missing Years, 1919–1941* (Berkeley: University of California Press, 2002), pp. 1–20.

35 Pierre Brocheux, *Ho Chi Minh: A Biography*, ed. Claire Duiker (New York: Cambridge University Press, 2007), p. 11.

36 Nguyễn Thụy Phương, "A French School in North Vietnam: The Lycée Albert-Sarraut from 1954 to 1965," *Journal of Vietnamese Studies* 10, no. 3 (2015): 1.

37 Tai, *Radicalism and the Origins of the Vietnamese Revolution*, p. 179.

38 *Les grèves d'écoliers*, 1937, p. 1, quoted in Kelly, "Conflict in the Classroom," 191.

39 Archives Nationales d'Outre-mer, Aix-en-Provence, France, fond B13917.

40 Peter Zinoman, *The Colonial Bastille: A History of Imprisonment in Vietnam, 1862–1940* (Berkeley: University of California Press, 2001), pp. 148–57.

41 Stuart Hall, "Race, Articulation and Societies Structured in Dominance," in *Sociological Theories: Race and Colonialism* (Paris: Unesco, 1980), p. 305; C. L. R. James, *The Black Jacobins: Toussaint L'Ouverture and the San Domingo Revolution*, 2nd ed., rev. ed. (New York: Vintage Books, 1963), pp. 85–118.

42 Gary Wilder, *The French Imperial Nation-State: Negritude & Colonial Humanism between the Two World Wars* (University of Chicago Press, 2005), p. 155; Brent Hayes Edwards, *The Practice of Diaspora: Literature, Translation, and the Rise of Black Internationalism* (Cambridge, MA: Harvard University Press, 2003); Alice Conklin, *A Mission to Civilize: The Republican Idea of Empire in France and West Africa, 1895–1930* (Stanford University Press, 1997), pp. 142–73.

43 James C. Scott, *Weapons of the Weak: Everyday Forms of Peasant Resistance* (New Haven: Yale University Press, 1985), pp. 148–57.

44 Stuart Hall and Ferial Ghazoul, "Cultural Identity and Diaspora," *Alif: Journal of Comparative Poetics* no. 32 (2012): 257; Antonio Gramsci, *Prison Notebooks* (New York: Columbia University Press, 1992), pp. 120–225.

CHAPTER 7

1 Vassilis Fouskas, *The Fall of the US Empire: Global Fault-Lines and the Shifting Imperial Order*, ed. Bülent Gҟay (London: Pluto, 2012), pp. 38–55.

2 W. E. B. Du Bois, note on the Bretton Woods Conference, c. 1945. W. E. B. Du Bois Papers (MS 312). Special Collections and University Archives, University of Massachusetts Amherst Libraries.

3 Eric Helleiner, *Forgotten Foundations of Bretton Woods: International Development and the Making of the Postwar Order* (Ithaca, NY: Cornell University Press, 2014).

4 www.cadtm.org/Crisis-deepens-as-global-South-debt-payments-increase-by-85

5 See Jonathan Israel, *The Dutch Republic and the Hispanic World, 1606–1661* (Oxford University Press, 1982), p. 41; also his *Conflicts of Empires: Spain, the Low Countries and the Struggle for World Supremacy, 1585–1713* (London: Hambledon Press, 1997).

6 Lodewijk Petram, *The World's First Stock Exchange* (New York: Columbia Business School Publishing, 2014), p. 42.

7 Françoise Vergès, "Racial Capitalocene," in *Futures of Black Radicalism*, ed. Gaye Theresa Johnson and Alex Lubin (London: Verso, 2017), pp. 72–82.

8 Ian Baucom, *Specters of the Atlantic: Finance Capital, Slavery, and the Philosophy of History* (Durham, NC: Duke University Press, 2005), p. 80.

9 Karl Marx, *Capital: A Critique of Political Economy*, ed. Ben Fowkes (New York: Vintage Books, 1977).

10 Andrew Carl Sobel, *Birth of Hegemony: Crisis, Financial Revolution, and Emerging Global Networks* (University of Chicago Press, 2012).

11 Dutch forts included (in alphabetical order): Batticaloa 1638; Cannonore 1662; Cochin 1663; Colombo 1656; Cranganore 1663; Fort Nassau 1609; Fort Zeelandia 1623–61; Galle 1640; Jaffna 1658; Macassar 1666; Malacca 1641; Negapatnam 1660; Pulicat 1613; Sultanate of Bantam (under Dutch control since 1682); Ternate 1605; Tidore 1605; Tuticorin 1658.

12 P. G. M. Dickson, *The Financial Revolution in England: A Study in the Development of Public Credit, 1688–1756* (Aldershot: Ashgate Publishing, 1993), p. 317; Hubert Bonin and Nuno Valério, *Colonial and Imperial Banking History* (London: Taylor and Francis, 2015).

13 On economic penetration and incorporation, see Immanuel Maurice Wallerstein, *The Modern World-System* (Berkeley: University of California Press, 2011), pp. 165–89; J. E. Inikori and Stanley L. Engerman, *The Atlantic Slave Trade: Effects on Economies, Societies, and Peoples in Africa, the Americas, and Europe* (Durham, NC: Duke University Press, 1992).

14 Helen J. Paul, *The South Sea Bubble: An Economic History of Its Origins and Consequences* (London: Routledge, 2011), p. 37.

15 Paul McKittrick, "Modernity and the Spirit of the Sea: Maritime Influences on Early Modern English State Institutions and Society, 1485–1763" (Georgia Institute of Technology: PhD Dissertation, 2018).

16 Charles P. Kindleberger, *A Financial History of Western Europe*, 2nd ed. (New York: Oxford University Press, 1993), pp. 50–51.

17 This is a major theme in J. G. A. Pocock, *The Machiavellian Moment: Florentine Political Thought and the Atlantic Republican Tradition*, 2nd pbk. ed., with a new Afterword (Princeton University Press, 2003), p. 31.

18 Bruce G. Carruthers, *City of Capital: Politics and Markets in the English Financial Revolution* (Princeton University Press, 1999), p. 115.

19 Carl Wennerlind, *Casualties of Credit: The English Financial Revolution, 1620–1720* (Cambridge, MA: Harvard University Press, 2011), pp. 4, 242.

20 Dickson, *The Financial Revolution in England*, p. 16.

21 Inikori and Engerman, *The Atlantic Slave Trade*.

22 Sanjay Subrahmanyam, *The Political Economy of Commerce: Southern India, 1500–1650* (Cambridge University Press, 1990), pp. 281–98; H. V. Bowen, *The Business of Empire: The East India Company and Imperial Britain, 1756–1833* (Cambridge University Press, 2006), pp. 84–117; H. V. Bowen, Elizabeth Mancke, and John G. Reid, *Britain's Oceanic*

Empire: Atlantic and Indian Ocean Worlds, c. 1550–1850 (Cambridge University Press, 2012).

23 Lauren A. Benton, *Law and Colonial Cultures: Legal Regimes in World History, 1400–1900* (Cambridge University Press, 2004), p. 3.

24 Michael P. Costeloe, *Bubbles and Bonanzas: British Investors and Investments in Mexico, 1821–1860* (Lanham: Lexington Books, 2011), pp. 8, 172.

25 Om Prakasch, "The Trading World of India and Southeast Asia in the Early Modern Period," *Archipel* 56 (1998).

26 Daniel Defoe, "Money All-Powerful," *Defoe's Review* (October 16, 1707), p. 422.

27 Kari Polanyi Levitt, *The Great Transformation* (Boston: Beacon Press, 1957), pp. 59–70.

28 *Ibid.*, pp. 60–64.

29 Dickson, *The Financial Revolution in England*, p. 6; Christine Desan, *Making Money: Coin, Currency, and the Coming of Capitalism* (Oxford University Press, 2014), p. 267.

30 John Frederick Martin, *Profits in the Wilderness: Entrepreneurship and the Founding of New England Towns in the Seventeenth Century* (Chapel Hill: University of North Carolina Press, 1991), p. 111.

31 Wallerstein, *The Modern World-System*, p. 191.

32 Amiya Bagchi, "Anglo-Indian Banking in British India," in *Money, Finance, and Empire, 1790–1960*, ed. A. N. Porter and R. F. Holland (London: F. Cass, 1985), p. 95; Geoffrey Jones, *Merchants to Multinationals: British Trading Companies in the Nineteenth and Twentieth Centuries* (Oxford University Press, 2000), p. 29.

33 Stanley D. Chapman, *The Rise of Merchant Banking* (London: Allen & Unwin, 1984).

34 Marcello De Cecco, *Money and Empire: The International Gold Standard, 1890–1914* (Oxford: B. Blackwell, 1974), p. 42.

35 John Maynard Keynes, *The General Theory of Employment, Interest and Money* (New York: Harcourt, Brace, 1936), p. 40.

36 Jonathan Levy, *Freaks of Fortune: The Emerging World of Capitalism and Risk in America* (Cambridge, MA: Harvard University Press, 2012), p. 191.

37 See Amiya Kumar Bagchi, "Contested Hegemonies and Laissez-Faire: Controversies over the Monetary Standard in India at the High Noon of the British Empire," *Review (Fernand Braudel Center)* 20, no. 1 (1997): 19; also his *Money & Credit in Indian History: From Early Medieval Times* (Delhi: Tulika, 2012).

38 David Sunderland, *Financing the Raj: The City of London and Colonial India, 1858–1940* (Rochester: Boydell & Brewer, 2013), p. 116; G. Balachandran, *India and the World Economy 1850–1950* (New Delhi; New York: Oxford University Press, 2003), pp. 12–14.

39 Odette Lienau, *Rethinking Sovereign Debt: Politics, Reputation, and Legitimacy in Modern Finance* (Cambridge, MA: Harvard University Press, 2014), p. 226.

40 David Graeber, *Debt: The First 5,000 Years* (New York: Melville House Publishing, 2012), p. 6.

41 The "Société de Régie de Monopoles de Grèce," established in 1887, was led by the Comptoire d'Escompte of France and the Hambro Bank of Britain. See John Levandis, *The Greek Foreign Debt and the Great Powers, 1821–1898* (New York: Columbia University Press, 1944), pp. 68, 69.

42 Jeff A. King, "Odious Debt: The Terms of the Debate," *North Carolina Journal of International Law and Commercial Regulation* 32, no. 4 (2007): 616.

43 Daniel Immerwahr, *How to Hide an Empire: A History of the Greater United States* (New York: Farrar, Straus, Giroux, 2019); Ellen D. Tillman, *Dollar Diplomacy by Force: Nation-Building and Resistance in the Dominican Republic* (Chapel Hill: University of North Carolina Press, 2016), pp. 11–27; Randy Martin, *An Empire of Indifference: American War and the Financial Logic of Risk Management* (Durham, NC: Duke University Press, 2007), pp. 124–68.

44 Ronald Cox, *Power and Profits: US Policy in Central America* (Lexington: The University Press of Kentucky, 2015), pp. 20–47.

45 Peter James Hudson, *Bankers and Empire: How Wall Street Colonized the Caribbean* (University of Chicago Press, 2017), p. 84; Liliana Obregón, "Empire, Racial Capitalism and International Law: The Case of Manumitted Haiti and the Recognition Debt," *Leiden Journal of International Law* 31, no. 3 (2018): 597; Laurent Dubois, *Haiti: The Aftershocks of History* (New York: Henry Holt and Co., 2012); Pompée-Valentin Vastey, *The Colonial System Unveiled*, ed. Chris Bongie (Liverpool University Press, 2014).

46 Kari Polanyi Levitt, *From the Great Transformation to the Great Financialization: On Kari Polanyi Levitt and Other Essays* (London; New York: Zed Books, 2013), pp. 141–58.

47 On legacies of financialized conquest, see Kari Polanyi Levitt, *Silent Surrender: The Multinational Corporation in Canada* (Toronto: Macmillan, 1970), p. 92; Murat Birdal, *The Political Economy of Ottoman Public Debt: Insolvency and European Financial Control in the Late Nineteenth Century* (New York: Palgrave Macmillan, 2010); Şevket Pamuk, *The Ottoman Empire and European Capitalism, 1820–1913: Trade, Investment, and Production* (Cambridge University Press, 1987); Jonathan Conlin, "Debt, Diplomacy and Dreadnoughts: The National Bank of Turkey, 1909–1919," *Middle Eastern Studies* 52, no. 3 (2016): 525.

48 Suraiya Faroqhi, "Ottoman Cotton Textiles," in *The Spinning World: A Global History of Cotton Textiles, 1200–1850*, ed. Giorgio Riello and Prasannan Parthasarathi (Oxford University Press, 2009), p. 89; Candan Badem, *The Ottoman Crimean War, 1853–1856* (Boston: Brill, 2010); Seda Ozekicioglu, "First Borrowing Period at Ottoman Empire (1854–1876): Budget Policies and Consequences," *Business and Economic Horizons* 3 (2010): 33.

49 Birdal, *The Political Economy of Ottoman Public Debt*, p. 167.

50 Alexander Schälch and Alexander Schölch, "Wirtschaftliche Durchdringung und politische Kontrolle durch die europäischen Mächte im osmanischen Reich (Konstantinopel, Kairo, Tunis)," *Geschichte und Gesellschaft* 1, no. 4 (1975): 404.

51 On "reputation" in international lending, see Michael Tomz, *Reputation and International Cooperation: Sovereign Debt across Three Centuries* (Princeton University Press, 2011).

52 Gerardo Marti, "Argentina – The 1890 Crisis: External Debt and the Financial Crash," *Trimestre económico* 57:4, no. 228 (1990): 933.

53 Lienau, *Rethinking Sovereign Debt*; Hudson, *Bankers and Empire*, pp. 222–52.

54 C. K. Hobson, *The Export of Capital* (London: Constable and Co. Ltd., 1914), pp. xx, xxi.

55 Edhem Eldem, "Ottoman Financial Integration with Europe: Foreign Loans, the Ottoman Bank and the Ottoman Public Debt," *European Review* 13, no. 3 (2005): 431–45.

56 Stefania Ecchia, "La politique économique à la fin de l'empire ottoman," *Anatoli* (October 1, 2014): 91.

57 Hobson, *The Export of Capital*, p. xx.

58 John G. Williamson, *Karl Helfferich, 1872–1924: Economist, Financier, Politician* (Princeton University Press, 1971), pp. 66–88.

59 Fritz Fischer, *Germany's Aims in the First World War* (New York: W. W. Norton, 1967), p. 11.

60 Latin American economists were leaders in studying the depleting impacts of the Bretton Woods system. See Raúl Prebisch, *La cooperación internacional en la política de desarrollo latinoamericana* (New York: United Nations, 1954), pp. 10–18. In the 1960s and 1970s, the New World school of economic thinkers in the Caribbean studied these processes extensively. See Norman Girvan, *Foreign Capital and Economic Underdevelopment in Jamaica* (Mona: University of the West Indies, 1971).

61 W. E. B. Du Bois, "The Winds of Time: The Meaning of Bretton Woods," *Chicago Defender*, March 17, 1945, p. 12.

62 *Ibid.*

63 *Ibid.*

64 Adom Getachew, *Worldmaking after Empire: The Rise and Fall of Self-Determination* (Princeton University Press, 2019), p. 142; Christopher J. Lee, *Making a World after Empire: The Bandung Moment and Its Political Afterlives* (Athens, GA: Ohio University Press, 2010), pp. 1–19.

65 Norman Girvan, "Expropriation and Compensation from a Third World Perspective," in his *Corporate Imperialism: Conflict and Expropriation* (New York: M. E. Sharpe, 1976), pp. 200–32.

66 Amiya Kumar Bagchi, "Contested Hegemonies and Laissez-Faire," 135.

67 Nils Gilman, "The New International Economic Order: A Reintroduction," *Humanity: An International Journal of Human Rights, Humanitarianism, and Development* 6, no. 1 (2015): 1–16.

68 See "Macroeconomic Developments and Prospects in Low-Income Developing Countries – 2018," Report of the International Monetary Fund, March 22, 2018 at: www.imf.org/en/Publications/Policy-Papers/Issues/2018/03/22/pp021518macro economic-developments-and-prospects-in-lidcs

69 Samba Sylla, "The CFA Franc: French Monetary Imperialism in Africa." Blog of the London School of Economics, October 27, 2017 at: http://blogs.lse.ac.uk/africaatlse/

70 Vanessa Ogle, "Archipelago Capitalism: Tax Havens, Offshore Money, and the State, 1950s–1970s," *The American Historical Review* 122, no. 5 (2017): 1431.

71 See Polanyi Levitt's classic study of interventions by banks and corporations of the United States of America in Canadian fiscal and monetary policy, *Silent Surrender*, pp. 19–25. On the effects of financialization across the Global South, see Polanyi Levitt, *Great Transformation to the Great Financialization*, pp. 181–92.

72 Thomas Piketty, *Capital in the Twenty-First Century*, ed. Arthur Goldhammer (Cambridge, MA: The Belknap Press of Harvard University Press, 2014), p. 430.

73 Getachew, *Worldmaking after Empire*, p. 177.

CHAPTER 8

1 See report on: www.greenleft.org.au/content/pilger-reveals-british-us-conspiracy-steal-nation

2 David Vine and Laura Jeffrey, "Give Us back Diego Garcia," in *The Bases of Empire: The Global Struggle against US Military Posts*, ed. Catherine Lutz (New York University Press, 2009), pp. 181, 189; David Vine, *Island of Shame: The Secret History of the US Military Base on Diego Garcia* (Princeton University Press, 2011), p. 164.

3 Amahl A. Bishara, "Palestinian Acts of Speaking Together, Apart: Subalterneities and the Politics of Fracture," *Journal of Ethnographic Theory* 6, no. 3 (2016): 305. See Charles Tilly, *Regimes and Repertoires* (University of Chicago Press, 2006), p. 30.

4 Bishara, "Palestinian Acts of Speaking Together, Apart," 309.

5 A. I. Asiwaju, *Partitioned Africans: Ethnic Relations across Africa's International Boundaries, 1884–1984* (New York: St. Martin's Press, 1985), p. 2.

6 Lisa Lowe and Kris Manjapra, "Comparative Global Humanities after Man: Alternatives to the Coloniality of Knowledge," *Theory, Culture, and Society* 36, no. 5 (2019).

7 J. B. Harley, *The New Nature of Maps: Essays in the History of Cartography* (Baltimore: Johns Hopkins University Press, 2001), pp. 109–47.

8 See Luciana de Lima Martins, "Mapping Tropical Waters: British Views and Visions of Rio de Janeiro," in *Mappings*, ed. Denis E. Cosgrove (London: Reaktion Books, 1999), pp. 147–57; Denis Wood, *Rethinking the Power of Maps* (New York: Guilford Press, 2010), pp. 44–51.

9 See Henri Lefebvre on the many scales of "capitalist space" and production of "sectors" for conquest and appropriation, *The Production of Space* (Oxford: Blackwell, 1991), pp. 321–40.

10 On "full spectrum dominance," see Ian G. R. Shaw, *Predator Empire: Drone Warfare and Full Spectrum Dominance* (Minneapolis: University of Minnesota Press, 2016), p. 4.

11 Ann Rogers, *Unmanned: Drone Warfare and Global Security*, ed. John Hill (Toronto: Pluto Press, 2014), pp. 83–110.

12 Derek Gregory, "Dirty Dancing: Drones and Death in the Borderlands," in *Life in the Age of Drone Warfare*, ed. Lisa Parks and Caren Kaplan (Durham, NC: Duke University Press, 2017), p. 30; Achille Mbembe, "Necropolitics," *Public Culture* 15, no. 1 (2003); Georges Bataille, *Visions of Excess: Selected Writings, 1927–1939*, ed. Allan Stoekl (Minneapolis: University of Minnesota Press, 1985), pp. 118–29.

13 See the dialectic of exploitation and creative response under colonialism as discussed in Neferti X. M. Tadiar, *Things Fall Apart: Philippine Historical Experience and the Makings of Globalization* (Durham, NC: Duke University Press, 2009), pp. 232–61.

14 C. C. Eldridge, *The Imperial Experience: From Carlyle to Forster* (New York: St. Martin's Press, 1996), p. 151.

15 Caroline Elkins, "Race, Citizenship, and Governance: Settler Tyranny and the End of Empire," in *Settler Colonialism in the Twentieth Century: Projects, Practices, Legacies*, ed. Caroline Elkins and Susan Pedersen (New York: Routledge, 2005), p. 214.

16 Talal Asad, *On Suicide Bombing* (New York: Columbia University Press, 2007), pp. 29–38; Jasbir K. Puar, *Terrorist Assemblages: Homonationalism in Queer Times* (Durham, NC: Duke University Press, 2007), p. 51.

17 J. A. Hobson, *Imperialism: A Study* (New York: Gordon Press, 1975), p. 46.

18 Howard Zinn, *A People's History of the United States* (New York: Harper, 1999), p. 14.

19 Mahmood Mamdani, *Good Muslim, Bad Muslim: America, the Cold War, and the Roots of Terror* (New York: Three Leaves Press, 2005), pp. 108, 109.

20 Daniel Immerwahr, *How to Hide an Empire: A History of the Greater United States* (New York: Farrar, Straus, Giroux, 2019), p. 372.

21 B. D. Hopkins and Magnus Marsden, *Beyond Swat: History, Society and Economy along the Afghanistan–Pakistan Frontier* (New York: Columbia University Press, 2013), p. 143.

22 Shaw, *Predator Empire*, p. 125.

23 On "biological conquest" see Elinor G. K. Melville, *A Plague of Sheep: Environmental Consequences of the Conquest of Mexico* (Cambridge, MA: Cambridge University Press, 1994), pp. 13–16.

24 James Onley, *The Arabian Frontier of the British Raj: Merchants, Rulers, and the British in the Nineteenth-Century Gulf* (New York: Oxford University Press, 2007), pp. 62–103.

25 Valeska Huber, *Channelling Mobilities: Migration and Globalisation in the Suez Canal Region and Beyond, 1869–1914* (Cambridge University Press, 2013), p. 24; Robert D. Aguirre, *Mobility and Modernity: Panama in the Nineteenth-Century Anglo-American Imagination* (Columbus: Ohio State University Press, 2017), p. 13.

26 John Marlowe, *World Ditch: The Making of the Suez Canal* (New York: Macmillan, 1964); Huber, *Channelling Mobilities*, p. 35.

27 Ricardo Salvatore, "The Enterprise of Knowledge: Representational Machines of Informal Empire," in *Close Encounters of Empire: Writing the Cultural History of US–Latin American Relations*, ed. Gilbert Joseph and Catherine Legrand (Durham, NC: Duke University Press, 1998), p. 80; Michael Conniff, *Black Labor on a White Canal: Panama, 1904–1981* (University of Pittsburgh Press, 1985).

28 María Josefina Saldaña-Portillo, *Indian Given: Racial Geographies across Mexico and the United States* (Durham, NC: Duke University Press, 2016), p. 114.

29 Roxanne Dunbar-Ortiz, *An Indigenous Peoples' History of the United States* (Boston: Beacon Press, 2014), p. 132; John Grenier, *The First Way of War: American War Making on the Frontier, 1607–1814* (Cambridge University Press, 2005), p. 8.

30 Noel Maurer, *The Big Ditch: How America Took, Built, Ran, and Ultimately Gave Away the Panama Canal* (Princeton University Press, 2011), p. 98.

31 Dirk van Laak, *Weisse Elefanten: Anspruch und Scheitern technischer Grossprojekte im 20. Jahrhundert* (Stuttgart: Deutsche Verlag-Anstalt, 1999), p. 66.

32 Maurer, *The Big Ditch*, p. 102.

33 *Ibid.*, p. 108.

34 David G. McCullough, *The Path between the Seas: The Creation of the Panama Canal, 1870–1914* (New York: Simon and Schuster, 1977), p. 489.

35 Julie Greene, *The Canal Builders: Making America's Empire at the Panama Canal* (New York: Penguin Press, 2009), p. 144.

36 Lok Siu, "At the Intersection of Nations: Diasporic Chinese in Panama and the Cultural Politics of Belonging" (Stanford University: PhD Dissertation, 2000), p. 83.

37 Maurer, *The Big Ditch*, p. 51.

38 *Ibid.*, p. 59.

39 *Ibid.*, p. 60.

40 On continuities with plantation labor, see Cindy Hahamovitch, *No Man's Land: Jamaican Guestworkers in America and the Global History of Deportable Labor* (Princeton University Press, 2011), pp. 30, 31; Michael Donoghue, *Borderland on the Isthmus: Race, Culture, and the Struggle for the Canal* (Durham, NC: Duke University Press, 2014).

41 Wendy Brown, *Walled States, Waning Sovereignty* (Cambridge, MA: MIT Press, 2010), pp. 73–95.

42 Thomas Bassett, "Cartography and Empire Building in Nineteenth-Century West Africa," *Geographical Review* 84, no. 3 (1994): 317; Christopher Prior, *Exporting Empire: Africa, Colonial Officials and the Construction of the British Imperial State, c. 1900–1939* (Manchester University Press, 2013); Winichakul Thongchai, *Siam Mapped: A History of the Geo-Body of a Nation* (Honolulu: University of Hawaii Press, 1994); Matthew H. Edney, *Mapping an Empire: The Geographical Construction of British India, 1765–1843* (University of Chicago Press, 1997).

43 Sean Kelly, "How Far West?: Lord Curzon's Transcaucasian (Mis)Adventure and the Defence of British India, 1918–23," *The International History Review* 35, no. 2 (2013): 274.

44 Magnus Marsden and Benjamin Hopkins, *Fragments of the Afghan Frontier* (Oxford University Press, 2018), p. 23; Vazira Fazila-Yacoobali Zamindar, *The Long Partition and the Making of Modern South Asia: Refugees, Boundaries, Histories* (New York: Columbia University Press, 2007); Brian Hanley, *The Impact of the Troubles on the Republic of Ireland, 1968–79: Boiling Volcano?* (Manchester University Press, 2018).

45 Ahmad Sa'di, "Afterword," in *Nakba: Palestine, 1948, and the Claims of Memory*, ed. Ahmad Sa'di and Lila Abu-Lughod (New York: Columbia University Press, 2007), p. 292.

46 Brown, *Walled States, Waning Sovereignty*, p. 36.

47 Ruth Wilson Gilmore, *Golden Gulag: Prisons, Surplus, Crisis, and Opposition in Globalizing California* (Berkeley: University of California Press, 2007), p. 242; Miriam Tlali, "Fud-U-U-A!," in *Soweto Stories* (London: Pandora, 1989); Carole Boyce Davies, "Finding Some Space: Black South African Women Writers," *A Current Bibliography on African Affairs* 19, no. 1 (1986): 31.

48 Steve Pickering, *Understanding Geography and War: Misperceptions, Foundations, and Prospects* (New York: Palgrave Macmillan, 2017).

49 See the presentation here: www.youtube.com/watch?v=W88lXtRWkic

CHAPTER 9

1 Alondra Nelson, *Body and Soul: The Black Panther Party and the Fight against Medical Discrimination* (Minneapolis: University of Minnesota Press, 2011), p. 5.

2 Michel Foucault, *The Archaeology of Knowledge*, 1st American ed. (New York: Pantheon Books, 1972), p. 137.

3 Ann Laura Stoler, *Carnal Knowledge and Imperial Power: Race and the Intimate in Colonial Rule* (Berkeley: University of California Press, 2002); Neel Ahuja, *Biosecurities: Disease Interventions, Empire, and the Government of Species* (Durham, NC: Duke University Press, 2016).

4 Octavia Butler, *Lilith's Brook: The Complete Xenogenesis Trilogy* (New York: Open Road Media, 2012).

5 Anne McClintock, *Imperial Leather: Race, Gender, and Sexuality in the Colonial Contest* (New York: Routledge, 1995), pp. 207–8.

6 David Arnold, *Colonizing the Body: State Medicine and Epidemic Disease in Nineteenth-Century India* (Berkeley: University of California Press, 1993), p. 89.

7 Rajnarayan Chandavarkar, "Plague Panic and Epidemic Politics in India, 1896–1914," in *Epidemics and Ideas: Essays on the Historical Perception of Pestilence* (Cambridge University Press, 1992), p. 203.

8 See Suman Seth on the commonplace notion of European physical fragility: Suman Seth, *Difference and Disease: Medicine, Race, and the Eighteenth-Century British Empire* (Cambridge University Press, 2018), p. 93. See also Martin Lynch, *Mining in World History* (London: Reaktion Books, 2002), p. 51.

9 Seth, *Difference and Disease*, pp. 91–111.

10 Harriet A. Washington, *Medical Apartheid: The Dark History of Medical Experimentation on Black Americans from Colonial Times to the Present* (New York: Doubleday, 2006), p. 52.

11 Mark Harrison, *Medicine in an Age of Commerce and Empire: Britain and Its Tropical Colonies, 1600–1830* (Oxford University Press, 2019).

12 Alison Bashford, ed., *Quarantine: Local and Global Histories* (London: Macmillan, 2016), p. 2; Eric Tagliacozzo, *The Longest Journey: Southeast Asians and the Pilgrimage to Mecca* (Oxford University Press, 2013), p. 133; Mark Harrison, *Contagion* (New Haven: Yale, 2013), pp. 50–79, 284.

13 From the 1866 Constantinople conference on international sanitation, quoted in Valeska Huber, "The Unification of the Globe by Disease? The International Sanitary Conferences on Cholera, 1851–1894," *History Journal* 49, no. 2 (2006): 455.

14 Tagliacozzo, *The Longest Journey*, p. 150; John Booker, *Maritime Quarantine: The British Experience, c. 1650–1900* (Aldershot: Ashgate, 2007).

15 Quoted in Huber, "The Unification of the Globe by Disease?," 462.

16 Alison Bashford, *Imperial Hygiene: A Critical History of Colonialism, Nationalism and Public Health* (Houndsmills: Palgrave Macmillan, 2004), p. 84.

17 Nayan Shah, *Contagious Divides: Epidemics and Race in San Francisco's Chinatown* (Berkeley: University of California Press, 2001), p. 185.

18 Kelly Lytle Hernandez, *City of Inmates: Conquest, Rebellion, and the Rise of Human Caging in Los Angeles, 1771–1965* (Chapel Hill: University of North Carolina Press, 2017), p. 139.

19 Hagar Kotef, *Movement and the Ordering of Freedom: On Liberal Governances of Mobility* (Durham, NC: Duke University Press, 2015), p. 87.

20 Frank Fenner, *Smallpox and Its Eradication* (Geneva: World Health Organization, 1988), p. 232.

21 Jean-Pierre Dedet, "The Overseas Pasteur Institutes, with Special Reference to Their Role in the Diffusion of Microbiological Knowledge: 1887–1975," *Research in Microbiology* 159, no. 1 (2008): 31.

22 Biswamoy Pati, *South Asia from the Margins: Echoes of Orissa, 1800–2000* (Manchester University Press, 2012), p. 63; Arnold, *Colonizing the Body*, p. 121.

23 Anna Lowenhaupt Tsing, *Friction: An Ethnography of Global Connection* (Princeton University Press, 2005), p. 86. See Anna Davin, "Imperialism and Motherhood" in *Tensions of Empire: Colonial Cultures in a Bourgeois World*, ed. Frederick Cooper and Ann Laura Stoler (Berkeley: University of California Press, 1997), pp. 87–151.

24 Arnold, *Colonizing the Body*, p. 107.

25 Clare Anderson, "Colonization, Kidnap and Confinement in the Andamans Penal Colony, 1771–1864," *Journal of Historical Geography* 37, no. 1 (2011) p. 68. See Michael Ignatieff, *A Just Measure of Pain: The Penitentiary in the Industrial Revolution, 1750–1850* (New York: Pantheon Books, 1978), p. 11.

26 Kerry Ward, *Networks of Empire: Forced Migration in the Dutch East India Company* (Cambridge University Press, 2009), p. 247.

27 Éric Fougère, *Île-prison, bagne et déportation: Les murs de la mer, éloigner et punir* (Paris: L'Harmattan, 2002); Katherine Roscoe, "A Natural Hulk: Australia's Carceral Islands in the Colonial Period, 1788–1901," *International Journal of Social History* 63, no. S26 (2018), p. 45.

28 Satadru Sen, *Disciplining Punishment: Colonialism and Convict Society in the Andaman Islands* (Delhi: Oxford University Press, 2000), pp. 83–100.

29 *Ibid.*; Anderson, "Colonization, Kidnap and Confinement in the Andamans Penal Colony," 130.

30 Anderson, "Colonization, Kidnap and Confinement in the Andamans Penal Colony," 12, 34–58; Peter Zinoman, *The Colonial Bastille: A History of Imprisonment in Vietnam, 1862–1940* (Berkeley: University of California Press, 2001), p. 84; Douglas Blackmon, *Slavery by Another Name* (New York: Anchor, 2008), p. 8; Michelle Alexander, *The New Jim Crow* (New York: The New Press, 2010), p. 30; Sarah Haley, *No Mercy Here* (Chapel Hill: University of North Carolina Press, 2016), p. 58.

31 Stoler, *Carnal Knowledge and Imperial Power*, p. 19.

32 Kyla Schuller, *The Biopolitics of Feeling: Race, Sex, and Science in the Nineteenth Century* (Durham, NC: Duke University Press, 2018); Naoroji, *Poverty and Un-British Rule in India* (London: S. Sonnenschein & Co., 1901).

33 Laura Briggs, *Reproducing Empire: Race, Sex, Science, and US Imperialism in Puerto Rico* (Berkeley: University of California Press, 2002), pp. 22, 28, 38.

34 Lenore Manderson, "Shaping Reproduction: Maternity in Early Twentieth-Century Malaya," in *Maternities and Modernities: Colonial and Postcolonial Experiences in Asia and the Pacific*, ed. Kalpana Ram and Margaret Jolly (Cambridge University Press, 1998), p. 26; Narin Hassan, *Diagnosing Empire: Women, Medical Knowledge, and Colonial Mobility* (Burlington: Ashgate, 2011).

35 Ahuja, *Bioinsecurities*, p. 217.

36 Ellen Amster, "The Syphilitic Arab?: A Search for Civilization in Disease Etiology, Native Prostitution, and French Colonial Medicine," in *French Mediterraneans: Transnational and Imperial History*, ed. Patricia Lorcin and Gee Sphard (Lincoln, NE: University of Nebraska Press, 2016), p. 320.

37 Harald Fischer-Tiné, *Low and Licentious Europeans: Race, Class, and "White Subalternity" in Colonial India* (Delhi: Oriental BlackSwan, 2009), p. 186.

38 Philippa Levine, *Prostitution, Race, and Politics: Policing Venereal Disease in the British Empire* (New York: Routledge, 2003), p. 16.

39 Briggs, *Reproducing Empire*, p. 23.

40 Karen Kruse Thomas, *Deluxe Jim Crow: Civil Rights and American Health Policy, 1935–1954* (Athens, GA: University of Georgia Press, 2011), p. 9.

41 Washington, *Medical Apartheid*, p. 157.

42 Alexander G. Weheliye, *Habeas Viscus: Racializing Assemblages, Biopolitics, and Black Feminist Theories of the Human* (Durham, NC: Duke University Press, 2014), p. 55; Nelson, *Body and Soul*; James H. Jones, *Bad Blood: The Tuskegee Syphilis Experiment*, ed. Tuskegee Institute (New York: Collier Macmillan, 1981), p. 4.

43 Ruha Benjamin, *People's Science: Bodies and Rights on the Stem Cell Frontier* (Stanford University Press, 2013), p. 152.

44 See the *Farmer-Paellmann v. FleetBoston* lawsuit filed in 2002. Alondra Nelson, *The Social Life of DNA* (Medford, MA: Digital Collections and Archives, Tufts University, 2017), pp. 121–40.

EPILOGUE

1 James Baldwin, *The Fire Next Time* (New York: Dell, 1988 [1963]).

2 Toni Morrison, *Beloved* (New York: Alfred A. Knopf, 1987).

3 Ruth Wilson Gilmore, *Golden Gulag: Prisons, Surplus, Crisis, and Opposition in Globalizing California* (Berkeley: University of California Press, 2007); Michelle Alexander, *The New Jim Crow: Mass Incarceration in the Age of Colorblindness* (New York: New Press, 2010).

4 Nick Estes, *Our History Is the Future: Standing Rock versus the Dakota Access Pipeline, and the Long Tradition of Indigenous Resistance* (New York: Penguin Random House, 2019).

5 Arundhati Roy, *Walking with the Comrades* (New York: Penguin Books, 2012).

6 Adam Branch, *Africa Uprising: Popular Protest and Political Change*, ed. Zachariah Cherian Mampilly (London: Zed books, 2015); Partha Chatterjee, *Lineages of Political Society: Studies in Postcolonial Democracy* (New York: Columbia University Press, 2011).

7 Denis Wood, *Rethinking the Power of Maps* (New York: Guilford Press, 2010).

8 Sylvia Wynter, "Towards the Sociogenic Principle: Fanon, the Puzzle of Conscious Experience, of 'Identity' and What It's Like to Be 'Black,'" in *Latin America between Marginalization and Integration*, ed. Mercedes Durán-Cogan and Antonio Gómez-Moriana (New York: Routledge, 2013), p. 23; Frantz Fanon, *Black Skin, White Masks*, ed. Richard Philcox and Anthony Appiah (New York: Grove Press, 2008).

9 These practices of liberation are Fanon's theme in Frantz Fanon, *The Wretched of the Earth*, ed. Constance Farrington (New York: Grove Press, 1968).

10 Alberto Alonso-Fradejas, "Anything but a Story Foretold: Multiple Politics of Resistance to the Agrarian Extractivist Project in Guatemala," *Journal of Peasant Studies* 42, nos. 3–4 (2015).

11 Judith Butler, *Frames of War: When Is Life Grievable?* (London: Verso, 2010).

12 Naomi Shihab Nye, "Cross That Line," in *You and Yours*, ed. Naomi Shihab Nye (New York: BOA Editions, 2005).

13 Paul Robeson, "A Lesson from Our South African Brothers and Sisters (1952)," in *Paul Robeson Speaks: Writings, Speeches, and Interviews, 1918–1974*, ed. Philip Sheldon Foner (Secaucus, NJ: Citadel Press, 1978).

Select Bibliography

Bagchi, Amiya Kumar. "Contested Hegemonies and Laissez-Faire: Controversies over the Monetary Standard in India at the High Noon of the British Empire." *Review (Fernand Braudel Center)* 20, no. 1 (1997): 19–76.

Balachandran, G. *India and the World Economy 1850–1950.* New Delhi; New York: Oxford University Press, 2003.

Baldwin, James. *The Fire Next Time.* New York: Dell, 1988 [1963].

Bhabha, Homi K. *The Location of Culture.* London; New York: Routledge, 2004.

Blaut, J. "Colonialism and the Rise of Capitalism." *Science and Society* 53, no. 3 (1989): 260–96.

Branch, Adam, and Zachariah Cherian Mampilly. *Africa Uprising: Popular Protest and Political Change.* London: Zed Books, 2015.

Byrd, Jodi A. *The Transit of Empire: Indigenous Critiques of Colonialism.* Minneapolis: University of Minnesota Press, 2011.

Césaire, Aimé. *Discourse on Colonialism.* Translated by Joan Pinkham. New York: Monthly Review Press, 2000.

Chakravartty, Paula, and Denise Ferreira Da Silva. "Accumulation, Dispossession, and Debt: The Racial Logic of Global Capitalism – An Introduction." *American Quarterly* 64, no. 3 (2012): 361–85.

Chatterjee, Partha. *Nationalist Thought and the Colonial World: A Derivative Discourse.* Minneapolis; London: University of Minnesota Press, 1993.

Chaudhuri, K. N. *Asia before Europe: Economy and Civilisation of the Indian Ocean from the Rise of Islam to 1750.* Cambridge University Press, 1990.

Comaroff, Jean, and John L. Comaroff. *Law and Disorder in the Postcolony.* University of Chicago Press, 2006.

Conklin, Alice. *A Mission to Civilize: The Republic Idea of Empire in France and West Africa, 1895–1930.* Stanford University Press, 1997.

Crosby, Alfred W. *Ecological Imperialism: The Biological Expansion of Europe, 900–1900.* 2nd ed. Cambridge, MA: Cambridge University Press, 2004.

Du Bois, W. E. B. *Black Reconstruction in America: An Essay toward a History of the Part Which Black Folk Played in the Attempt to Reconstruct Democracy in America, 1860–1880.* New York: Oxford University Press, 2007.

Eldem, Edhem. "Ottoman Financial Integration with Europe: Foreign Loans, the Ottoman Bank and the Ottoman Public Debt." *European Review* 13, no. 3 (2005): 431–45.

Fabian, Johannes. *Time and the Other: How Anthropology Makes Its Objects.* New York: Columbia University Press, 1983.

Fanon, Frantz. *The Wretched of the Earth.* Edited by Constance Farrington. New York: Grove Press, 1968.

Field, Kendra Taira. *Growing up with the Country: Family, Race, and Nation after the Civil War.* New Haven: Yale University Press, 2018.

Fischer, Fritz. *Germany's Aims in the First World War.* New York: W. W. Norton, 1967.

Foucault, Michel. *The Archaeology of Knowledge.* 1st American ed. New York: Pantheon Books, 1972.

Furtado, Celso. *Accumulation and Development: The Logic of Industrial Civilization.* Oxford: M. Robertson, 1983.

Development and Underdevelopment. Berkeley: University of California Press, 1964.

Galeano, Eduardo. *Open Veins of Latin America: Five Centuries of the Pillage of a Continent.* 25th anniversary ed. Foreword by Isabel Allende. New York: Monthly Review Press, 1997.

Getachew, Adom. *Worldmaking after Empire: The Rise and Fall of Self-Determination.* Princeton University Press, 2019.

Gilmore, Ruth Wilson. *Golden Gulag: Prisons, Surplus, Crisis, and Opposition in Globalizing California.* Berkeley: University of California Press, 2007.

Girvan, Norman. "Expropriation and Compensation from a Third World Perspective." In his *Corporate Imperialism: Conflict and Expropriation*, 200–28. New York: M. E. Sharpe, 1976.

Goldstein, Alyosha. *Formations of United States Colonialism.* Durham: Duke University Press, 2014.

Guha, Ranajit. *Dominance without Hegemony: History and Power in Colonial India.* Cambridge, MA: Harvard University Press, 1997.

"The Prose of Counter-Insurgency." In *Selected Subaltern Studies*, edited by Ranajit Guha and Gayatri Spivak Chakravorty. New York: Oxford University Press, 1998.

Gunder Frank, Andre. *Reorient: Global Economy in the Asian Age.* Berkeley: University of California Press, 1998.

Hall, Stuart. "Race, Articulation and Societies Structured in Dominance." In *Sociological Theories: Race and Colonialism*, ed. Unesco, 305–45. Paris: Unesco, 1980.

Hardt, Michael, and Antonio Negri. *Empire*. Cambridge, MA: Harvard University Press, 2000.

Hartman, Saidiya V. *Scenes of Subjection: Terror, Slavery, and Self-Making in Nineteenth-Century America*. New York: Oxford University Press, 1997.

Ho, Engseng. *The Graves of Tarim: Genealogy and Mobility across the Indian Ocean*. Berkeley: University of California Press, 2006.

Hudson, Peter James. *Bankers and Empire: How Wall Street Colonized the Caribbean*. University of Chicago Press, 2017.

Inikori, J. E. *The Atlantic Slave Trade: Effects on Economies, Societies, and Peoples in Africa, the Americas, and Europe*. Durham, NC: Duke University Press, 1992.

Jalal, Ayesha. *Partisans of Allah: Jihad in South Asia*. Cambridge, MA: Harvard University Press, 2008.

James, C. L. R. *The Black Jacobins: Toussaint L'Ouverture and the San Domingo Revolution*. 2nd ed., rev. ed. New York: Vintage Books, 1963.

Jennifer, L. Morgan. *Laboring Women: Gender and Reproduction in the Making of New World Slavery*. Philadelphia: University of Pennsylvania Press, 2004.

Kelley, Robin D. G. *Freedom Dreams: The Black Radical Imagination*. Boston: Beacon Press, 2002.

Kish, Zenia, and Justin Leroy. "Bonded Life: Technologies of Racial Finance from Slave Insurance to Philanthrocapital." *Cultural Studies* 29, nos. 5–6 (2015): 630–51.

Kopf, David. *The Brahmo Samaj and the Shaping of the Modern Indian Mind*. Princeton University Press, 1979.

Lee, Christopher J. *Making a World after Empire: The Bandung Moment and Its Political Afterlives*. Athens, GA: Ohio University Press, 2010.

Look Lai, Walton. *Indentured Labor, Caribbean Sugar: Chinese and Indian Migrants to the British West Indies, 1838–1918*. Baltimore: Johns Hopkins University Press, 1993.

Lowe, Lisa. *The Intimacies of Four Continents*. Durham, NC: Duke University Press, 2015.

Maldonado-Torres, Nelson. *Against War: Views from the Underside of Modernity*. Durham: Duke University Press, 2008.

Mamdani, Mahmood. *Good Muslim, Bad Muslim: America, the Cold War, and the Roots of Terror*. New York: Three Leaves Press, 2005.

Mantena, Karuna. *Alibis of Empire: Henry Maine and the Ends of Liberal Imperialism*. Princeton University Press, 2010.

Marx, Karl. *Capital: A Critique of Political Economy*. Edited by Ben Fowkes. New York: Vintage Books, 1977.

Mbembe, Achille. *On the Postcolony*. Berkeley: University of California Press, 2001.

McKittrick, Katherine. *Demonic Grounds: Black Women and the Cartographies of Struggle.* Minneapolis: University of Minnesota Press, 2006.

Mehta, Uday Singh. *Liberalism and Empire: A Study in Nineteenth-Century British Liberal Thought.* University of Chicago Press, 1999.

Miles, Tiya. *Ties That Bind: The Story of an Afro-Cherokee Family in Slavery and Freedom.* 2nd ed. Oakland: University of California Press, 2015.

Mintz, Sidney W. *Sweetness and Power: The Place of Sugar in Modern History.* New York: Viking, 1985.

Morrison, Toni. *Song of Solomon.* New York: Knopf, 1977.

Ngai, Mae M. *Impossible Subjects: Illegal Aliens and the Making of Modern America.* Princeton University Press, 2004.

O'Brien, Jean M. *Dispossession by Degrees: Indian Land and Identity in Natick, Massachusetts, 1650–1790.* Cambridge, MA: Harvard University Press, 1997.

Patterson, Orlando. *The Sociology of Slavery: An Analysis of the Origins, Development, and Structure of Negro Slave Society in Jamaica.* 1st American ed. Rutherford: Fairleigh Dickinson University Press, 1969.

Piketty, Thomas. *Capital in the Twenty-First Century.* Edited by Arthur Goldhammer. Cambridge, MA: The Belknap Press of Harvard University Press, 2014.

Pitts, Jennifer. *A Turn to Empire: The Rise of Imperial Liberalism in Britain and France.* Princeton University Press, 2005.

Pratt, Mary Louise. *Imperial Eyes: Travel Writing and Transculturation.* London: Routledge, 1992.

Robinson, Cedric J. *Black Marxism: The Making of the Black Radical Tradition.* Chapel Hill: University of North Carolina Press, 2000.

Roediger, David R. *The Wages of Whiteness: Race and the Making of the American Working Class.* London; New York: Verso, 1991.

Said, Edward W. *Orientalism.* 25th anniversary ed. with a new preface by the author. New York: Vintage Books, 1994.

Saldaña-Portillo, María Josefina. *Indian Given: Racial Geographies across Mexico and the United States.* Durham, NC: Duke University Press, 2016.

Scott, James C. *Weapons of the Weak: Everyday Forms of Peasant Resistance.* New Haven: Yale University Press, 1985.

Sharpe, Christina. *In the Wake: On Blackness and Being.* Durham, NC: Duke University Press, 2016.

Simpson, Audra. *Mohawk Interruptus: Political Life across the Borders of Settler States.* Durham, NC: Duke University Press, 2014.

Singh, Nikhil. *Race and America's Long War.* Oakland: University of California Press, 2017.

Smallwood, Stephanie E. *Saltwater Slavery: A Middle Passage from Africa to American Diaspora.* Cambridge, MA: Harvard University Press, 2008.

Stoler, Ann. *Carnal Knowledge and Imperial Power: Race and the Intimate in Colonial Rule.* Berkeley: University of California Press, 2002.

Taylor, Diana. *The Archive and the Repertoire: Performing Cultural Memory in the Americas.* Durham, NC: Duke University Press, 2003.

Tinker, Hugh. *A New System of Slavery: The Export of Indian Labour Overseas, 1830–1920.* London: Oxford University Press, 1974.

Tomich, Dale. *Through the Prism of Slavery: Labor, Capital, and World Economy.* Lanham: Rowman & Littlefield, 2004.

Tsing, Anna Lowenhaupt. *Friction: An Ethnography of Global Connection.* Princeton University Press, 2005.

Vizenor, Gerald Robert. *Manifest Manners: Narratives on Postindian Survivance.* Hanover: University Press of New England, 1994.

Walcott, Derek. *Omeros.* New York: Farrar, Straus, Giroux, 1990.

Wallerstein, Immanuel Maurice. *The Modern World-System.* Berkeley: University of California Press, 2011.

Williams, Eric. *Capitalism and Slavery.* Chapel Hill: University of North Carolina Press, 2014.

Wolfe, Patrick. *Traces of History: Elementary Structures of Race.* London: Verso, 2016.

Woods, Clyde Adrian. *Development Arrested: The Blues and Plantation Power in the Mississippi Delta.* London: Verso, 1998.

Wynter, Sylvia. *Black Metamorphosis: New Natives in a New World.* New York: Schomburg Center for Research in Black Culture, n.d.

——— "Unsettling the Coloniality of Being/Power/Truth/Freedom: Towards the Human, after Man, Its Overrepresentation – An Argument." *CR: The New Centennial Review* 3, no. 3 (2003).

Zinn, Howard. *A People's History of the United States.* New York: Harper, 1999.

Index

Printed in Great Britain
by Amazon

81254067R00169